DICTIONARY
for
School Library Media
Specialists

DICTIONARY
for
School Library Media Specialists

A Practical and Comprehensive Guide

Mary Maude McCain
and
Martha Merrill

2001
Libraries Unlimited
A Division of Greenwood Publishing Group, Inc.
Greenwood Village, Colorado

We dedicate this dictionary to our individual mentors and models in the profession. Martha Merrill to Dr. Margaret Tassia and Dr. Blanche Woolls. Mary Maude McCain to Mildred Johnston and Dr. Mary Sue McGarity. Together we wish to thank Dr. Jane Bandy Smith for her professionalism and leadership.

LIBRARIES UNLIMITED
A Division of Greenwood Publishing Group, Inc.
7730 East Belleview Avenue, Suite A200
Greenwood Village, CO 80111
1-800-255-5800
www.lu.com

Library of Congress Cataloging-in-Publication Data

McCain, Mary Maude.
  Dictionary for school library media specialists : a practical and comprehensive guide / Mary Maude McCain and Martha Merrill.

      p. cm.
    ISBN 1-56308-696-4 (softbound)
      1. Library science--Dictionaries. 2. School libraries--Dictionaries. 3. Instructional materials centers--Dictionaries. I. Merrill, Martha. II. Title.

  Z1006 .M43 2001
  020'.3--dc21

                                                          2001016506

CONTENTS

PREFACE

This dictionary is the outgrowth of a need we have observed in the school library media profession. A practical, up-to-date, and comprehensive guide to the basic terminology used in the daily operation of a K–12 school library media center is nonexistent.

Many books on topics such as education, cataloging, management, technology, and reference contain glossaries, and there are dictionaries devoted to each of these subjects. However, many of these glossaries and dictionaries are fragmented in scope, and other resources are out of date or are not designed exclusively for use by school library media specialists.

There is no one source that contains all the types of terminology that school library media specialists must know. We believe that a single source of terminology and definitions is a much-needed resource.

This dictionary reflects a consolidation of all the terminology that we determined would benefit school library media specialists into one volume. This up-to-date reference text should be helpful to both the beginning and the experienced school library media specialist.

We extend our thanks to our Advisory Committee, composed of Phyllis Heroy, Pat Scales, Jane Bandy Smith, Margaret Tassia, and Nancy Teger, who offered guidance and suggested terminology for inclusion. We also thank Betty Morris, former Acquisitions Editor, Rich Lane, Project Editor, and Edward Kurdyla, General Manager of Libraries Unlimited, for assistance and advice with this project.

Mary Maude McCain

Martha Merrill

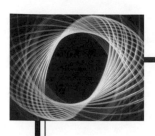

AUTHOR BIOGRAPHIES

Mary Maude McCain recently retired as a library media specialist with 30 years of experience in public education and public libraries. She has also served as an adjunct professor of library media management and children's literature for the University of Alabama and the University of Alabama at Birmingham. McCain developed award-winning media programs in two Alabama schools, one of which was included in the 1986 publication of the U.S. Department of Education, *Check These Out: Exemplary Media Programs.* She has also lectured and consulted at the local, state, and national levels in the areas of library media management, flexible scheduling, automation, and educational technology. In addition, she has served in many leadership positions with library-related associations, including president of the Alabama Library Association. She was a delegate to the 1991 White House Conference on Libraries. McCain was named Outstanding Educator of the Year by the University of Alabama at Birmingham in 1984 and in 1998 was named Librarian of the Year by the Alabama Beta Kappa Chapter of Beta Phi Mu.

Martha Merrill is a professor of instructional media at Jacksonville State University where she coordinates and teaches in the graduate-level school library media program. She received her doctorate in library science from the University of Pittsburgh and has 27 years of experience in the library science profession. Merrill has chaired and served on numerous professional committees at the national, regional, and state levels. She has served as president of the Alabama Library Association. Merrill has made numerous state presentations on intellectual freedom and has written journal articles for state and national publications, primarily on intellectual freedom issues. She served as editor for *The Reference Librarian* issue and also the monograph entitled *Reference Services and Media.* Merrill's honors include the Alabama/SIRS Intellectual Freedom Award in 1992, the Alabama Library Association Distinguished Service Award in 1995, and the Alabama Beta Kappa Chapter Beta Phi Mu Librarian of the Year Award in 1997.

INTRODUCTION

This dictionary is designed to be a useful and convenient work for its primary target audience—building-level library media specialists. The purpose is to identify and define the various terms and consolidate them into a single reference work. The dictionary should also be valuable to library media students and as a quick reference guide to media center paraprofessionals and clerks.

School library media contains the components of many disciplines. This dictionary assimilates definitions of terms that relate not only to the school library media profession, but also to computer science, counseling, educational administration, educational psychology, educational technology, educational testing, instructional design, literature, and special education.

It was difficult to decide what to include from the constantly changing and diverse field of school library media. Criteria for including entries had to be loosely defined because the subject of school library media is so broad and because it overlaps so many other fields. Many resources, including books, periodicals, and the World Wide Web, were examined to identify terms. In most cases, the terms included appeared in more than one source. An Advisory Committee was consulted for suggestions for additional terms to be included, and editors at Libraries Unlimited also reviewed all terms and definitions.

This dictionary concentrates on terms and definitions of central importance across the entire breadth of library media and education practice. It includes terms of enduring value as well as those that have emerged more recently. Technological advances have greatly influenced and changed the library media field. An entirely new vocabulary has evolved as have entirely different methods of providing service in library media programs.

No dictionary of terminology can be all-inclusive because the terminology constantly changes and expands. It is inevitable, then, that some terms are not defined in this dictionary. Commercial companies and products were eliminated because these terms could not be all-inclusive.

Two types of definitions are included: 1. Those given brief glossary descriptions, and 2. Those given more comprehensive coverage. Deciding how much to include about each term was difficult, and equal treatment was not given to all terms. Judgments on the relative significance of the terms were made, and terms were defined according to the information available and the need for a better understanding of certain terms, particularly in the area of technology. In some cases, multiple definitions were included for a term.

The objectives of this dictionary are:

1.   To assist library media personnel in understanding the terminology associated with the profession.

2.   To enable library media students to understand the terminology related to the field of library media.

3.   To give readers in any field a better understanding of the various terminology included in this dictionary.

HOW TO
USE THIS
DICTIONARY

The terms in this dictionary are listed in alphabetical order in the letter-by-letter style. Hyphenated words are considered one word in the alphabetical sequence. Alphabetical order ignores spaces, punctuation, and numbers in the entry titles.

Acronyms and abbreviations are generally in full uppercase letters. *RAM* and *ROM* are examples. They are not defined, and the reader is referred to the full term for the definition. If more than one definition is related to the term, the entry is itemized to reflect the various meanings.

Cross-references are used to refer the reader to other entries. Because acronyms and abbreviations refer the reader to the full term, they appear in boldface type with a *See* reference to the full term. For example, **MARC**: See *Machine-readable cataloging*. A cross-reference appears in boldface italics when defined terms are found in the body of the text. If a term is not included in the body of the text, a *See also* cross-reference is used to refer the reader to additional defined terms in boldface italics at the end of the definition. If two or more terms have essentially the same meaning, the term in wider use is defined; the less widely used term has a cross-reference to the defined term. For example, **School library media specialist**: See *Library media specialist*.

AACR2R: See *Anglo-American Cataloging Rules*, 2nd edition, 1998 Revision.

AASL: See *American Association of School Librarians*.

ABA: See *American Booksellers Association*.

ABBY Awards: Awards given annually by the *American Booksellers Association* for *book* titles that the members most enjoyed handling in the past year.

Ability grouping: See *Homogeneous grouping*.

Abridged edition: A condensed version of a *book*. See also *Edition*.

Abstract: A *summary* of an article, a *book*, or any other *format* of *information*. See also *Full text*.

AC: See *Annotated Card program*.

AC headings: See *Annotated Card headings*.

AC program: See *Annotated Card program*.

Acceptable Use Policy (AUP): Written rules and responsibilities, usually published by a *network* operator, that establish the conditions under which users may access network services. Breaches of an AUP may result in the termination of user privileges. Schools often request that the students and their parents sign a form agreeing to the appropriate use of the *Internet* and to the imposition of penalties for the misuse of the Internet.

Access: 1. The process of choosing and formulating headings for a *bibliographic record*. Also refers to the larger processes of providing *bibliographic* access (i.e., *cataloging*), intellectual access (i.e., classification and indexing), and physical access to material. 2. The process of using a computer *directory* or *file*. 3. The retrieval of *data* from a *disk drive*. 4. Ability to communicate with, enter, or approach.

Access point: Any name, *word*, or phrase by which a *catalog* record for an item can be retrieved from the catalog; also known as an *entry*, *heading*, or *retrieval* point. Main entries, added entries, and subject entries are examples of access points. See also *Added entry*, *Main entry*, and *Subject entry*.

Access time: The amount of time required to retrieve *data* from the *internal memory* of a *computer* or from *secondary storage* such as a *floppy disk*. See also *Random access memory* and *Response time*.

Access to Electronic Information, Services, and Networks: An interpretation of the *Library Bill of Rights* prepared by the *American Library Association* that states that users should not be restricted or denied *access* for expressing or receiving constitutionally protected speech and that electronic *information* and services should be equally, readily, and equitably available to all *library* users.

Access to Resources and Services in the School Library Media Program: An interpretation of the *Library Bill of Rights* prepared by the *American Library Association* that specifically addresses the school library media *program*. It includes *collection development*, *resources*, and services, and describes how *intellectual freedom* principles apply to these elements.

Accession book: A book or ledger that maintains a record of *bibliographic* and ordering *information* as well as the *accession number*. *Automation* of library media centers has eliminated the need for accession books.

Accession number: A number assigned to each item as it is received in the *library media center*. Accession numbers may consist of continuous numbering such as 10,251, 10,252, 10,253 or a coded system generally referring to the year and the sequence of receipt such as 98-100, 98-101, 98-102. The numbers are recorded in an *accession book*. In automated library media centers, the *barcode* replaces the accession number.

Accompanying materials: Materials intended for use in conjunction with the primary cataloged item. For example, books may be accompanied by materials such as a *cassette tape*, a CD-ROM, a teacher's *manual*, or a print.

Accountability: A concept in education that holds a *school system* responsible for student performance.

Accountable talk: Discussion that is purposeful and polite as well as discussion that demonstrates reasoning and increases knowledge. A *library media specialist* uses this method of speaking when asking students to discuss their information-seeking activities such as explaining their reasoning, justifying their conclusions, and substantiating the sources used to obtain the *information*.

Accreditation: Approval of a program of study or an institution for meeting certain *standards* set by an external organization. For example, the *National Council for Accreditation of Teacher Education* accredits undergraduate and graduate *teacher* education programs. State departments of education may accredit an individual *school* or a *school system*. Regional associations may accredit K-12 schools or postsecondary institutions. The Southern Association of Colleges and Schools is an example of such a regional association. See also *Accreditation standards*.

Accreditation standards: The requirements that accrediting agencies establish and review for a *program* of study or an institution. The accrediting agencies use these requirements to determine if approval (*accreditation*) is warranted.

Achievement test: A type of examination that measures a student's knowledge or skill, or both, in one or more subjects. These tests are generally norm-referenced, multiple-choice tests, and the results are used to compare the scores of students and schools with those of other students and schools. The *Stanford Achievement Test* is an example. See also *Norm-referenced assessment*.

ACLU: See *American Civil Liberties Union*.

Acquisition: The process of obtaining *hardware* and *resources* for a library *collection*. Materials may be obtained through purchase, gifts, or lease plans.

ACRL: See *Association of College and Research Libraries*.

Acronym: A *word* formed from the letters of the name of an entity or a term; for example, ALA—*American Library Association* or MARC—*Machine-readable cataloging*.

ACT: See *American College Testing Program*.

Action research: A form of *research* that applies the scientific method to the solution of practical problems. In education, practitioners investigate educational problems in actual educational settings. A problem is identified, and relevant *data* are analyzed. The focus is to improve *school* practices.

Active learning: Activities that actively engage the student. *Learning* is believed to increase if a student is actively involved in a learning activity rather than listening to a *teacher* lecture or completing a worksheet. Acting out a play or using math manipulatives are examples. See also *Constructive teaching* and *Manipulative*.

Ad hoc committee: A temporary committee charged with completing a specific assignment. Once the task is completed, the committee is dissolved.

ADA: See *Americans with Disabilities Act*.

Adapter: A device used to achieve compatibility between two items of equipment such as a connecting cord between a *videocassette recorder* and a *television*.

ADD: See *Attention deficit disorder*.

Added entry: Any catalog *entry* except the *main entry* or *subject entry*. Added entries consist of joint authors, illustrators, editors, compilers, translators, and series. See also *Access point*, *Corporate entry*, and *Title entry*.

Addendum: Additional material added to a *book*. The supplement is generally added after the book has been typeset or "laid out" in a *desktop publishing* program. The plural form of the word is addenda.

Address: The location of an *electronic mail* or *Internet* site.

ADHD: See *Attention deficit hyperactivity disorder*.

Administrator: The head of an agency; for example, a *principal* of a school or the superintendent of a *school system*. See also *Superintendent of schools*.

ADSL: See *Asymmetrical digital subscriber line*.

Adult education: An educational *program* designed for adults, offering them the opportunity to pursue knowledge and skills for personal or job-related growth, or both.

Advanced placement classes (AP classes): College-level courses offered in many high schools to above-average students. If a student attains a sufficient score on a standardized AP *test*, most colleges will award credit for the equivalent college course.

Advisory committee: A school-wide committee formed to assist the *library media specialist* by suggesting *resources* for purchase. The committee typically includes *teacher*, student, and parent representation.

AECT: See *Association for Educational Communications and Technology*.

Affective domain: One of the three domains included in a *taxonomy* developed by Benjamin Bloom. This domain includes behaviors that relate to emotions, feelings, and attitudes. See also *Bloom's taxonomy*, *Cognitive domain*, and *Psychomotor domain*.

AFT: See *American Federation of Teachers*.

ALA: See *American Library Association*.

Alex Awards: Awards that honor the top ten books enjoyed by young adults ages 12 through 18 that were published in the preceding year. These annual awards began in 1998. They are cosponsored by the *Young Adult Library Services Association*, a division of the *American Library Association*, and by *Booklist*. The award is named for Margaret Alexander Edwards, who was called Alex by her friends, and is funded by the Margaret Alexander Edwards Trust. See also *Edwards Award*.

Alliteration: Repetition of an initial consonant sound such as "Peter Piper picked a peck of pickled peppers." See also *Assonance*.

Almanac: A *summary* of *data* and statistics used to answer ready reference questions. Both general almanacs and subject almanacs are published and are available for *library* use. See also *Ready reference question*.

Alpha testing: Initial testing of new computer *software* conducted by the manufacturer. The second test is *beta testing*, which is performed by users in real-life situations.

Alphabet: Letters or characters that identify a certain *language* and in which that language is written.

Alphabet book: A juvenile *book* designed to teach children the *alphabet*. These books help children to learn the names and shapes of letters, and they can also help children to identify or name the objects portrayed in the illustrations. See also *Illustration*.

Alphanumeric characters: A set of characters found on a *keyboard*. These characters include the *alphabet* (A–Z), numbers (0–9), punctuation marks, and other keyboard symbols. See also *Character*.

ALSC: See *Association for Library Service to Children*.

Alternative school: A type of *school* that does not follow the design of a conventional school. These nonconventional schools may be public or private with a *curriculum* that meets the needs of the students enrolled. Magnet schools as well as schools for the *gifted and talented* or for disruptive students are examples. See also *Magnet school*.

Alternative title: A *title* following the *title proper* and preceded by the word "or" in any *language;* for example, the underlined item in the operetta by Gilbert and Sullivan titled: *Trial by jury,* or The lass who loved a sailor.

ALU: See *Arithmetic logic unit*.

American Association of School Librarians (AASL): A division of the *American Library Association* that represents school library media specialists. It advocates *research*, professionalism, *leadership*, and *continuing education* in the school library media field. The organization publishes *Knowledge Quest*, a *journal* for AASL members, five times a year, and *School Library Media Research* (formerly *School Library Media Quarterly Online*), an *online* research journal that accepts and publishes articles on its Web site at ⟨http://www.ala.org/aasl/SLMR⟩.

American Booksellers Association (ABA): A not-for-profit trade organization founded in 1900 with headquarters in Tarrytown, New York. ABA is devoted to meeting the needs of its core members—independently owned bookstores with storefront locations—through advocacy, education, *research*, and *information* dissemination. The organization supports free speech, *literacy*, and programs that encourage children to *read*.

American Civil Liberties Union (ACLU): An organization founded in 1920 and located in New York, New York. It defends the freedoms in the Bill of Rights to the United States Constitution. Its Web site is ⟨http://www.aclu.org⟩.

American College Testing Program (ACT): A nonprofit educational organization that offers several services related to college admissions. One service is the ACT, which is a *test* many colleges and universities use to determine admissions.

American Federation of Teachers (AFT): An organization founded in 1916 with headquarters in Washington, D.C. The group works at the state and local levels with teachers and other educational employees on issues such as organizing, collective bargaining, public relations, and other educational matters. Members receive *American Educator* quarterly and *AFT Action: A Newsletter for AFT Leaders* weekly.

American Library Association (ALA): The national professional *library* association located in Chicago, Illinois. Founded in 1876, it is the oldest and largest national library association in the world. The membership represents state, academic, public, *school*, and special libraries. Members receive *American Libraries*, a *journal* published 11 times a year. The ALA *Web site* is ⟨http://www.ala.org⟩.

American National Standards Institute (ANSI): A nonprofit organization founded in 1918 and located in New York, New York. It develops voluntary national *standards*, including information *technology* standards, to improve the productivity and competitiveness of industrial concerns in the United States. This group represents the United States to the *International Standards Organization*. See also *National Information Standards Organization* and *Z39.50*.

American Society for Information Science (ASIS): An organization founded in 1937 with headquarters in Silver Spring, Maryland. ASIS fosters the improvement of the *information* transfer process and focuses on *research* and education. Members include information specialists, librarians, and others interested in information *storage* and *retrieval*. The *Journal of the American Society for Information Science* is its monthly publication.

American Standard Code for Information Interchange (ASCII): (Pronounced ask-ee). A *binary code* for *text* as well as for the *storage* and *transmission* of *data*. ASCII is used for *information* interchange among *data processing* systems.

American Standard Code for Information Interchange file (ASCII file): A *file* that contains *data* made up of ASCII characters. As a *text file*, it is the opposite of a *binary file*. See also *Graphics file*.

Americans with Disabilities Act (ADA): A law passed in 1986 to protect the disabled from employment discrimination. Employers are required to offer reasonable accommodation to those with a disability. *Standards* for public *access* to buildings and services for the disabled are addressed. For example, shelving width and height of *computer* terminals are two issues related to the ADA standards for library media centers.

Amplifier: A sound system device used to enhance an electronic signal, such as loud speakers.

Analog: An electronic signal produced and transmitted according to a continuous and varying waveform. Conventional *television*, videocassette recorders, and telephones use analog *transmission*. *Digital* transmission is a more recent *technology*.

Analytic entry: A *catalog* record or *access point* for a *work* that is part of a larger *bibliographic* unit; for example, one song on a sound recording that contains several songs.

Andrew Carnegie Award: An award given to the most distinguished American *videotape* for children produced in the preceding year. It is presented annually by the *Association for Library Service to Children*, a division of the *American Library Association*.

***Anglo-American Cataloging Rules*, 2nd edition, 1998 Revision (AACR2R)**: The current standard rules for *descriptive cataloging* and for access points. These rules are more commonly referred to as *Anglo-American Cataloging Rules*, 2nd edition, revised. See also *Access point*.

Animation: A *film* technique of creating static figures that appear to move and seem alive. These still images are placed in motion by the juxtaposition of a series of pictures that have small, incremental changes from one picture to the next. See also *Image*.

Annotated Card headings (AC headings): A list of *subject* headings designated by the *Library of Congress* as suitable for assignment to children's materials. Headings are given in the first *volume* of *Library of Congress Subject Headings*. A separate publication of these headings is also available. See also *Annotated Card program* and *Subject heading*.

Annotated Card program (AC program): A *program* sponsored by the *Library of Congress* that provides variant *catalog* records for children's materials. Items cataloged under this program are given summaries; *subject* headings are assigned to works of imagination; and *Library of Congress Subject Headings* are supplemented with terms from a designated list of headings suitable for children's materials. See also *Annotated Card headings* and *Subject heading*.

Annotation: A *summary* of a *work*, such as a *book*, that may be a part of a *bibliography* or catalog *entry*.

Annual: A *serial* published once a year.

Annual report: A *document* that summarizes the activities, services, programs, expenditures, and *circulation* records, among other topics, of a *library media center* for a period of one year.

Annual review: A publication containing articles and *research* on a particular *topic* or a particular field during a one-year period.

Anonymous: An unidentified source; of unknown authorship or origin.

Anonymous file transfer protocol (Anonymous FTP): An *application* used to transfer files between two computers on the *Internet*. Many Internet sites have established publicly accessible material that can be obtained through FTP; the user logs on using the account name of *anonymous*. These sites are called anonymous FTP servers. See also *Archie* and *File transfer protocol*.

Anonymous FTP: See *Anonymous file transfer protocol*.

ANSI: See *American National Standards Institute*.

Anthology: A *collection* of literary pieces such as *poetry* or short stories. The collection may include works by several authors or be limited to a particular *subject*.

Anthropomorphism: Giving human qualities to animals. For example, *Charlotte's Web* contains anthropomorphism because the animals have the ability to communicate. See also *Personification*.

Antivirus software: Computer *software* that scans for viruses; the software removes any viruses and may repair damage they have caused. This software is continually updated because new viruses emerge constantly. The user needs to purchase the updates frequently to protect *computer* programs. See also *Virus*.

Antonym: A *word* that means the opposite of another word. For example, the opposite of *good* is *bad*. See also *Homonym* and *Synonym*.

AP classes: See *Advanced placement classes*.

Aperture: 1. The opening in a *scanner* through which the reflected light exits to read a *barcode*. 2. The opening of a camera *lens* through which light passes. See also *F-stop*.

Appendix: Supplementary material attached at the end of a *work*. Examples of this supplementary material are graphs, tables, clarifying examples, and additional *resources*.

Application: A computer *program* written to perform a specific function such as *word processing*, *acquisition*, *circulation*, or *cataloging*.

Approval plan: An arrangement with a *publisher* or *jobber* to supply material in a particular category as requested by the *library media specialist*.

Aptitude test: A type of examination that measures a student's potential ability for *learning* new *information* or skills. One example is the *Intelligence Quotient* (IQ) test, which is a *test* that measures a person's intellectual ability.

Arbuthnot Award: Named for May Hill Arbuthnot, an authority on *children's literature*, the award is given annually by the *International Reading Association* to an outstanding *teacher* of children's literature.

Arbuthnot Honor Lecture: The *Association for Library Service to Children*, a division of the *American Library Association*, annually selects a distinguished *author*, critic, librarian, historian, or *teacher* of *children's literature* to present a free public lecture at a site chosen by ALSC.

Archie: A search *program* used to *search* files indexed and stored on any anonymous FTP sites. See also *Anonymous file transfer protocol*.

Architectural barrier: Any obstacle in or near a building that makes the building or its *resources* inaccessible to the physically disabled.

Archive copy: A *copy* of a *computer* program or *file* to be stored while using the original *program*. *Data* are copied onto a *disk* or *streaming tape* as a *backup* or a historical copy.

Archives: 1. Historical records of an organization. 2. The area where historical documents are stored. Some public libraries have an Archives Department. 3. The agency responsible for selecting, preserving, and providing *access* to historical records. Some states have an archives agency.

Archivist: The person who collects and maintains historical records and documents.

Area of description: One of the eight parts of a *bibliographic description* designated by *International Standard Bibliographic Description* (ISBD) and *Anglo-American Cataloging Rules, 2nd edition, 1998 Revision* (AACR2R); for example, the *Edition area* (Area 2) or the Series area (Area 6). The eight areas to address for the *descriptive cataloging* of an item are: Area 1: *Title* and *statement of responsibility*; Area 2: Edition; Area 3: *Material specific details*; Area 4: Publication, distribution, etc.; Area 5: Physical description; Area 6: *Series*; Area 7: *Notes*; Area 8: *Standard number* and terms of availability. See also *Physical description area* and *Publication and distribution area*.

Arithmetic logic unit (ALU): The portion of a computer's *central processing unit* that does calculating and comparing. It makes all the decisions for the *microprocessor* based on the mathematical computations and logic functions it performs.

ASCD: See *Association for Supervision and Curriculum Development*.

ASCII: See *American Standard Code for Information Interchange*.

ASCII file: See *American Standard Code for Information Interchange file*.

ASIS: See *American Society for Information Science*.

AskERIC: A service provided on the *Internet* to educators. It began in 1992 as a project by the ERIC Clearinghouse at Syracuse University. *Resources* include answers to questions, search of the ERIC *database*, *collection* of lesson plans, *full text* of ERIC digests, and InfoGuides to Internet resources for education. Responses to messages for education *information* occur within 48 hours. The e-mail address is (askeric@askeric.org). The *Web site* is (http://www.askeric.org).

Aspect ratio: The width to height ratio of a display *screen* or of an *image*. It can refer to a *television* screen or to a computer *monitor*. The enlargement, reduction, or transferring of images may force images into different aspect ratios and cause distortion. For example, converting a *motion picture* for television viewing may result in distortion.

Assessment: 1. An *evaluation* of a *collection* or a school library media *program*. It may be formal or informal and may measure effectiveness, quality, or both. 2. An evaluation of student or staff performance. A variety of techniques and instruments measure the *learning* and performance of students and teachers. Some types of assessment are *authentic assessment, criterion-referenced assessment, needs assessment, norm-referenced assessment, performance assessment, portfolio assessment, qualitative assessment*, and *quantitative assessment*. See also *Performance appraisal*.

Association for Educational Communications and Technology (AECT): An organization founded in 1923 and located in Washington, D.C. The association is concerned with the use of educational *technology* and its application to the *learning* process. Members include teachers, instructional media specialists, *audiovisual* personnel, and others. Publications include *Educational Technology Research and Development*, a quarterly, and *TechTrends*, published six times a year. See also *Division of School Media and Technology*.

Association for Library Service to Children (ALSC): A division of the *American Library Association* concerned with *library* services to children in all types of libraries. Members receive the quarterly *ALSC Newsletter* and the quarterly *Journal of Youth Services in Libraries*, which is issued jointly with the *Young Adult Library Services Association*.

Association for Supervision and Curriculum Development (ASCD): An organization founded in 1943 with headquarters in Alexandria, Virginia. ASCD focuses on *research* and *professional development* in *curriculum* and supervision. Members include supervisors, curriculum coordinators, education professors, classroom teachers, principals, superintendents, and others. Publications include *Educational Leadership*, published eight times a year, and the quarterly *Journal of Curriculum and Supervision*.

Association of College and Research Libraries (ACRL): A division of the *American Library Association* whose members include academic and *research* librarians. It encourages *professional development* among the membership and promotes the improvement of library *resources* and services. Publications include *Choice,* eleven times a year; *College & Research Libraries,* bimonthly; and *College & Research Libraries News,* eleven times a year.

Assonance: Repetition of vowel sounds. The "e" sound in the *poem* "Don't Ever Seize a Weasel by the Tail" is an example. See also *Alliteration*.

Asymmetrical digital subscriber line (ADSL): A method of *data* communication through telephone lines. A high-quality *audio* and *video* signal can be delivered at 1.5 *megabits per second*.

Asynchronous communication: Electronic communication characterized by a time delay between the posting and the receipt of *information*. The opposite of this is *synchronous communication*, where two or more parties are communicating simultaneously and interactively; that is, in *real time*.

Atlas: A *collection* of maps that often includes some geographical *information*. See also *Map*.

At-risk: A term used to refer to students who have a higher than average possibility of dropping out of or failing *school*. These students may include inner-city, low-income, and special-needs children as well as those for whom English is not a native *language*.

Attachment: A *file* that is transmitted through an *electronic mail* message.

Attention deficit disorder (ADD): A condition of an individual marked by inattention, problems staying on task, and difficulty focusing on conversations and activities. See also *Attention deficit hyperactivity disorder*.

Attention deficit hyperactivity disorder (ADHD): A condition of an individual marked by hyperactivity, inability to control behavior, and constant movement as well as the symptoms of *attention deficit disorder*.

Attention span: The length of time an individual is able to concentrate on a task such as listening, taking notes, or using a skill.

Audio: The sound portion of various forms of *media* such as *television*, computers, *videotape*, or *film*. See also *Video*.

Audio dub: An *editing* technique used to erase the *audio* track on a *videotape* and replace it with another audio *track*.

Audio head: A magnetic element in a *cassette tape* recorder that records or plays back sound.

Audio mixer: An electronic component that combines sound from two or more sources.

Audiocassette: A tape that has only sound (*audio*) and is contained inside a plastic cover. It is played by using an audiocassette player. See also *Micro/minicassette*.

Audioconferencing: A teleconference using voice-only communications. A telephone call links two or more sites. In most cases standard telephone lines and speaker phones are used. Formerly called a conference call. See also *Teleconferencing*.

Audiotape: Mylar plastic tape on which sound (*audio*) is encoded. Because the tape is covered with iron oxide, the sound can be encoded as magnetic signals.

Audio/video mixer (A/V mixer): An electronic component that can combine *audio* and *video* and may also permit *editing*, the creation of special effects, and the addition of *graphics* and *text*.

Audiovisual (AV): Refers to both the *audiovisual hardware* such as a *cassette tape* player or *videocassette recorder* and the *audiovisual software* such as CD-ROM or *cassette tape*.

Audiovisual hardware: Refers to the equipment, such as the *filmstrip* projector, *cassette tape* player, *videocassette recorder*, or *computer*, that either plays or accesses *information* from the *audiovisual software*.

Audiovisual material: See *Audiovisual software*.

Audiovisual software: Nonprint materials, such as *videotape*, CD-ROM, or *filmstrip*, that need specific *hardware* to be used. Synonymous with audiovisual material. See also *Audiovisual hardware*.

Audiovisual specialist: The person in the *library media center* who is responsible for the *audiovisual software* and the *audiovisual hardware* necessary for using the *audiovisual* software.

Auditory learner: Refers to a type of learner who learns primarily by hearing. Lectures, audiotapes, and records are useful to this type of learner. See also *Learning style*.

AUP: See *Acceptable Use Policy*.

Authentic assessment: A type of student *evaluation* involving a performance by the student that demonstrates the desired outcome or behavior in the context of a real-life situation. The student is required to perform a task or learn a body of material. Portfolios, interviews, performances, and tests can be examples of authentic assessment. See also *Assessment*.

Authentic learning: Refers to meaningful *learning* in which students solve real-world problems or challenging tasks. *Higher order thinking skills* are required instead of rote memorization. Students are able to organize and prioritize, to demonstrate problem-solving skills, and to work with others.

Author: The person chiefly responsible for the intellectual or artistic content of a *work*. Examples of a personal author are a writer of a *book*, an artist, or a composer. See also *Joint author*.

Author entry: The name of the *author* of a *work* used as an *entry* in the library *catalog*. In most cases, this is used as the *main entry* for a *bibliographic record*.

Author number: A system used in most library media centers to arrange items in alphabetical order on the shelf. Typically, the first three letters of the *main entry*, which is usually the author's last name (Blu for Blume), are used with the *classification number*. It is sometimes called the *book number*.

Authoring language: A computer *language* used for creating *computer-assisted instruction* quickly and easily. Two examples are Authorware and HyperCard.

Authoring system: See *Authoring language*.

Authority control: The process of establishing consistent access points. Various forms of headings are grouped under a designated *heading* to ensure consistency. The process is used with personal names, corporate bodies, titles, series, and subject headings. See also *Access point*.

Authority file: A *file* containing the official forms of names, uniform titles, series titles, or *subject* headings, or all of these, used as access points in a library *catalog*. The purpose is to maintain consistent headings. Cross-references to variant forms not used as access points are indicated. See also *Access point* and *Cross-reference*.

Autobiography: The story of a person's life written by the *subject* of the *book*. See also *Biography*.

Automatic focus: A feature on most cameras, video cameras, and camcorders that automatically makes minor adjustments to the *focal length*; this feature eliminates the need to focus the *camera* manually.

Automation: The use of computers to manage library media operations such as *circulation* and *cataloging*. See also *Integrated Library System*.

Auxiliary table: In classification of materials, a table of subdivisions intended to be used with numbers from the main *schedules*. There are several auxiliary tables. Two examples are the Table of Standard Subdivisions and the Table of Geographic Areas and Persons.

AV: See *Audiovisual*.

A/V mixer: See *Audio/video mixer*. ■

Baby N connector (BNC): A twist lock device that is used to connect *coaxial cable*. It can be used for a video connector.

Back issue: An issue of a *periodical* that precedes the current *issue*.

Back light: 1. Light used in photography that is used behind the subject or is focused on the background. It adds contrast and creates a three-dimensional effect. 2. A feature on some camcorders that will increase the *video* signal to compensate for subjects who are not well lighted. See also *Fill light* and *Key light*.

Back order: An order to purchase material that is not currently available. The *publisher* or distributor will supply the item(s) at a later date.

Backbone: The primary, highest level infrastructure of an electronic *network* where secondary network systems feed in and out. For example, a K-12 school *local area network* might feed into (and take from) a state-operated backbone.

Back-to-Basics: A movement whose advocates stress a return to the basic subjects such as *reading*, *writing*, and mathematics. The number of electives should be reduced, and all courses should have high *standards*. Declining *test* scores and the lowering of academic standards led to these concerns.

Backup: A procedure for making a duplicate *copy* of a software *program* or a data *file*. The duplicate copy is available in case the original is corrupted, destroyed, or lost. Library media specialists should maintain backup records of *circulation* daily and *cataloging* records biweekly or as often as possible after each cataloging session. Automatic backups may be set on the *computer* so that, for example, after 50 circulation transactions, the *data* are automatically backed up on the internal *disk drive*. Backup data may be stored on floppy disks or *streaming tape*. See also *Floppy disk*.

Backup power supply: A battery-powered device that provides power to a *computer* when the normal AC power fails.

Balance: 1. The harmonious arrangement of the visual elements in a *work* of art. 2. The proper relationship between the level of two sound sources or among the level of more than two sound sources.

Ballad: Developed during the Middle Ages in Europe, the ballad is a form of *narrative* folk song. Modern ballads are poems that are *read* instead of sung. See also *Poetry*.

Band: A range of frequencies used for transmitting a signal. A band is identified by its lower and upper limits. For example, a 10-MHz band in the 100- to 110-MHz range. See also *Frequency*.

Bandwidth: The amount of *information* that a cable or electronic system can transmit at one time. For example, a telephone cable with a narrow bandwidth might be able to handle only one telephone call at a time; a cable with a wide bandwidth might handle 100 calls at one time. Higher bandwidths can carry more information than lower bandwidths. It is the difference between the highest and lowest frequencies that a system can transmit. The difference is measured in cycles per second (*hertz*) or *bits per second* (bps).

Banned book: A *book* that has been removed or prohibited from a *library media center*. See also *Challenged material*.

Banned Books Week: An annual promotion celebrating the freedom to *read*. It is sponsored by the *American Booksellers Association*, the American Booksellers Foundation for Free Expression, the *American Library Association*, the American Society of Journalists and Authors, the Association of American Publishers, and the National Association of College Stores. The event is also endorsed by the Center for the Book of the *Library of Congress*. These groups sponsor this week, typically in September, to draw attention to the importance of *access* to all types of *information* in a free society.

Barcode: Small, parallel vertical lines that a *scanner* can *read* and interpret. Items and patrons in the *library media center* are assigned barcode numbers. Barcodes can be entered into the *computer* either electronically using a scanner or by manually keying in the numbers. See also *Dumb barcode* and *Smart barcode*.

Barcode reader: See *Barcode scanner*.

Barcode scanner: A device used to *read* or enter, or both, a *barcode* number into a *computer*. Also called a barcode reader. See also *Scanner*.

Base number: A number designated in *Dewey Decimal Classification* to which a number from the auxiliary tables may be added. See also *Auxiliary table*.

Batch processing: A process in which *computer* records are grouped together and processed together at one time. In a *library media center*, the printing of *overdue* notices may be a batch process.

Batchelder Award: An award given annually by the *Association for Library Service to Children*, a division of the *American Library Association*, to a U.S. *publisher* of the year's most outstanding *book* that is a translation of a book first published in another country. The award, which began in 1966, is named for Mildred L. Batchelder, a former executive director of the Association for Library Service to Children.

Baud rate: The number of bits a modem can send or receive per second. It is a redundant reference to baud because baud is a rate. The term is derived from the name of Emil Baudot, a nineteenth-century inventor. The higher the number for the baud rate, the faster *data* are transmitted. Only at slower speeds are the baud rate and the *bits per second* (bps) synonymous. At higher speeds, more bps can be transmitted than the baud rate. Therefore, baud is outdated, and bits per second is the more current term. See also *MOdulator-DEModulator*.

BBS: See *Bulletin board system*.

Beast tale: A type of *folktale* in which animals act and talk like human beings. "Little Red Hen," "Three Little Pigs," and "Three Billy Goats Gruff" are examples.

Behavior modification: Techniques used to attempt to change the behavior of individuals or groups. Desirable behavior is reinforced with rewards, and undesirable behavior is usually eliminated by lack of reward or by punishment.

Behavioral objective: See *Performance objective*.

Behaviorism: A school of psychology that believes only observable behavior should be objectively studied. It is opposed to the subjective study of introspection. John Watson and B. F. Skinner were two well-known psychologists who promoted behaviorism.

Belpre Award: An award given biennially to a children's *book* published in the United States or Puerto Rico to recognize an outstanding original *work* written or illustrated by a Latino/Latina *author* or *illustrator* that portrays and celebrates the Latino/Latina cultural experience. It is cosponsored by the *Association for Library Service to Children* and the National

Association to Promote Library Services to the Spanish Speaking (REFORMA). Named for Pura Belpre, the first Latina librarian from the New York Public Library, the award began in 1996.

Beta: A half-inch *videotape* format that was formerly made primarily for home use. However, the VHS *format* is the current one in use. See also *Video home system*.

Beta Phi Mu: A national professional honor society for *library science* founded in 1948. Annual meetings are held in conjunction with the *American Library Association*. With chapters organized in most states, the society provides scholarships and bestows the annual Distinguished Service to Library Education Award.

Beta testing: The second test of a *software* product performed by users in real situations. These tests are performed after the manufacturers have conducted alpha tests. Beta testing is the final *test* before the product is released for sale by the manufacturer. See also *Alpha testing*.

BI: See *Bibliographic instruction*.

Biannual: A *serial* that is published twice a year.

Bibliographer: One who prepares bibliographies (i.e., lists of items) on a specific *topic* or by a specific *author*. See also *Bibliography*.

Bibliographic: Refers to the creation and management of records describing items in a *library* or *database*.

Bibliographic citation: The complete *information* about an item written according to the *format* listed in a recognized *style manual*.

Bibliographic control: The process of creating, organizing, and maintaining records of items in the *library media center* to facilitate *access* to the items by the users.

Bibliographic data: See *Bibliographic information*.

Bibliographic database: Contains *author*, *title*, source, *subject*, and related *information* about a *document*, but not the *full text* of the document. An *abstract* may or may not be included.

Bibliographic description: The part of a *catalog* record that identifies the item it represents exclusive of access points, *call number*, and control number other than the *International Standard Book Number* and the *International Standard Serial Number*. See also *Access point* and *Library of Congress Control Number*.

Bibliographic information: The *information* that comprises a *bibliographic record*. Also referred to as bibliographic *data*.

Bibliographic instruction (BI): *Instruction* that is designed to teach *library* users effective ways to locate and use *information* in a *library media center*. Sometimes called library instruction.

Bibliographic level: 1. One of three standard styles of description prescribed by AACR2R, each containing varying amounts of *bibliographic information* from the least (level 1) to the most (level 3). 2. In MARC *format*, a *fixed field* identified by the prefix "Bib lvl," which indicates whether an item is monographic or serial. See also *Machine-readable cataloging*.

Bibliographic network: A group of libraries that shares a computerized *database* of *bibliographic information* or whose individual *bibliographic* databases are electronically linked, or both.

Bibliographic record: A *catalog* record that contains complete *cataloging* information for an item in the *library media center*. See also *Bibliographic information*, *Entry*, and *Machine-readable cataloging record*.

Bibliographic utility: A group of electronically linked libraries that generates new *catalog* records. This group comprises a *network* to provide a *bibliographic database* to members. The *database* may be used for verifying *information*, for *cataloging*, for *retrospective conversion*, and for *interlibrary loan*. Examples of bibliographic utilities include *OCLC Online Computer Library Center, Inc.* and *Research Libraries Information Network* (RLIN).

Bibliography: A list of items such as books and periodicals on a particular *subject* or by a specific *author*. For lists that contain material in other formats, the term *mediagraphy* is sometimes used. See also *Subject bibliography* and *Webliography*.

Bibliophile: One who loves books.

Bibliotherapy: Using books to address the intellectual, emotional, and personality development of the reader. The readers often gain insights that assist in understanding themselves and others.

Bid: An offer by a company to provide goods or services at a particular price. Generally, state laws govern which goods and services must be bid. For example, *library media center* books may be exempt from a bid law, but furniture and equipment may have to be bid.

Bidding: The process of obtaining prices for goods or services from various companies to purchase the desired goods or services at the best price. See also *Formal bidding* and *Informal bidding*.

Bidirectional microphone: A type of *microphone* that picks up sound in front of and behind itself, but does not pick up sound from the side.

Biennial: A *serial* published every two years.

Big Six: A *model* that assists students with *problem solving* and is used in the *teaching* of *information literacy skills*. The six steps in the model are Task Definition, Information Seeking Strategy, Location and *Access*, Use of *Information*, *Synthesis*, and *Evaluation*. The model, developed by Michael Eisenberg and Robert Berkowitz, was presented in their 1990 book entitled *Information Problem-Solving: the Big Six Skills Approach to Library & Information Skills Instruction*. See also *Information literacy process models*.

Bilingual education: An educational *program* that uses two languages for *instruction*. One *language* is the student's native language, and the other is English.

Binary code: A code that represents any *information* with only two digits, 0 and 1. Once the information is converted to the binary code, it can be read by a *computer*.

Binary file: Any *computer* file that is not a *text file*. The *file* contains *data* or *program* instructions in a computer-readable *format*. The opposite of a binary file is an ASCII file. See also *American Standard Code for Information Interchange file* and *Graphics file*.

Binary number system: A numbering system with a base of 2. The binary numbers of 0 and 1 are used to encode *information* to be *read* by a *computer*.

Bindery: A company that binds periodicals or rebinds books. See also *Binding*, *Book*, and *Periodical*.

Binding: A method of placing a cover on the pages of a *book* or on a *volume* (several issues) of a *periodical*. See also *Bindery*, *Library binding*, and *Trade book*.

Biographical dictionary: An alphabetical list of selected individuals. Entries are primarily in *data* format with brief *information*. People are included based on the scope and purpose of the resource. *Webster's New Biographical Dictionary* is an example.

Biographical directory: An alphabetical list of selected individuals. Entries are primarily in *data* format and often contain more *information* than a *biographical dictionary*. People are included based on the scope and purpose of the resource. The directories are among the most frequently used of all the biographical *resources*. *Who's Who in America* is an example.

Biographical sources: Materials used to locate *information* about an individual. Sources may include individuals who are alive or deceased. The scope and the purpose of the source indicate the coverage. Entries may be in *data* format, which is brief, factual information such as birth date and address. The *Who's Who* series is an example of this *format*. Entries may also be in essay format, which is a long, *narrative* article. *Current Biography* is an example of this format.

Biography: The story of a person's life written by another individual. See also *Autobiography* and *Collective biography*.

Bit: A term that is a contraction for BInary DigiT. It is the smallest unit of *information* in a digital *computer*. A binary digit represents either 0 or 1. Generally, 8 bits form a *byte* or one *character*.

Bitmap: The representation of a graphic *image* as a set of bits. The image is stored in the computer's *memory* as a pattern of dots. Each dot in a pattern corresponds to a *bit*. Images scanned into a *computer* are turned into bitmaps, and any picture on a *Web page* is a bitmap.

Bits per second (bps): The speed at which *data* are transferred. The higher the speed, the faster the *transmission* of data. The use of bps is a common method of measuring the speed of a modem; it describes how many bits a modem can send or receive per second. A 28.8 modem transmits data at speeds up to 28,800 bits per second. See also *Baud rate*, *Bit*, and *MOdulator-DEModulator*.

Block grant: A type of *grant* that does not specify or earmark funds for a specific purpose, used mainly by state and federal governments. The recipient has considerable latitude over how the funds will be allocated and spent.

Block scheduling: Class periods that have been increased from the traditional 45 or 50 minutes to longer periods such as 1.5 hours. The students take fewer courses per day for only one semester.

Blocking software: *Software* that electronically screens out network-supplied material deemed offensive, indecent, or obscene. When such software is used, targeted material will not appear on the user's *desktop computer*. Some computer software prohibits *access* to certain *Internet* sites or prohibits searching Internet sites using specific keywords. The software is also known as a filter or filter software. The *American Library Association* opposes the use of blocking software. *Access to Electronic Information, Services, and Networks*, one of the Association's interpretations of the *Library Bill of Rights*, states its position on access to electronic *resources*. See also *Keyword*.

Bloom, Benjamin: See *Bloom's taxonomy*.

Bloom's taxonomy: A classification of educational *objectives* that Benjamin Bloom developed in the 1950s. The classification divides *learning* into three domain areas of *cognitive domain*, *affective domain*, and *psychomotor domain*.

Blurb: The description of a *book* that is usually located on the dust jacket of a *hardback* book or on the back of a *paperback* book. The blurb may also contain *author* information. See also *Book jacket*.

BNC: See *Baby N connector*.

Board: See *Circuit board*.

Board of education: The elected or appointed officials responsible for governing a *school system*. The *superintendent of schools* reports to this body. School board is a commonly used term for this entity.

Board of Education, Island Trees (New York) Union Free School District 26 v. *Pico*: A 1982 Supreme Court case related to the free speech issue in the First Amendment. Five students (including Stephen Pico) challenged the *school* board's removal of nine *library* books in 1975. The district court granted a summary judgment (a decision based on the facts without a trial) in favor of the *board of education*. The Second Circuit Court of Appeals reversed the decision and remanded the case for trial. In a 5-4 vote, the Supreme Court affirmed that decision for a trial. In so doing, the justices wrote varied opinions. The plurality opinion stated that students have the right to *information*. Books cannot be removed simply because the school board disagrees with the ideas in them. Although the case was never tried in the lower courts, it is still cited as an affirmation of the First Amendment in relation to books in a school *library media center*.

Book: A written or printed *work* on consecutive sheets of paper, parchment, or other material fastened or bound together. A book may be bound with hard covers or paper covers. See also *Binding*, *Electronic book*, *Hardback*, and *Paperback*.

Book card: The card used in library media centers that are not automated to record the name of the *borrower* and the date on which the *book* is due to be returned to the *library media center*. It generally contains the *title, author, call number*, and *accession number* of the book. When used in library media centers that are not automated, the card is kept in the *book pocket* when the book is not checked out, and it is filed in file drawers by *date due* when the book is checked out.

Book catalog: A *catalog* printed in a *book* format.

Book fair: An exhibit of books for sale. Many library media centers schedule book fairs to encourage *reading* and to raise money. Several companies and some bookstores provide books and services for book fairs.

Book jacket: The paper cover that fits around and is detachable from a *hardback* book. It may be called a jacket or dust jacket. It usually contains the *blurb* with the description of the *book* and sometimes, information about the *author*.

Book jobber: See *Jobber*.

Book number: Part of a *call number*. It is used to arrange materials with the same *classification number* in alphabetical order. Most library media centers use an *author number*, which is the first three letters of the *main entry*. Larger libraries use a *Cutter number* composed of letters and numbers.

Book pocket: A paper pocket glued onto the rear endpaper or inside the rear cover of a *book* in library media centers that are not automated. The *book card* is placed in the book pocket when the book is not in *circulation*. See also *End papers*.

Book review: A critique of a *book*. *Literary elements* such as *plot, theme, setting*, and *characterization* are discussed for a *work* of *fiction*. Objectivity, accuracy, authenticity, and *writing* style are elements covered in the *review* of a *nonfiction* work. Published reviews are important *resources* for the *selection* of materials and for *collection development* in school library media centers.

Book talk: A short, oral presentation of a *book* designed to entice listeners to *read* the book.

Book truck: A cart that contains two or three shelves for holding *library* materials. Because it is on wheels, the cart can be moved to various locations within the *library media center*.

Bookmark: 1. A piece of material, such as paper, leather, or ribbon, placed between the pages of a *book* to mark one's place of *reading*. 2. A feature in *Gopher* and the *World Wide Web* browsers that allows users to "mark" frequently visited locations so that they may revisit without searching for or reentering the identifying *address*. See also *Browser*.

Bookmobile: A vehicle that carries books and other materials to various areas in or near a community. Many public libraries offer bookmobile services to patrons who do not live near the main *library* or its branches.

Boolean logic: A system of logic named for George Boole, a British mathematician. Most *online searching* uses Boolean logic to develop *search* strategies. Logical operators—AND, OR, and NOT—are used to indicate relationships among search terms or sets of citations. Venn diagrams are used to indicate the relationships that result from using these logical operators. The operators are commonly referred to as *Boolean operators*. See also *Citation*, *Search strategy*, and *Venn diagram*.

Boolean operators: The logical functions AND, OR, and NOT used as part of a *search strategy* that allows users to define and limit the scope of their searches. The operator AND retrieves only items with both terms; OR retrieves items with either term, and NOT retrieves items with one term and not the other. See also *Implied Boolean operators* and *Nested Boolean logic*.

Boolean search: Using the logical functions AND, OR, and NOT to expand or narrow a *search* in an electronic *database*. The operators AND and NOT narrow a search. The operator OR expands a search. Searches that use these operators, such as between keywords, tend to produce a relevant and manageable list of hits. See also *Hit* and *Keyword search*.

Boot: Abbreviated from the term bootstrap, it means to start or restart the *computer*. Bootstraps help to pull boots on; booting the computer helps it to receive its initial instructions. To boot the computer means to load the *operating system* that starts the computer. A boot may be a *cold boot* or a *warm boot*.

Borrower: A person who checks out material from a *library media center*.

Bounce: An *electronic mail* message that is returned because a delivery error "bounces" it back to the original sender. Mistakes in an e-mail *address* or a problem in a *network* may cause a delivery failure.

Bps: See *Bits per second*.

Brain-based learning: A term based on neuroscience *research* to indicate how *learning* occurs. Because the brain searches for meaning, patterns, and connections, these elements should be part of the *teaching* process. Because the brain can process different types of *information* at one time, integrated learning experiences are better than isolated details of information. Emotions are important because learning will be impeded if there is a threatening atmosphere; however, challenging experiences promote learning.

Brainstorm: A method of gathering the ideas of a group where all ideas are shared and may then be grouped and prioritized. The technique is useful in gaining the expertise of all members of the group to secure a maximum number of ideas for use in *problem solving*, innovation efforts, and design activities, among others.

Branching: The ability to jump or branch from one location in a software *program* to another.

Bridge: 1. A device, often leased through a telephone company, that links three or more telephone lines together for *audioconferencing*. 2. A *computer* or other device that links two or more local area networks (LANs). See also *Local area network*.

Broadband: *Telecommunications* channels that carry a wide range of frequencies at a high rate of speed. *Cable television*, for example, uses broadband *transmission*. See also *Narrowband*.

Broadcast television: Television stations that allow viewers to receive free programs on any *television* set with, perhaps, the addition of a special antenna. See also *Cable television* and *Public television*.

Broader term (BT): A *cross-reference* from one *subject heading* to another subject heading that is more general in nature. For example, under the subject heading Robins there may be a cross-reference or *see reference* to the *heading* Birds. See also *Narrower term* and *Related term*.

Brownout: A partial loss of electrical power to a *computer* (along with other equipment that relies on electricity), usually caused by excessive electrical demand.

Browser: Computer *network* interface *software* that enables navigation (browsing) of the *World Wide Web* on the *Internet*. Browsers can be either *text* or *graphics* based. A graphical browser can display graphics as well as text. Two graphical browsers are Netscape Navigator and Internet Explorer. Synonymous with Web browser.

Browsing: 1. Viewing *file* names in a disk *directory*. 2. Viewing file contents. 3. Examining *library* materials in a random and unsystematic fashion. 4. Moving from one *hyperlink* to another on the *World Wide Web*. Navigating the Web may be unstructured or it may be structured by using a hierarchical *subject* list in a directory.

BT: See *Broader term*.

Buckley Amendment: See *Family Educational Rights and Privacy Act*.

Budget: A financial plan that reflects the goals, *objectives*, and priorities of a *library media center*. A budget is developed for a specified time period (such as *fiscal year*, calendar year, or *school* year) to indicate the planned expenditures for that year based on anticipated income. Some types of budgets are *equipment budget, expansion budget, incremental budget, line-item budget, lump-sum budget, maintenance budget, object-of-expenditure budget, performance budget*, and *zero-based budget*. See also *Budget record keeping, Fiscal year, Long-range budget plan*, and *Planning, Programming, Budgeting System*.

Budget record keeping: Maintaining accurate *budget* records for the *library media center*. Good records enable the *library media specialist* to be informed of the status of budget expenditures. Manual records may be kept using paper forms to reflect expenditures. A computer *spreadsheet* is an alternative method for maintaining accurate records.

Buffer: A *memory* area where electronic *information* is temporarily stored as it is being transmitted between devices with different operating speeds. For example, *printer* buffers take information from the *computer, store* it, and gradually send it to be printed. See also *Operating speed*.

Bug: A *programming* error that causes a *computer* system to malfunction. Bugs may produce incorrect results, cause the system to perform erratically, or lead to failure of the entire system. A *hardware* problem is called a *glitch*. See also *Debug*.

Bulletin board system (BBS): An electronic messaging system or clearinghouse where account holders may post public notices in much the same manner as paper notices are posted on a conventional bulletin board. Some BBS systems are local in scope; others, such as USENET newsgroups, are very broad-based BBS systems. These systems can be reached via a modem. See also *MOdulator-DEModulator* and *Newsgroup*.

Bus: 1. A channel between multiple devices that allows electronic signals to be sent from one connected component to any others. The term is named for a bus that stops at all bus stops on the route; all the electronic signals on the bus go to all the devices connected to it. The size of the bus (its width) determines the amount of *data* it can transmit at the same time. 2. A *topology* for a *local area network* in which there is a central cable to which all computers are connected. Data are transmitted simultaneously by one *workstation* through the central cable to all the other workstations. If one *node* fails, the rest of the local area network is not affected.

Button: 1. A *key* on the *keyboard* that is pushed to activate a function. 2. A part of a *mouse* that is clicked to perform a function.

Byte: A grouping or series of eight bits used as a unit of measurement with computers. A byte is treated as a single unit or *character* by a *computer;* it holds the equivalent of a single character such as the letter C or a question mark. It is the sequence of ones and zeroes in a byte that determines the character. See also *Bit.* ∎

Cable television: *Television* signals received locally with a *satellite dish* or a main antenna. The signals are sent through wires to cable subscribers who pay a monthly fee to *access* the programs. See also *Broadcast television*, *Interactive cable television*, and *Public television*.

Cache: (Pronounced "cash"). An area of *random access memory* (RAM) that stores frequently used *data* or *program* instructions. It allows for fast *information retrieval*.

Caddy: A plastic case or tray into which a CD-ROM *disc* is placed before it is inserted into a CD-ROM disc drive of some computers. Newer computer models may not require a caddy as the disc is placed in an open tray. See also *Compact disc-read only memory* and *Jewel box*.

CAI: See *Computer-assisted instruction*.

Caldecott Award: An award presented annually by the *Association for Library Service to Children*, a division of the *American Library Association*, to the *illustrator* of the most distinguished American *picture book* published in the preceding year. The award, which began in 1938, is named after Randolph Caldecott, a British illustrator of children's books.

Call number: The shelf address of an item made up of its classification number and shelf marks. The number is composed of the letters, numbers, or symbols used to identify and locate an item. Generally, the two parts of a call number are the *classification number* (such as the *Dewey Decimal Classification* number or *Library of Congress Classification* number) and the *book number* (such as an *author number* or a *Cutter number*).

Camcorder: A contraction of *camera* and *recorder*, this term refers to a *video camera* and *videocassette recorder* combined into one portable unit.

Camera: In photography, a device consisting of a *lens* attached to a lightproof enclosure that holds *film*. When light is admitted to the enclosure through the lens, images are formed.

Capital outlay: Money spent to acquire or replace fixed assets such as land, buildings, and equipment. See also *Fixed asset*.

Capture: The process of collecting and saving *text* or image *data* to a *computer* from a remote system. Capturing data, or saving to a *disk*, allows the user to view or print *online* data at a later time.

Card catalog: A library *catalog* of cards in which each *entry*, or *record*, is printed or typed on a card. The card catalog has been replaced in most library media centers by an automated catalog. See also *Online catalog*.

Career education: A program to prepare students for careers. Aptitude tests are often given to relate students' natural aptitudes and their academic courses to the world of work.

Carnegie Award: See *Andrew Carnegie Award*.

Carrel: An individual desk or cubicle designed for independent study or for viewing and listening purposes in a *library media center* or classroom. A carrel that is wired with electric power for viewing and listening is often called a wet carrel.

Cartography: The art of mapmaking. See also *Map*.

Cartridge: 1. A plastic single-core container for 16-mm or 35-mm microfilm. *Microfilm* from the cartridge is automatically threaded onto a take-up spool built into the reader. 2. A container for *magnetic tape* that is often used in microcomputer-based automated *library* systems to *backup* data from the *hard drive*. 3. A plastic cover for *audiotape*, *loop tape*, and *videotape*. 4. Various types of *computer* printers have a cartridge that holds ink or toner. See also *Ink cartridge* and *Toner cartridge*.

Caseload: The number of students assigned to *school* personnel, such as special education teachers and counselors, to receive a certain type of service.

Cassette tape: Thin strips of plastic tape enclosed in a double-core container with both a supply and take-up spool in a single housing. See also *Audiotape* and *Videotape*.

Catalog: 1. To create *bibliographic* records for items to be added to a *library media center*. 2. A set of bibliographic records that represents the holdings of a library *collection*. It may be arranged by *classification number*, *alphabet*, or *subject*. The catalog may be in various forms such as a *card catalog*, a *book catalog*, or an *online catalog*. See also *Classed catalog*, *Dictionary catalog*, *Divided catalog*, and *Omni catalog*.

Cataloger: A librarian who catalogs items by using descriptive *information*, *subject* headings, and a *classification system* to assign a *classification number*. See also *Descriptive cataloging* and *Subject heading*.

Cataloging: The process of preparing material for the *library* shelves. This process includes describing items for a *bibliographic record*; determining the *main entry*, and assigning added entries, *subject* headings, and a *call number*. See also *Added entry*, *Machine-readable cataloging*, and *Subject heading*.

Cataloging profile: Specification preferences requested by vendors of library media specialists to *catalog* and process newly ordered items so that they will be consistent with the remainder of the *collection*.

Cataloging workstation: A *computer* on a *network* that is dedicated to *cataloging* functions. Cataloging *information* can be found by accessing records on the network and by using CD-ROM *bibliographic* databases such as Precision One, Alliance Plus, or Bibliofile.

Cataloging-in-Publication (CIP): A *program* sponsored by the *Library of Congress* and cooperating publishers that makes partial *cataloging* information available before items are published. Each *book* has a partial *bibliographic description* on the *verso* of the *title page*.

Cathode ray tube (CRT): An electronic tube that displays visual images and *graphics*. When equipped with a *keyboard*, it can be used to input *data* into a *computer* and view the data *output*. Also called video display terminal. See also *Input*.

Cathode ray tube projector (CRT projector): A *monitor* that does not use liquid crystals but uses red, green, and blue tubes.

CAV: See *Constant Angular Velocity*.

CBC: See *Children's Book Council*.

CCTV: See *Closed circuit television*.

CD: See *Compact disc*.

CD-DA: See *Compact disc-digital audio*.

CD-I: See *Compact disc-interactive*.

CD-R: See *Compact disc-recordable*.

CD-ROM: See *Compact disc-read only memory*.

CD-ROM drive: See *Compact disc-read only memory drive*.

CD-ROM tower: See *Compact disc-read only memory tower*.

CD-RW: See *Compact disc-rewritable*.

Cell: 1. A small geographic area used in a cellular system. 2. The intersection of a row and a column in a *spreadsheet*. See also *Cellular phone*.

Cell phone: See *Cellular phone*.

Cellular phone: The first *wireless* telephone based on a *cellular system* that currently transmits by means of *digital* signals. This *technology* enables the cell phone to become a *smart phone* that can even provide *access* to the *Internet*. In a cell phone system, many base stations are used, with each one covering a *cell* or small geographic area that slightly overlaps adjacent cells at the borders. The multiple cells allow the same frequencies to be re-used in different cells within a same location. See also *Digital signal* and *Hand-held device*.

Cellular system: A communications system that currently transmits primarily by means of *digital* signals. The system uses multiple base stations or cells to cover a geographic area. Calls made by a *cellular phone* user are "handed off" to the next station as the mobile phone user travels to new locations. See also *Cell* and *Digital signal*.

Censorship: Limiting *access* to material as a result of a challenge. The limited access may include removing the item from the *library media center* or restricting the item's use (parental permission or reserve shelf, for example). The *American Library Association* opposes censorship, and the *Library Bill of Rights* with its various interpretations states the policy and philosophy of the national association. See also *Challenged material*, *Freedom to Read Foundation*, *Freedom to Read Statement*, *Freedom to View Statement*, *Intellectual freedom*, *National Coalition Against Censorship*, and *Office for Intellectual Freedom*.

Central office: The office of the superintendent of a *school system* and the personnel who staff that office. See also *Superintendent of schools*.

Central processing unit (CPU): The "brain" of a *computer*. The CPU is composed of the *arithmetic logic unit* (ALU), the *control unit* (CU), and *main memory* (RAM). These units work together to *store* information, execute instructions, and process *data*. Other names include *microprocessor*, microchip, or *chip*.

Central tendency: A statistical term used to indicate the single most typical score for a group of scores; it is the score around which other scores tend to cluster. The three measures of central tendency include the *mean*, *median*, and *mode*.

Centralized cataloging: See *Centralized processing*.

Centralized processing: The centralization of technical processes involved in preparing and *cataloging* items for use in library media centers. Materials for all school library media centers in a *school system* are processed at one central location. The term is synonymous with centralized cataloging.

Certificate of High School Equivalency: A type of diploma issued to an individual who did not complete formal high school but, by passing the *Tests of General Education Development* (GED), has fulfilled the requirements for high school graduation.

Certification: The process by which a state agency, generally the State Department of Education, grants a professional credential. Certification in library media typically requires either a bachelor's or master's degree and *teaching* experience.

Challenged material: Material that has received either or both of the following: (1) an oral complaint about the presence or appropriateness, or both, of the item in a *library media center* or (2) a written complaint, which is part of a formal process specified in a library media *selection policy*, about the item's presence or appropriateness. Materials are typically challenged because they contain sex, profanity, drugs, witchcraft, the occult, racism, ageism, sexism, lack of respect for authority, depressing scenes, and violence, among others. See also *Banned book* and *Censorship*.

Change agent: An individual who produces a change within a *school* or *school system*. The individual may be an outside professional or someone within the school or school system.

Character: A single letter, number, punctuation mark, or symbol. For a *computer*, a character is the equivalent of a *byte*.

Character education: Identified values that are taught as a part of the school *curriculum*. The objective is to encourage students to become responsible citizens.

Characterization: The literary element used by authors to develop characters in a story. Characters may be developed through narration, conversation, and action, among others. Believable characters that are real or lifelike are a sign of good *writing*. The more depth to a character, the more he or she seems to be human or real. Consistent characters are a sign of good writing. Whatever a character does should be consistent with the character's age, culture, and environment in the story. Growth and development of a character contributes to good characterization. As a story progresses, good writing will show that the characters change. Characters are often remembered long after the *plot, setting*, and *theme* have been forgotten. See also *Literary elements*.

Charge: To lend or to check out an item from a library media center's *collection*. See also *Circulation desk*, *Discharge*, *Loan*, and *Renew*.

Charging desk: See *Circulation desk*.

Chart: *Information* arranged in *outline*, graphic, or tabular *format*.

Chat: An *online* forum or conference that permits two or more users to conduct a "conversation" with each other. Each user takes a turn entering a *message* using the *keyboard*. Each keystroke is transmitted as it is pressed. Chats can take place on a *local area network*, a *bulletin board system*, or the *Internet*.

Chat room: An *online* location where "live" discussions or conversations occur via a computer *telecommunications* network (modem).

Check in: See *Discharge*.

Check out: See *Charge*.

Chief source of information: In *descriptive cataloging*, the main location from which *bibliographic* data are taken, such as the *title page* of a *book* or title *screen* of a computer *file*. AACR2R rules prescribe the places to look for this *bibliographic information* according to the type of material being cataloged. The chief source of information varies for different types of materials.

Children's Book Council (CBC): Founded in 1945 with headquarters in New York, New York, this group encourages the *reading* of children's books. Members are publishers of trade books for children and young adults. The group sponsors *Children's Book Week*, an annual celebration of *children's literature*, held in November. See also *Trade book*.

Children's Book Week: Sponsored by the *Children's Book Council*, a week in November is designated annually to publicize and promote *children's literature*.

Children's Choices Book Awards: Awards sponsored by the *International Reading Association* and the *Children's Book Council*. *School* children in different regions of the United States read newly published trade books and vote for their favorites. The list of winners for ages 5–13 is printed in the October issue of *The Reading Teacher*. See also *Trade book*.

Children's literature: Books and other materials in a diverse range of formats that are written or produced based on children's experience and understanding. See also *Young adult literature*.

Chip: A chip consists of a very small piece of silicon containing integrated circuitry with electrical paths of thin layers of gold or aluminum. Computers are made up of these chips placed on electronic boards called printed circuit boards. The set of electronic circuits is designed for use as processors and *memory* in computers. A CPU chip contains an entire processing unit. A *memory chip* contains blank memory. The term chip is used interchangeably with integrated circuit, microchip, and *microprocessor*. See also *Central processing unit* and *Circuit board*.

Chronological age: A person's actual age cited in years and months. The term is often used in evaluating *standardized test* results. For example, it is used in comparison with *mental age* to determine the IQ score of an individual. See also *Intelligence quotient*.

Cinquain: A five-line verse of *poetry* with specific structural requirements. Line 1—one *word* for the *title*; Line 2—two words that describe the title; Line 3—three words that express action related to the title; Line 4—four words that express a feeling about the title; and Line 5—one word that either repeats the title or expresses a word closely related to the title.

CIP: See *Cataloging-in-Publication*.

Circuit board: An insulated rigid card that holds chips and other electronic components. The main circuit board is also called a motherboard. The circuit board or motherboard contains slots into which smaller boards can be plugged. See also *Chip* and *Slot*.

Circuit breaker: A switch that automatically turns off the electrical current if there is an abnormal condition; for example, if the circuit becomes overloaded.

Circulation: The borrowing and returning of items in a *library media center*. See also *Charge* and *Discharge*.

Circulation desk: The area where items from the library media *collection* are checked out (charged) and checked in (discharged). See also *Charge* and *Discharge*.

Circulation system: The system that contains the *information* about an item, the *borrower*, and the *date due*. This may be either a manual or an automated system.

Citation: A reference to a source or to a part of a *text* from which a passage is quoted or used. See also *Bibliographic citation*, *Endnote*, and *Footnote*.

Claiming: The process of notifying a *jobber*, *publisher*, or *subscription agency* that *serial* issues have not been received.

Classed catalog: A *catalog* in which records are filed by classification numbers or subjects, such as a *shelflist*.

Classics: Books, stories, or audiovisuals that are of the highest quality and of enduring value and interest. These works have passed the test of time because people continue to purchase and *read* or view these outstanding works. Classics have memorable and believable characters that are genuinely entertaining, and the works convey feelings and thoughts in such a way that others can easily identify and place themselves in the place of the characters.

Classification: See *Classification system*.

Classification number: The number assigned to an item to indicate its *subject* and location in a *collection* of materials. Most library media centers use the *Dewey Decimal Classification* system. See also *Call number* and *Classification system*.

Classification schedule: The printed scheme of a particular *classification system*.

Classification system: A systematic scheme used to indicate the *subject* matter of the material as well as to assist in the physical placement of like subjects together on the shelf. Most library media centers use the *Dewey Decimal Classification* system, and large academic and public libraries use the *Library of Congress Classification* system.

Classify: To assign a *classification number* to a *library* item such as a *book*, *videotape*, *cassette tape*, or computer *program*.

Classroom management: A teacher *management* system that structures the daily operation of a classroom. This system enables the *teacher* to organize the daily schedule, the *instruction* program, and techniques for student discipline, among others, to facilitate *learning*.

Client: A computer *workstation* that runs programs and accesses *data* stored on another *computer* called a *file server*.

Client server network: A *computer* served by a *file server*. The server computer provides *resources* and file *storage* space for "*client*" computers to use interactively. Client programs interact with the user; the server programs operate in the background on behalf of multiple clients.

Clip art: Previously existing illustrations that can be used in a variety of publications. The art may be in a paper *format* or in an electronic format that allows the illustrations to be inserted into a *document*. Clip art, both paper and electronic, can be obtained from numerous commercial sources.

Clipboard: An area in a computer's *memory* where *cut* or copied *text* and *graphics* can be temporarily stored before being moved to another location in the same *document* or into a new document. This *information* stored in the clipboard is lost if not pasted to a document before other information is moved to the clipboard. See also *Copy* and *Paste*.

Clone: A term used to describe a *computer* that strongly resembles or is highly compatible with a major brand of computers. A "no-name clone" is a system assembled from standard components that are obtained from various companies.

Closed circuit television (CCTV): A *television* signal transmitted from a central site to television receivers connected to the central site by wires. It is often used in a *school* building or campus-wide.

Closed shelves: See *Closed stack*.

Closed stack: An area of shelves or a stack area containing materials that are not accessible to the public such as rare books and special collections. Synonymous with closed shelves. See also *Open stack*.

Close-up: A *camera* shot of a person's head and shoulders or a subject at close range. See also *Extreme close-up*.

Coaching: A *teaching* technique used to assist students in *learning* a skill. This technique permits a student to be actively involved in the learning process rather than being a passive receptor of *information*. The coach facilitates the learning process by helping a student ascertain what he or she needs to know and by encouraging the student to develop skills for himself or herself. See also *Peer coaching*.

Coaxial cable: Shielded metal cable capable of carrying large quantities of *data*, including *full-motion video*, over relatively long distances. This type of cable is typically used for *television* signal *transmission* by commercial *cable television* operations. It is also capable of carrying voice, *image*, and data signals and is used in a *local area network* to connect computers. See also *Fiber optic cable* and *Twisted pair cable*.

Code: 1. A set of machine symbols that represents *data* or instructions. 2. A representation of one set of data for another. 3. To write a *program*.

Code of Ethics: A *document* published by the *American Library Association* that is the standard of ethical conduct for all types of librarians. See also *Ethics*.

Cognition: Processes of knowing and perceiving. Cognition includes how knowledge is acquired; how people learn.

Cognitive development: Refers to the intellectual development of an individual. Jean Piaget, a Swiss psychologist, developed a theory of cognitive development that describes four stages of growth. See also *Concrete operations*, *Formal operations*, *Preoperational period*, and *Sensory-motor period*.

Cognitive domain: One of the three domains included in a *taxonomy* by Benjamin Bloom. This domain includes behaviors that relate to the mental processes of recall, reasoning, comprehension, and judgment. A hierarchical order of thinking skills includes knowledge—basic recall; comprehension—an understanding of the meaning of an idea; application—the ability to use an idea in another context or in *problem solving*; analysis—the ability to reduce *information* into basic components and then demonstrate skills such as comparing and contrasting; *synthesis*—the capacity for combining the components of information in a different way to create a new product; and *evaluation*—the capability for using criteria to judge ideas. See also *Affective domain*, *Bloom's taxonomy*, and *Psychomotor domain*.

Cognitive psychology: A branch of psychology that studies how individuals acquire, process, and use *information*.

Cold boot: The process for starting a *computer* by turning on the power switch. See also *Boot* and *Warm boot*.

Collaboration: 1. Refers to the cooperative efforts between teachers and library media specialists to plan, develop, and implement *information literacy skills* into the classroom *curriculum*. 2. Refers to the relationship between schools and business fostered to achieve educational goals. These partnerships may result in additional *school* funding and school volunteers. See also *Cooperative planning*, *Cooperative teaching*, and *School partnerships*.

Collaborative planning: See *Cooperative planning*.

Collaborative teaching: See *Cooperative teaching*.

Collation: See *Physical description area*.

Collection: 1. The materials (in a variety of formats) located in a *library media center*. 2. The total number of items in a library media center. 3. The number of items on a specific *subject*, by a certain *author*, or in a certain *format*. See also *Anthology*.

Collection development: A process that requires knowing the *collection*, the *school*, the community, and the informational and instructional needs of the users. It encompasses more than the *acquisition* of materials, and it involves more than having a *selection policy*. The process includes formulating collection development policies to serve as guides for the *selection*, *acquisition*, and *evaluation* of *resources*. See also *Collection maintenance* and *Selection criteria*.

Collection maintenance: Specific, ongoing functions designed to preserve the material in a library media center *collection*. The *mending* and *binding* of materials are two examples. These activities are an aspect of *collection development*.

Collection mapping: A visual indication of the strengths and weaknesses of the *collection*. The visual might be a poster or a *computer* printout of bar graphs, pie charts, or columns of numerical *data*. Collection mapping reflects how well the media center collection serves the *curriculum*; it shows the strengths of the collection in relation to various curriculum topics. The collection size for certain topics can be compared to suggested national selection lists and national numbers for a collection.

Collective biography: Biographical *information* about more than one person. See also *Biography*.

Collective title: A *title* given to an item that contains several works.

Collective work: A *work* that includes (1) three or more independent parts by one *author* or (2) two or more independent parts by more than one author.

Colophon: *Information* at the end of a printed item or on the *verso* of the *title page* about the printer, typeface, grade of paper, *binding*, or names of those who contributed to the production of the *book*.

Colorado Study: A 1991-1992 and a 1998-1999 *research* project conducted on Colorado schools. *The Impact of School Library Media Centers on Academic Achievement* by Keith Curry Lance, et al. published by Hi Willow Research & Publishing in 1993 and *How School Librarians Help Kids Achieve Standards: the Second Colorado Study* by Keith Curry Lance, et al. published by Hi Willow Research & Publishing in 2000 report a direct connection between well-trained media specialists with good *media* collections and programs and higher student *test* scores. It is also referred to as the Lance Study for the principal investigator. Similar studies in Alaska and Pennsylvania reached the same conclusion.

COM: See *Computer output microform*.

Command: Instruction the user gives to the *computer* to perform a specific task.

Communication skills: The ability to exchange *information* and ideas effectively. Eye contact, body *language*, articulation, and attitude all contribute to effective communication.

Communications software: *Software* that connects two computers, allowing them to transmit *information*.

Compact disc (CD): 1. A *digital* audio *disc* introduced in 1982. The plastic disc is 4.75 inches in diameter and is recorded on one side. It contains up to 74 minutes of hi-fi stereo sound. The individual selections may be played in any sequence. It is more formally known as *compact disc-digital audio*. 2. A term that is used loosely for all compact disc formats.

Compact disc-digital audio (CD-DA): The more formal term for the original *compact disc* format. The designation CD-DA refers to a music *disc* as opposed to other CD formats that contain *data* such as CD-ROM, CD-R, and CD-RW. See also *Compact disc-read only memory*, *Compact disc-recordable*, and *Compact disc-rewritable*.

Compact disc-interactive (CD-I): An *optical disc* that uses laser *technology* to store *text*, *audio*, and visual (still and motion) *data* that can be controlled by user commands. See also *Light Amplification by Stimulated Emission of Radiation*.

Compact disc-read only memory (CD-ROM): An *optical disc* format that holds *text*, *graphics*, and hi-fi stereo sound. It holds 650 MB of *data*, which is the approximate equivalent of 250,000 pages of text. Although it is similar to a *compact disc-digital audio*, it uses a different *track* format for data. A CD-ROM drive is needed to play it. CD-ROMs were originally used for reference works such as encyclopedias, but they are now used in *multimedia* applications and *software* distribution. Many *online* databases are also being produced on CD-ROM and are updated at regular intervals.

Compact disc-read only memory drive (CD-ROM drive): The drive on a *computer* that is used to *read* the *data* encoded on a CD-ROM *disc*. CD-ROM drives do not *retrieve* data as fast as computer *disk* drives. The speed of a CD-ROM drive is stated as a multiple of the original specification, which was a data transfer rate of 150 kilobytes per second. For example, if a drive functions at 16×, it is 16 times faster than the original specification. See also *Compact disc-read only memory* and *Disk drive*.

Compact disc-read only memory tower (CD-ROM tower): Multiple CD-ROM drives stacked together in one unit in which each drive is accessible over a *network*. See also *Compact disc-read only memory drive* and *Tower*.

Compact disc-recordable (CD-R): A *disc* that can be written only once. The disc can be *read* in a CD-ROM player. These discs are used for several purposes including archiving *data*.

Compact disc-rewritable (CD-RW): A *disc* that can be rewritten numerous times. The newer multiread CD-ROM drives are needed to *read* such a disc.

Compatible: A *computer* that is similar to or can be substituted for another. For example, a computer that is IBM PC-compatible can be substituted for an IBM PC.

Compendium: A *summary* of a larger *work*.

Compensatory education: Beginning in the 1960s, special programs were designed to reach children affected by poverty. Head Start is one such program.

Competency-based instruction: A type of *teaching* in which the goal is to enable learners to reach a satisfactory level of achievement by measuring their *learning* outcomes against the specific standard cited in the instructional *objectives*. May also be called performance-based *instruction* or criterion-referenced instruction.

Compiler: Someone who selects and puts together material written or produced by others.

Compound surname: A last name comprising two or more proper names, often connected by a hyphen, conjunction, or preposition.

Compressed file: A computer *file* that has been reduced in size by applying a *compression* program such as PKZIP. The user must decompress these files before using them. See also *Decompression* and *Unzip*.

Compression: Reduction of *data* (such as *video*, images, or *audio*) to allow for more efficient *storage* and *transmission*. Although compression saves *disk* space, it may also reduce the quality of the playback. See also *Decompression* and *Unzip*.

Compulsory school attendance age: The legal age span during which a child is required to attend *school*. A typical age range is ages 6–16.

Computer: A programmable machine that processes *data*. Its components include the *central processing unit* (CPU); *input* devices such as a *mouse* or *keyboard*; *storage* devices such as a *hard drive* and *secondary storage* such as a *floppy disk drive*; and *output* devices such as a *monitor* and a *printer*. Several types are *desktop computer*, *laptop computer*, *mainframe*, *microcomputer*, *notebook computer*, and *palmtop computer*.

Computer file: See *File*.

Computer hardware: See *Computer*.

Computer literacy: The knowledge of basic *computer* terminology, how they are used in society, and how to actually use a computer.

Computer multimedia system: See *Multimedia*.

Computer network: See *Network*.

Computer output microform (COM): The result of placing *information* produced by a *computer* onto *microfilm* or *microfiche*. See also *Microform*.

Computer software: See *Software*.

Computer virus: See *Virus*.

Computer-assisted instruction (CAI): A method of *teaching* by using *computer* programs. Generally, the *instruction* is self-paced using drills, tutorials, and tests with immediate feedback of the results.

Concept book: A juvenile *book* that describes various dimensions of an object, a class of objects, or an abstract idea. These books deal with such concepts as color, size, shapes, and opposites, among others.

Concordance: An alphabetical *index* of the principal words in a *book* or in the works of one *author*. The definitions and the *text* location are indicated, and the context of the words may be given.

Concrete operations: The third stage in Piaget's theory of *cognitive development*, covering approximately the 7–11 age period. Children in this age group are more flexible in their thinking. They can understand different points of view, and they are beginning to exercise reasoning and problem-solving skills. At this stage, children enjoy books that show young protagonists managing life experiences. See also *Formal operations*, *Preoperational period*, and *Sensory-motor period*.

Concrete poetry: A type of *poetry* in which the message of a *poem* is emphasized by the fact that the poem forms the shape of a picture. This arrangement of the words presents a shape that contributes to the meaning of the poem.

Condenser microphone: A type of *microphone* that has a diaphragm that moves in response to sound waves and then comes into contact with a metal disc. It picks up sound from any direction.

Conference: A meeting where two or more individuals convene to discuss various education-related issues such as staff and student *assessment* and behavior. Types of conferences include a combination of *teacher* and student, teacher and parent, *principal* and teachers, and principal and students, among others.

Conference call: See *Audioconferencing*.

Confidentiality of records: The concept that *library* files are not accessible to the public. Most states have a confidentiality of records law that prevents *circulation* records and *database* uses from being revealed unless a court subpoena is issued. Some of these state laws allow parents *access* to the records of their minor children.

Connect time: The length of time a user is connected to an *online service* such as America Online or Dialog.

Consequence: The result of a particular behavior. Desirable behaviors receive positive results, and negative behaviors receive negative results.

CONSER: See *Conversion of Serials*.

Consideration file: A list of items that have been identified by the *library media specialist* as short-range or long-range purchases.

Consortium: See *Library network*.

Constant Angular Velocity (CAV): A *videodisc* format that stores *information* in concentric rings of motion *video* and *audio* tracks on each side of the videodisc. This *format* allows users to *access* individual images by *frame* numbers. Videodiscs recorded in the CAV format can *store* a maximum of 30 minutes of motion on each side.

Constructive teaching: A *teaching* approach based on *research* that has indicated students learn best when their knowledge is obtained through *active learning*. Students "construct" knowledge and do not receive it from others. Therefore, this approach considers hands-on activities to be more beneficial than lectures. *Higher order thinking skills* are encouraged rather than memorization.

Constructivism: See *Constructive teaching*.

Content designation: The use of specific codes such as tags, indicators, and subfields to identify a particular item of *information* in a *machine-readable cataloging record* (MARC record). See also *Content designators*, *Indicator*, *Subfield*, and *Tag*.

Content designators: In the MARC *format*, characters or combinations of characters identifying specific parts of *bibliographic*, authority, or holdings records or the kinds of *data* held in them, or both. A *tag*, a *subfield code*, and an *indicator* are used to label and explain the *bibliographic record*. For example, 100 is the tag for the *author* field in a *machine-readable cataloging record* (MARC record). See also *Content designation*.

Contents page: The *page* at the front of a *book* or *serial* that lists the contents of the item and the sequence in which they appear. See also *Table of contents*.

Continuing education: *Instruction* designed to advance a person's knowledge after formal education has been completed.

Continuum: 1. A *serial* published on an irregular basis. 2. A list of suggested skills or *objectives* for specific grades, ages, or subjects.

Contrast ratio: The range of gray between the darkest and brightest part of a *television* screen. This comparison between the darkest and brightest part of the *screen* is expressed in a ratio such as 20:1.

Control field: A *field* in the MARC *format* identified by a *tag* beginning with the number 0. Control fields contain *information* such as *call number*, *International Standard Book Number* (ISBN), and *Library of Congress Control Number* (LCCN). See also *Machine-readable cataloging*.

Control unit: The area of the *central processing unit* (CPU) that controls all *computer* operations and the operations of the *input* and *output* devices.

Controlled vocabulary: A list of terms authorized for indexing such as a *subject heading* list or *thesaurus*. See also *Subject authority*.

Convergent thinking: Refers to a commonly used *test* that is scored for the "right" or "best" answer. Facts and reason produce a correct answer. It is the opposite of *divergent thinking*.

Conversion of Serials (CONSER): A program originally administered at the *Library of Congress* but later shifted to *OCLC Online Computer Library Center, Inc.*, whose objective is to build a national *database* of *catalog* records for serials and holdings. See also *Serial*.

Cookie: *Data* created by a *World Wide Web* server that are stored on a computer's *hard drive* without the user's permission. Cookies permit the *Web site* to follow a user's patterns and preferences. These data enable one *Web page* to give *information* to other Web pages. Because direct marketing companies are compiling information about a user's browsing habits, many are concerned about privacy issues.

Cooperative learning: A way of structuring student-to-student interaction so that students work together in groups. Students receive specific *instruction* in the organization and social skills necessary for the group to succeed. Students have the opportunity to evaluate how well their group is working. See also *Learning*.

Cooperative planning: *Collaboration* between teachers and library media specialists to integrate *information literacy skills* into the classroom *curriculum*. The term is used interchangeably with collaborative planning.

Cooperative teaching: Implementation of *information literacy skills* into classroom *instruction* by both the *teacher* and the *library media specialist*. The term is used interchangeably with collaborative teaching.

Copy: 1. A reproduction or a duplication of an original *work*. 2. To make a reproduction or duplicate. 3. In *word processing*, to reproduce *text* or *graphics* from one *document* to another. The *information* is copied to the *clipboard* to *paste* it into another document.

Copy stand: A vertical or horizontal device used to accurately position a *camera* for the photographing of flat subjects.

Copyright: A legal right given to authors, composers, or publishers to publish a *work* for a specified number of years. Copyright offers protection from the work being copied by others without permission. See also *Face-to-face teaching exemption*, *Fair use*, *Intellectual property*, and *License*.

Copyright date: The date a *copyright* is issued. This date is located on the *verso* of the *title page* in a *book*.

Core collection: A minimum number of titles in all formats that should be included in the library media center *collection*.

Core curriculum: Common course requirements for all students in areas such as English, math, science, or history. See also *Curriculum*.

Coretta Scott King Award: An award given annually to one African American *author* and one African American *illustrator* for outstanding contributions to *children's literature*. The award began in 1970 and is administered by the *Social Responsibilities Round Table*, a unit of the *American Library Association*.

Corporate body: A named group of people that acts as an entity; may include associations, conferences, institutions, and governments.

Corporate entry: The name of a *corporate body* used as a *main entry* or *added entry* in a *catalog*.

Counting book: A juvenile *book* that contains numbers and corresponding objects such as the number 3 with a picture of three clowns.

Course of study: A written guide that indicates what knowledge and skills are to be taught in a particular discipline at a particular grade level.

CPU: See *Central processing unit*.

Crash: 1. The physical destruction of a *hard disk*. Misalignment or dust contamination may cause the *read/write head* to collide with the disk's surface. As a result, *data* are destroyed, and both the *disk* platter and head must be replaced. 2. An abnormal termination of *program* execution. The computer locks up and must be rebooted. See also *Reboot*.

Criterion: A standard by which something can be judged. For example, it may be a standard with which scores on a testing instrument are compared or against which they are evaluated. For example, a criterion may be a standard in a *performance objective* that denotes how acceptable performance is judged; this standard might require a number of correct responses, or a time limit, or some qualitative judgment based on the satisfaction of the *teacher*.

Criterion-referenced assessment: Generally, a *test* that measures how well a student has learned a *subject*. The test score is compared to a standard or a criterion of performance. No comparison is made with other students. Many schools use criterion-referenced tests throughout the *curriculum*. An example is solving math problems with a certain degree of accuracy in a given time period. Another example is a road test taken to obtain a driver's license. See also *Assessment*, *Norm-referenced assessment*, and *Standardized test*.

Criterion-referenced instruction: See *Competency-based instruction*.

Critical thinking skills: The process of evaluating *information* and reaching an objective and logical conclusion. See also *Higher order thinking skills*.

Cross-platform: A software *program* that can run in both Macintosh and Windows environments.

Cross-reference: A *message* that directs a reader or user from one term to another. Cross-references are used in *library* catalogs and in reference materials such as an *encyclopedia*, a telephone book, and a *thesaurus*. Two types of cross-references are a *See reference* and a *See Also reference*. See also *Broader term*, *Narrower term*, and *Related term*.

CRT: See *Cathode ray tube*.

CRT projector: See *Cathode ray tube projector*.

Cultural literacy: Defined by E.B. Hirsch in the 1987 book *Cultural Literacy* as the body of knowledge about a culture that those of the culture should know to function in society.

Culture bias: A characteristic found in several segments of society. In educational testing, a *test* may contain items that are more familiar for one cultural subgroup than for others. *Media* formats, such as *literature* or videotapes, may contain subjective, stereotypical *information* or characters. The bias may be intentional or unintentional.

Cumulative index: An *index* in which several previously published indexes are combined to form a single, comprehensive index.

Cumulative tale: A type of *folktale* that features repetition of details with a quick ending. "The House That Jack Built" is an example.

Current: An up-to-date or timely item.

Current selection aids: Professional periodicals, published on a regular basis, which contain reviews of new *book* titles, periodicals, and *software* products. See also *Retrospective selection aids* and *Review*.

Curriculum: 1. The totality of ideas and activities designed by an educational institution to meet the *learning* needs of students and to achieve the desired educational goals. 2. A written plan that states the content of what students will be taught. 3. All the courses offered at a specific *school*. For example, an elementary school might have a curriculum of *language* arts, mathematics, science, and social studies. 4. All the courses offered at a school in a particular area of study. For example, a history curriculum might contain such courses as world history, U.S. history, and ancient history. See also *Core curriculum* and *Curriculum development*.

Curriculum development: A plan to establish educational goals; to decide course content, the *teaching* methods, and the *resources* needed to meet the goals; to implement the *curriculum* activities with the learners; and to evaluate the effectiveness of the curriculum and make adjustments when needed.

Curriculum integration: See *Integrated instruction*.

Cursor: A marker on a computer *monitor* that usually blinks or flashes to indicate where new *data* may be entered or where data may be changed or deleted. The *mouse* or the arrow keys will move the cursor on the *screen*. See also *Key*.

CU-See Me: A popular, public domain *videoconferencing* tool for the *Internet* developed at Cornell University.

Cut: To remove part of *text* or *graphics* and *store* it in the *clipboard*. See also *Cut and paste.*

Cut and paste: To *cut* or move *text* or *graphics* in one *document* and *paste* it into another place in the same document or in another document.

Cutter number: An alphanumeric code designed to arrange items in alphabetical order on the shelf. Originated by Charles A. Cutter, it is sometimes called the *book number*. See also *Cutter table*.

Cutter table: The alphanumeric list assigned to authors' names to create the *Cutter number*. The table was constructed by Charles A. Cutter.

Cutter-Sanborn table: An extension of the *Cutter table* constructed by Kate E. Sanborn. ■

Daisy chain: A method of connecting peripheral devices to a *computer*. For example, a CD-ROM drive, a *hard disk*, and a *scanner* can be connected in a daisy chain to one SCSI *port*. For example, several CD-ROM drives can be connected to a single SCSI port on a single computer by connecting one drive to the computer and then connecting a second drive to the first drive and so forth. See also *Peripheral device* and *Small computer system interface*.

Daisy-chained network: A type of unconnected *ring* network *topology* in which computers are connected in a series, one after another. *Data* are transmitted to the first *workstation*, then to the second, and so on. See also *Network*.

Data: 1. Factual *information*. 2. Information, such as measurements or statistics, often gathered through *research* techniques to analyze, explain, or calculate. 3. Information such as *text*, numbers, sounds, and images that can be processed by a *computer*. The word data is plural; datum is its singular form. See also *Code* and *Metadata*.

Data conferencing: A teleconference in which *data* are shared among participants in different locations. The participants write and draw on an on-screen notepad that everyone can view. The participants can also work interactively in a software *application* that is only loaded on one person's machine. Although all participants can view the *document*, only one person can edit it. Data conferencing is often used with *audioconferencing* or *videoconferencing*. See also *Teleconferencing*.

Data processing: Preparation, *storage*, and *retrieval* of *data* and *information*.

51

Database: *Information* (data) in a *machine-readable* format that can be searched by a *computer*. The information is organized in files that contain records consisting of *data* that have been input into fields. For example, an address *file* may have one *record* for each individual whose address is included. Each record may have one *field* for a name, another field for a street address, another field for a ZIP code, and another field for a telephone number. These files can be organized, retrieved, searched, and changed by using a *database management system*. See also *Online database*.

Database management system (DBMS): A computer software *program* that manages a *database* so that the *information* in the database can be organized, retrieved, searched, and changed. Database management systems vary; some, such as dBase, run on personal computers, and others, such as Oracle, run on mainframes.

Date due: The date by which circulating materials should be returned to the *library media center*. See also *Fine* and *Overdue*.

Date of publication: The year in which a *work* was published.

Date slip: A piece of paper glued to an inside cover or an end paper of a *book* on which the date the item is to be returned to the *library media center* is stamped. See also *End papers*.

DBMS: See *Database management system*.

DDC: See *Dewey Decimal Classification*.

Debug: To eliminate errors in computer *software* or *hardware*. See also *Bug*.

Decode: To convert coded *data* back into their original form. A *hardware* device or *software* used for this process is called a *decoder*. See also *Digital theater system* and *Encode*.

Decoder: A *hardware* device or *software* that converts coded *data* back into their original form. See also *Decode*, *Digital theater system*, and *Encoder*.

Decompression: The restoration of *data* that have been compressed back to the original size. See also *Compression.*

Dedicated: *Hardware* such as a *computer* or a telephone line assigned exclusively for a specific purpose.

Dedicated line: A regular telephone line that is only used for the *transmission* of *data* such as *facsimile*, *electronic mail*, and *Internet* access.

Dedicated service: See *Dedicated line*.

Dedication: The author's inscription about the person(s) to whom the *book* is dedicated.

Deductive reasoning: The logical process of making a conclusion drawn from general premises. Inferences are made from a general principle or principles to a particular case; for example, all men are mortal; Socrates is a man; therefore, Socrates is mortal. It is the opposite of *inductive reasoning*.

Default: The setting a *computer* uses unless different instructions are entered. For example, a *word processing* program has a default *font* size that will be used automatically unless a different font is specified.

Defragmentation: To reorganize the files on a *hard disk*; the files are placed in contiguous sectors on the hard disk. In normal use, files are fragmented; they are spread out across the *disk*. *Retrieval* time slows when the *read/write head* has to move over the entire disk. The speed of *data* retrieval increases when files are defragmented. See also *File, Fragmentation,* and *Sector*.

Delete: To erase or remove *data*. See also *Save*.

Delimiter: In the MARC *format*, a symbol identifying the start of a *subfield*. Delimiters may print as dollar signs ($), "at" symbols (@), or double daggers (‡). See also *Machine-readable cataloging*.

Density: A measurement of the tightness of bits of *data* that are packed together onto a *hard disk* or a *floppy disk*. The measurement is expressed in megabits per square inch. Floppy disks can be single-density (the lowest density), double-density, high-density, and extra high-density. The higher the density, the more tightly the bits are packed, which creates more *memory* than in the lower density disks. Not all disk drives can accommodate all the varying disk densities. See also *Bit*.

Depository: A place where items are stored.

Depository library: 1. A *library* specified by law to receive free copies of all or of a select amount of government documents printed by the *Government Printing Office* (GPO) and distributed by the *Superintendent of Documents*. 2. A library specified by law to receive free copies of state documents published by state agencies. See also *Government document*.

Depth of field: In photography, this is the distance in a scene between the nearest and farthest points that are in sharp focus.

Descriptive: Defines words in a *dictionary* and indicates how they are used in the *language*. See also *Prescriptive*.

Descriptive cataloging: Identifying and recording the areas (elements) that describe an item and establishing access points. See also *Access point* and *Area of description*.

Descriptive research: A type of *research* that does not use variable manipulation. *Data* are collected on existing variables, and the results are interpreted. This research describes and interprets a current situation; it is primarily concerned with the present.

Descriptor: 1. In a *database management system*, a *word* used to classify a data *record* so that any record containing the word can be retrieved. 2. A term describing the *subject* content of a *work*. See also *Subject heading*.

Desensitize: To reverse the magnetic field on security tape placed in an item that is properly checked out so that the library media center's alarm will not activate. See also *Security system* and *Sensitize*.

Desktop: The representation on a computer *screen* of the top of a desk. A *graphical user interface* allows the user to view a desktop full of documents. The desktop contains icons that represent files, folders, and documents. The icons can be moved around on the *computer* screen just as items may be rearranged on a real desktop. In Microsoft Windows the term refers to the background of the screen on which windows, icons, and dialog boxes appear. See also *Dialog box*, *Icon*, and *Window*.

Desktop computer: A *computer* that is small enough to fit on the top of a desk.

Desktop publishing: The use of computers to design and produce *text* and graphic publications such as newsletters and brochures.

Detracking: To eliminate the practice of grouping students with similar *learning* abilities into a common class or groups within a class. See also *Heterogeneous grouping*.

Dewey Decimal Classification (DDC): A classification scheme for materials that uses numbers to represent subjects. DDC was devised by Melvil Dewey and published in 1876. Knowledge is divided hierarchically into ten main classes, which are divided into ten more subclasses, and so on, using the ten digits of the Arabic numeral system. See also *Classification system* and *Dewey, Melvil*.

Dewey, Melvil: This *library* pioneer (1851–1931) played a major role in the development of librarianship. He conceived the idea of relative location to supplant the fixed location method in which a book's physical location was fixed on a specific shelf. His relative location used decimal fractions to number the contents of books rather than the physical books themselves. The *Dewey Decimal Classification* scheme was published in 1876. Dewey was instrumental in founding the *American Library Association* in 1876 and served as its secretary for 14 years. He served as president in 1890 and 1892–1893. In 1876, he was instrumental in the publication of *Library Journal* and served as editor for five years. Also in 1876, he established the Library Bureau, a firm that worked to standardize library supplies and equipment. Dewey founded the first library school at Columbia College (now Columbia University) with the first class of 20 professional librarians graduating in 1887.

Diacritic: A mark used with a letter or a syllable to indicate the correct pronunciation.

Dialog box: A *window* in a computer software *program* that asks a question or allows users to *input* information.

Dial-up access: Using a *computer*, telephone line, and a modem to connect to another computer. *Data* can be transmitted or received. See also *MOdulator-DEModulator*.

Diamante: A seven-line verse of *poetry* with specific structural requirements. Line 1—one noun; Line 2—two adjectives; Line 3—three action words; Line 4—four-*word* phrase that captures some feeling about the *topic*; Line 5—three action words; Line 6—two adjectives; and Line 7—one contrasting noun. When written, the *poem* resembles a diamond shape.

Dictionary: An alphabetical arrangement of words with their definitions, spelling, pronunciation, and usage. See also *Descriptive* and *Prescriptive*.

Dictionary catalog: A *catalog* in which all records (such as *author, title, subject*, and *series*) are filed alphabetically.

Digital: Representation of *data* in the form of discrete numbers or pulses. Computers are digital because they use the digits 0 and 1 for data representation. *Text*, images, and sound can be transmitted in a digital *format*. Digital *technology* is an improvement over *analog* technology.

Digital camera: A *camera* that records images in a true *digital* form. The images are usually downloaded directly into a *computer* through its *serial port*.

Digital recording: A method of recording in which samples of an original *analog* signal are encoded as bits and bytes. See also *Bit, Byte*, and *Digital*.

Digital signal: An electronic signal that is transmitted in binary digits to reduce the effect of errors introduced by signal noise. See also *Binary code*.

Digital subscriber line (DSL): A *technology* that allows for ultrafast *Internet* access using regular telephone lines at speeds up to 50 times faster than conventional service received from a traditional *Internet Service Provider*.

Digital theater system (DTS): An optional *audio* encoding *format*. The player or external receiver must have a *decoder* to play this format. See also *Encode*.

Digital versatile disc (DVD): Also referred to as digital video *disc*. For some people, the *acronym* itself has become its name. Although it has the same dimensions of a *compact disc*, it has higher capacities. A DVD is double-sided; a CD is single-sided. See also *Digital versatile disc-read only memory* and *Digital versatile disc-video*.

Digital versatile disc-audio (DVD-audio): A CD-sized *disc* that contains *audio*. It will likely become the standard music *format* in the future because it offers higher sound quality than the CDs available now.

Digital versatile disc-read only memory (DVD-ROM): A CD-sized *disc* that can be digitally recorded with *data*, *interactive* material, *audio*, and *video*. It has a *storage* capacity from 4.7 GB to 17 GB depending on whether both sides are used and how many layers on a side are used. A DVD-ROM drive is required to use the disc.

Digital versatile disc-video (DVD-video): A CD-sized *disc* that has been digitally recorded with picture and sound of motion pictures. MPEG-2 *compression* allows approximately 133 minutes of *video* per side of the disc. The picture and the *audio* are of higher quality than *videotape*. DVD-videoplayers are needed to attach to a *television* to use the disc. See also *Moving Picture Experts Group*.

Digital versatile disk-random access memory (DVD-RAM): A type of rewritable DVD *disk*. A single-sided disk has a capacity of 2.6 GB, and a double-sided disk has a capacity of 5.2 GB. DVD+RW is a competing rewritable DVD standard that is fragmenting this emerging market. See also *Digital versatile disk+rewritable*.

Digital versatile disk+rewritable (DVD+RW): A type of rewritable DVD *disk*. It has a *storage* capacity of 3 GB per side in contrast to the DVD-RAM, which has a capacity of 2.6 GB per side. See also *Digital versatile disk-random access memory*.

Digital video: *Video* that is stored in bits and bytes on a *computer*. It can be manipulated and displayed on a computer *screen*. See also *Bit* and *Byte*.

Digital video disc (DVD): See *Digital versatile disc*.

Digital video interactive (DVI): A *technology* for compressing and decompressing *video* and *audio* to create *multimedia* applications. DVI can *store* more than an hour of *full-motion video* on a *compact disc*. See also *Compression* and *Decompression*.

Digitize: To convert an *analog* data or signal into a *digital* form. For example, sound can be digitized onto a CD-ROM, and optical scanners digitize images. The *computer* can recognize and use this digital *data*. See also *Compact disc-read only memory* and *Optical scanner*.

Diorama: A three-dimensional scene reproduced in miniature.

DIP switches: The name is derived from the casing for the switches, which is called a dual-in-line package. They are *toggle* switches because there are only two possible positions— "on" or "off." The switches permit configuration of computers and peripherals; they can set operating and *default* modes.

Direct cost: An expense that is directly associated with a specific program or activity. The salary of a program manager is an example. See also *Indirect cost*.

Direct entry: 1. An *access point* in which the desired name or *word* is the first part of the *heading* without naming a larger unit of which it is part. For example, the correct heading is ONTARIO, not CANADA—ONTARIO, or the correct heading is WHALES, not MAMMALS—WHALES. 2. Also used to indicate that a multiword heading is given in the order in which it would be spoken (i.e., "natural order") without reversing the order of the words. For example, the correct heading is LIBRARY CATALOGS, not CATALOGS, LIBRARY, or JAPANESE LITERATURE, not LITERATURE, JAPANESE. See also *Indirect entry*.

Directional question: A type of general reference question such as "Where is the *catalog*?" or "Where is the copier?" See also *Ready reference question* and *Research question*.

Directory: 1. An *index* of files stored on a computer *disk*. 2. A list of personal names or organizations providing such details as addresses, telephone numbers, officers, and functions. See also *Internet directory*.

Disc: Usually refers to a *videodisc, compact disc*, or *digital versatile disc*. *Computer* diskettes are generally referred to as disks (with a k), and videodiscs, other optical *storage* media, and compact discs are known as discs (with a c). However, the two words are often used interchangeably. See also *Disk*.

Discharge: To check in an item that was charged (checked out) from a *library media center*; to cancel the *loan* record of a borrowed item from the library media center when it is returned. See also *Charge* and *Circulation desk*.

Discipline: A term used for a broad group of subjects in a *classification system*; for example, *Technology*, Social Sciences, or Humanities.

Discovery learning: A *teaching* technique that allows students to experiment and explore on an independent basis to acquire *subject* matter knowledge or to "discover" a concept or a principle. May also be called inquiry learning. See also *Learning*.

Discovery method: See *Discovery learning*.

Discretionary funds: Money available that is not specifically allocated. For example, a monetary gift may be made to a *school*. Legislators often have discretionary funds ("pork") that can be used in their districts for whatever purpose they choose.

Discussion group: A group of people interested in a specific *topic* who communicate on the *Internet* through *electronic mail* messages.

Disk: *Computer* diskettes and some types of *digital* video disks are generally referred to as disks (with a k), and videodiscs, other optical *storage* media, and compact discs are referred to as discs (with a c). However, the two words are often used interchangeably. See also *Disc*.

Disk drive: A device that can *read* data stored on a *disk* and *write* data to a disk for *storage*. A hard disk drive reads and writes *data* to a *hard disk*, and a *floppy disk drive* reads and writes to a *floppy disk*. See also *Compact disc-read only memory drive*, *Hard drive*, *Jaz drive*, *Laser Servo-120 disk drive*, and *Zip drive*.

Disk operating system (DOS): See *MicroSoft-Disk Operating System*.

Disk storage: The storing of *data* onto *hard disk* or a *floppy disk*, or both. See also *Storage*.

Diskette: See *Floppy disk*.

Display: See *Monitor*.

Dissertation: A required written *work* based on original *research*. A doctoral student pursuing a doctoral degree writes a dissertation. See also *Thesis*.

Dissolve: An optical effect in *television* or *film* that produces a gradual change in scenes. There is a progressive blending of the end of one shot into the beginning of the next shot as one scene fades out and the next scene fades in. See also *Dissolve unit*, *Fade*, *Transition*, and *Wipe*.

Dissolve unit: The equipment used to create a *dissolve* effect.

Distance education: See *Distance learning*.

Distance learning: Any *learning* that occurs at a site other than the classroom where the *teacher* is present. *Satellite* or *cable television* courses, *videotape*, and the *Internet* are various forms of *technology* used with this process. An example is the *Star Schools* developed through the U.S. Department of Education.

Divergent thinking: Refers to a *test* in which creative responses are desirable. The thinking takes different directions. It is the opposite of *convergent thinking*.

Divided catalog: A *catalog* in which different types of records are gathered into separate files such as *author* headings in one *file*, *title* headings in a second file, and *subject* headings in a third file; or author and title headings in one file and topical subject headings in a separate file.

Division of School Media and Technology (DSMT): A unit within the *Association for Educational Communications and Technology* that promotes communication among school media specialists and technology coordinators. It strives to improve *instruction* through the use of *media* and *technology*.

Document: 1. *Journal* article, report, *book*, or other item that is cited in a *database* and can be retrieved by a computer *search*. 2. A computer *file*. 3. A written item that conveys *information*, such as a brochure, pamphlet, or statement. A printed *government document* and statements of professional associations are examples. See also *Document delivery* and *Document imaging*.

Document delivery: 1. The electronic transfer of a *document* at the request of a *computer* user. 2. The delivery of a document from the library media center *collection* at the request of a *library* user. 3. The transfer of a document through *interlibrary loan* at the request of a library user.

Document imaging: A process of scanning and storing a *document* on *computer* files. The document can then be viewed, printed, or faxed.

Documentary film: A nonfiction *film* or *television* program that deals with actual events.

Documentation: The instruction materials such as guides, user manuals, and tutorials that accompany computer *hardware* and *software*. See also *Manual* and *Tutorial*.

Dolly: A platform of either wheels or tracks on which a *camera* is placed for forward and backward movement. Moving the dolly while the camera is running results in a dolly shot. See also *Tripod dolly*.

Domain: *Internet* address that is subdivided by type of organization such as commercial (.com) or educational (.edu).

Domain name: The unique name assigned to each of the Internet's member computers or *computer* systems. The domain name allows each member *node* to be accurately addressed by users from remote locations.

DOS: See *MicroSoft-Disk Operating System*.

Dot matrix printer: An inexpensive and often noisy impact *printer* that forms images or characters consisting of close patterns of small dots (matrix) by the hammering of print heads against a ribbon. An *ink jet printer* or a *laser printer* is a superior printer that provides better quality.

Dot pitch: The size of the dots (pixels) displayed on a *monitor*. Given in millimeters, pitch determines the *resolution* used on the display *screen*. The higher the dot pitch, the lower the resolution on the display screen. The lower the dot pitch, the higher the resolution. A high resolution monitor uses a .31-mm dot pitch; the best ones use .28-mm or less. See also *Pixel*.

Dots per inch (DPI): Measures *printer* resolution by counting the dots that fit into a linear inch. The fewer dots per inch, the lower the *resolution*. The more dots per inch, the higher the resolution.

Down: Refers to a time when a *computer* or computer system is not working because of a malfunction.

Downlink: A communications channel from a *satellite* to an earth station. See also *Telecommunications* and *Uplink*.

Download: The process of receiving *data* sent from one *computer* to another computer usually at remote sites. The data can then be printed or stored on a *disk*. See also *Upload*.

DPI: See *Dots per inch*.

Drill-and-practice method: A *teaching* technique that involves constant repetition for mastering certain skills. For example, using flash cards for spelling words or math problems gives students practice in *learning* these skills. *Software* drill-and-practice programs are widely used in education as a teaching technique; however, their use is often controversial because some educators view them as expensive electronic worksheets.

Dry mounting: A process that uses a special tissue and heat to seal an item (such as a *picture* or a *map*) onto a cardboard background. Dry mount tissue is attached to the back of the item in several areas with a *tacking iron*. After the tissue is trimmed away, the item and the tissue are tacked to the mounting board. A heat process of a hand iron or a dry mount press is used to press the entire surface to the mounting board. See also *Wet mounting*.

DSL: See *Digital subscriber line*.

DSMT: See *Division of School Media and Technology*.

DTS: See *Digital theater system*.

Dumb barcode: A type of *barcode* that contains bars and the associated number. The barcode on a *book* must be matched to the corresponding *bibliographic record* in the automated *catalog*. Smart barcodes are preferable. See also *Smart barcode*.

Dumb terminal: A computer *workstation* on a *network* that cannot function as a *stand-alone* computer. This type of *terminal* can accept *data* from or transmit data to another *computer* but cannot function as an independent computer. For example, because it has no *memory*, it cannot *store* a *program*. See also *Intelligent terminal*, *Smart terminal*, and *Terminal host*.

Dump: 1. To transfer *data* from one *storage* device to another. The contents of *memory* are copied onto a *printer* or a *disk*. The contents can be examined or preserved. 2. Automatic entry of data in a computerized system. Also called loading or mounting data.

Duplicate: 1. An additional *copy* of an item that is already part of a library media center *collection*. 2. To make additional copies of an original item.

Dust cover: Covering for a turntable or a *printer* to reduce the accumulation of dust.

Dust jacket: See *Book jacket*.

DVD: See *Digital versatile disc*.

DVD-audio: See *Digital versatile disc-audio*.

DVD-RAM: See *Digital versatile disk-random access memory*.

DVD-ROM: See *Digital versatile disc-read only memory*.

DVD+RW: See *Digital versatile disk+rewritable*.

DVD-video: See *Digital versatile disc-video*.

DVI: See *Digital video interactive*.

Dyslexia: A *learning* disability that impairs the ability to *read*. An individual with this disability often reverses letters in words.

Dystopia: A type of *literature* that deals with a place of unhappiness. Generally, the stories are set in the future. Although *technology* plays a role, sociological, psychological, and emotional aspects are the focus of the story. See also *Utopia*. ■

Easy-to-read book: See *Picture book*.

E-book: See *Electronic book*.

ECIA: See *Education Consolidation and Improvement Act*.

ECU: See *Extreme close-up*.

Edgar Awards: These awards are given annually by the Mystery Writers of America honoring the best in *fiction*, *nonfiction*, *television*, and *film*. Named for Edgar Allen Poe, the awards begin in 1946 for works published or produced in the preceding year.

Editing: Altering, correcting, or revising a *manuscript*, a *film*, a *videotape*, or any other *work*.

Editing control unit: A system that controls *audio* and *video* recording to achieve a finished production.

Edition: 1. In the case of *nonbook material*, all the copies made from one master *copy* and issued by a particular agency. 2. In the case of books, all copies of a *book* published in one typographical *format*, printed from the same typesetting, and issued at one time or at intervals without alteration. See also *Abridged edition*, *Limited edition*, and *Revised edition*.

Edition area: The part of the *bibliographic description* that indicates the particular *edition* of the *work*. It appears in the second *area of description* on a *catalog* record.

Editor: A person who supervises or prepares another person's *work* for publication.

Education Consolidation and Improvement Act (ECIA): A 1981 law that consolidated numerous individual education programs into a single block *grant*; this legislation took the place of the 1965 *Elementary and Secondary Education Act*. The legislation allowed for local discretion to fund any of these earlier individual programs. Chapter II funds were available to library media centers only if a decision was made at the local administrative level to use some of this federal money for media centers. A 1990 reauthorized version of the Elementary and Secondary Act superseded the ECIA.

Education for All Handicapped Children Act (Public Law 94-142): Defines handicapped children to mean mentally retarded, hard of hearing, deaf, speech-impaired, visually handicapped, seriously emotionally disturbed, orthopedically impaired, other health-impaired, deaf-blind, multihandicapped, or with specific *learning* disabilities that require special education and related services. See also *Individualized Education Program* and *Individuals with Disabilities Education Act*.

Educational Resources Information Center (ERIC): A nationwide information *network* that collects and disseminates materials related to education. The network consists of 16 clearing houses. Materials include *journal* articles, lesson plans, *teaching* guides, and conference proceedings, among others. ERIC items can be accessed through print, CD-ROM, *microfiche*, and the *Internet*. The Internet *address* is (http://www.accesseric.org:81/home.html).

Educational technology: See *Instructional technology*.

Edwards Award: An award presented annually by the *Young Adult Library Services Association*, a division of the *American Library Association*, to an *author* for his or her lifetime of outstanding contribution to *young adult literature*. The award, which began in 1988, is named for Margaret A. Edwards, who was an administrator of young adult programs at Enoch Pratt Free Library in Baltimore, Maryland, for more than 30 years. *School Library Journal* sponsors the award. See also *Alex Awards*.

Effective schools: Several studies have identified a variety of characteristics for successful schools. Some of the characteristics are: (1) a safe and orderly climate; (2) a *school* mission shared by all the staff members; (3) strong instructional *leadership*; (4) high expectations of all students; (5) high time on task for students to learn important skills; (6) frequent monitoring of student progress; and (7) positive home–school relations.

E-journal: See *Electronic journal*.

Electronic book (E-book): 1. A *computer* device that is about the size of a printed *book*. It has a high-resolution *screen* and a few simple buttons for tasks such as turning pages, selecting books or documents, and enlarging the *font* size. It can *store* the equivalent of several books in *memory*. In the future, when e-books are mass produced, they will be cheaper and of better quality than they are now. 2. A book published in an electronic *format* and available on the *Internet*. See also *Electronic publishing*.

Electronic journal (E-journal): A *periodical* published in an electronic *format* and available on the *Internet*. An example is *School Library Media Research* (formerly *School Library Media Quarterly*) available at the *Web site* of the *American Association of School Librarians*. See also *Electronic publishing* and *Journal*.

Electronic mail (E-mail): Messages that are composed on a *computer* and sent electronically over a telecommunications *network* to the e-mail address of another. Each e-mail *message* is stored until the addressee accesses the system and retrieves all the stored messages. See also *Electronic mail address*, *Smart phone*, and *Telecommunications*.

Electronic mail address (E-mail address): A series of characters that specifically identifies the location of an individual's electronic *mailbox*. Typically, the *address* will consist of a name or number followed by the @ sign and the computer's *domain* name (jdoe@auburn.edu). See also *Electronic mail*.

Electronic publishing: 1. Use of computer *software* such as *desktop publishing* to produce documents with *text* and *graphics* that have the same quality as those prepared by a printing company. 2. Books, journals, and other documents that can be accessed *online*. See also *Electronic book* and *Electronic journal*.

Elementary and Secondary Education Act (ESEA): A law passed in 1965 to provide federal funds for books and equipment for school library media centers. Various sections of this law were given title numbers (such as Title II funds), which helped to develop many K-12 *library media center* collections. This law was superseded by the *Education and Consolidation Improvement Act* in 1981. However, ESEA was reauthorized in 1990 and continues to be reauthorized periodically. Title VI may be used for *library* services and instructional and media materials if there is a local administrative decision to do so.

Elements of description: See *Area of description*.

E-mail: See *Electronic mail*.

E-mail address: See *Electronic mail address*.

Embedded training: Training that is integrated into a computer application *program*. A user can call up the training as needed without exiting the *application*.

Emoticons: Emotions and actions expressed with symbols in *electronic mail* messages. These informal expressions are not used in formal communications. For example, happy is :-) kiss is :-* angry frown or upset is >:-(yell is :-O.

Empowerment: Giving educators, parents, and students a voice in the decision-making process of school *management* and operations.

Enabling objective: States what the learner must be able to do to meet a *performance objective*. Activities and *instruction* enable or assist the learner to meet this primary or terminal objective. See also *Objectives*.

Encapsulated PostScript (EPS): High-resolution graphic images stored in the PostScript page description *language*. Various *graphics* programs permit EPS images to be created and printed.

Encode: 1. To assign a *code* to represent *data*, such as a parts code. 2. To convert from one *format* or signal to another. The *hardware* device or *software* used for this process is called an *encoder*. See also *Decode*, *Decoder*, and *Digital theater system*.

Encoder: A *hardware* device or *software* used to assign a *code* to represent *data* or to convert from one *format* or signal to another. See also *Decoder*, *Digital theater system*, and *Encode*.

Encrypt: Coding procedure that bars remote *access* to confidential networked material or that bars access by certain classes of users to networked materials deemed inappropriate. For example, a *password* may be encrypted.

Encryption: The process of transforming *information* into gibberish to prevent unauthorized users from accessing the *data*.

Encumbrance: Financial obligation to purchase an item. A *purchase order* commits or encumbers funds for a specific purchase.

Encyclopedia: Comprehensive summaries on all fields of knowledge. It may also include pictures, bibliographies, or maps, among others, that accompany various topics. Formats may include print, CD-ROM, and *Internet* versions.

End matter: The leaves at the end of a *work* containing *bibliography*, *appendix*, and *index*, among others.

End papers: The leaves that join the front and back covers of a *book* to the *text* of the book.

Endnote: A statement at the end of a chapter or a *work* that contains explanatory *information* or is a *citation* for the source used.

Engagement: Holding a student's attention during *instruction*. Engagement is a concept based on building internal *motivation* as the key to *learning* rather than an external source of motivation such as grades.

English as a second language (ESL): The *teaching* of English to people with a different native *language*.

Enhancements: Additions or add-ons to *software* or *hardware* that will result in improved performance; for example, faster *processing* or enhanced compatibility with another *computer*.

Entry: Narrowly defined, an *access point* to a library *catalog*; broadly defined, a *bibliographic record*.

Entry word: The first *word* used to arrange an *entry* in a *catalog*. The articles *A*, *An*, and *The* are never used as the first word.

Ephemera: Materials of transitory interest. These materials, such as pamphlets and clippings, are usually found in a *vertical file* and are retained only for a limited time.

Epic: A *legend* that was transmitted verbally for centuries and is now a long narrative *poem* about human heroes; examples are *The Iliad* and *The Odyssey*. See also *Traditional literature*.

EPS: See *Encapsulated PostScript*.

Equipment budget: Allocating funds in the *planning* for obsolete equipment and equipment repairs. Most *audiovisual hardware* has a life expectancy of approximately five years before maintenance and repair costs become excessive. Often a *formula budget* technique is used to prepare an equipment *budget*.

E-rate: A federal discount program created by the Telecommunications Act of 1996 to help schools and libraries obtain *telecommunications* services. E-rate provides affordable *Internet* access and internal connections for eligible school and public libraries, especially those in rural and inner-city areas. E-rate is also known as the Universal Service Fund, and surcharges designated for this fund are added to telephone bills to defray the cost. *Grant* applications for subsidies are available.

Ergonomics: The science of designing machines and furniture so that they will be comfortable, safe, and efficient to use.

ERIC: See *Educational Resources Information Center*.

Errata: A list of corrections printed on a *page* that is added to the original *work*. The insertion of corrections is necessary when errors are discovered after a *book* has been printed.

ESEA: See *Elementary and Secondary Education Act*.

ESL: See *English as a second language*.

ET: See *Expansion technology*.

Ethernet: A type of *network architecture* that is the oldest and most widely used of the three types. It is reliable, inexpensive, and supports very fast data *transmission* speeds.

Ethics: The *standards* that guide the ethical conduct of a profession. The *American Library Association* has endorsed the *Code of Ethics* for the *library science* profession.

Etymology: The derivation of a *word* in which the origin and the history of the word are cited; found primarily in a *dictionary*.

Evaluation: The systematic process of gathering *information* to use for decision making or to use for accountability. See also *Assessment, Formative evaluation*, and *Summative evaluation*.

Expansion budget: A type of *budget* used if major developments are expected for the immediate future. The plan for a new *library media center* would involve an expansion budget to plan for the anticipated large expenditures.

Expansion card: A printed circuit card, such as a *video* or sound card, that plugs into an *expansion slot* and extends the capabilities of a *computer* system.

Expansion slot: A compartment inside a *computer* that accepts an *expansion card*. The slots are connected to the *bus*. Future expansion depends on the number of slots available. See also *Slot*.

Expansion technology (ET): A special type of circuitry that allows *video* users to *record* a super-VHS signal onto a high-grade VHS tape instead of having to use an S-VHS tape for recordings. See also *Super-video home system* and *Video home system*.

Experimental research: A type of *research* in which an independent variable is manipulated. The manipulation is done to determine if it will cause any difference in the dependent variable. The research provides *data* on cause-and-effect relationships. In education an independent variable may be a type of *teaching* method, and the dependent variable may be a *test* score. Generally, an experimental group receives a particular treatment, and the control group receives no treatment.

Export: The sending of *data* from one system or *program* to another. If necessary, the first program converts the *format* of the data so that the second program can *access* and *read* the *information*. See also *Import*.

Expository learning: A *teaching* technique in which the concept is presented, examples are given, and the knowledge is applied to the students' experiences. See also *Learning*.

Exposure: 1. Subjecting light-sensitive materials to light. The process is used to develop *film*. 2. A *camera* measurement based on the speed of the film and the intensity of the light necessary for shooting a quality *picture*.

Expurgate: To delete or remove parts of a *work* that are deemed objectionable.

Extension name: A suffix of three letters added after the *file name* to describe the type of *file*. The file name and the extension name are separated by a dot (e.g., LETTER.DOC). For example, EXE denotes an executable file; DOC denotes a *document*; and TXT denotes ASCII *text*. See also *American Standard Code for Information Interchange*.

Extent: The total amount of an item's physical manifestation, such as the pages of a *book*, reels of *microfilm*, cassettes of a *video recording*, or disks of a computer *file*; may also include additional *data* for some materials such as the number of frames and duration.

Extracurricular activities: School-sponsored activities for which academic credit is generally not given. Examples include football, band, and French Club.

Extreme close-up (ECU): A *camera* shot of just a face or a single feature, or a shot of just a part of an object. See also *Close-up*. ■

Fable: A type of *traditional literature* that presents a brief, moral tale in which animals or sometimes the elements (such as the sun or the wind) speak and act like human beings.

Face-to-face teaching exemption: A provision in the Copyright Law, Title 17, Section 110 of the U.S. Code. The exemption permits a performance or display of a *work* by instructors or pupils in the course of face-to-face *teaching* activities of a nonprofit educational institution in a classroom or similar place devoted to *instruction* unless the performance or display is given using an unlawful *copy* and the person responsible knew it was an unlawful copy. See also *Copyright*, *Fair use*, and *Intellectual property*.

Facilitator: 1. Normally, a neutral party who is trained to encourage and enhance discussion and *problem solving*. 2. A classroom *teacher* or *library media specialist* who encourages and enhances *learning* activities in the *library media center* or classroom.

Facility: The physical environment of a *library media center* that encompasses areas such as the office, workroom, and main *reading* room, among others.

Facsimile (Fax): Transmitting the *image* of a *document* between two locations using telephone lines. The document is scanned to create an image that is transmitted and then reconstructed at the receiving *terminal*. See also *Scanner*.

Facsimile machine (Fax machine): An electronic device that transmits written or graphic material over telephone lines to receivers in other locations.

Fade: A *video* or *television* procedure that (1) gradually replaces an *image* with a background color; for example, fade to black (fade out) or (2) that gradually replaces a background color with an image (fade in). See also *Dissolve*, *Transition*, and *Wipe*.

Fading: The systematic reduction in help the *teacher* gives to the student so that the student can learn to work independently.

Fair use: A provision in the Copyright Law, Title 17, Section 107 of the U.S. Code, which allows others to make reasonable uses of copyrighted materials without the specific consent of the *author*. Section 107 describes four factors defining fair use: (1) the purpose and character of the use; (2) the nature of the copyrighted *work*; (3) the amount and substantiality of the portion used in relation to the copyrighted work as a whole; and (4) the effect of the use on the potential market for or value of the copyrighted work. See also *Copyright*, *Face-to-face teaching exemption*, and *Intellectual property*.

Fairy tale: See *Wonder tale*.

Family Educational Rights and Privacy Act: A 1974 federal law that gives students or the parents of minor students the right to review the student's records on file at any educational institution. It stipulates that federal funds will be denied to any institution that refuses to reveal student records to the student or to the parent. It also requires authorization by the student or parent before any part of the records can be released to an outside party. The law is referred to as the Buckley Amendment because it was sponsored by James L. Buckley of New York.

Fantasy: A type of *literature* that deals with the imaginary or the make believe. Good authors in this *genre* permit readers to suspend their disbelief to accept the possibility that the story could have happened. See also *Science fiction*.

FAQ: See *Frequently asked questions*.

Fax: See *Facsimile*.

Fax machine: See *Facsimile machine*.

Fax modem: The combination of a fax board and a *data* modem that can be an external peripheral to plug into the *serial port* of a *computer* or an expansion board to install internally. A switch then allows a computer to send and to receive faxes. See also *Expansion card* and *Facsimile*.

Fax transmission: See *Facsimile*.

FDDI: See *Fiber Distributed Data Interface*.

Feasibility study: An analysis to determine the need for and projected success of a newly proposed *program*.

Festschrift: A publication generally containing the writings of different authors issued in honor of a person or an organization.

Fiber distributed data interface (FDDI): A type of *network architecture* that is the most expensive of the three types. FDDI uses a token-passing *technology* with a speed of 100 Mbps. It can be used for a distance of 60 miles.

Fiber optic cable: Cable capable of transmitting *video*, voice, and *data* signals over long distances. Signals are transmitted as light pulses through microscopically thin strands of flexible glass. Light, not electricity, is conducted through the cable. See also *Coaxial cable* and *Twisted pair cable*.

Fiction: A literary *work*, such as a novel, that contains imaginary or fictionalized characters and events. See also *Nonfiction*.

Field: 1. In a *database* management *program*, a space reserved for a specified segment of *information* in a data *record*. 2. In the MARC formats, one part of a record corresponding to one *area of description*, one *subject heading*, or one *call number*, for example. A field may contain one or more subfields. See also *Control field*, *Fixed field*, *Machine-readable cataloging*, *Subfield*, and *Variable field*.

Field searching: A computer *search strategy* that limits a *search* to a particular *field*. For example, a search may be made on the *author* field or a *subject* field in an *online public access catalog*.

File: 1. A *collection* of related records organized in such a way that they may be stored and retrieved easily. 2. A computer *document* or a collection of related *data* stored as a unit such as a file of library patrons. Files are given names so that they can be accessed. See also *File format* and *File name*.

File format: The arrangement or the structure of *data* inside a *file*.

File name: A name assigned to a computer *file* to identify it. See also *Extension name*.

File server: A *microcomputer* in a *local area network* that stores all the *data* used by the automated system on a large *hard disk* and acts as the *host computer* to the other connected computers. It stores and distributes the files for the workstations. A file server should have a larger disk *storage* capacity than the *client* computers it serves. See also *Client server network* and *Workstation*.

File transfer protocol (FTP): A standard procedure that allows files to be transferred between networked computer systems. It is a special way to *log on* to another *Internet* site to *retrieve* or send files, or both. Many Internet sites have established publicly accessible material that can be obtained through FTP; the user logs on using the account name *anonymous*. These sites are called anonymous FTP servers. The need to accurately transfer files was one of the driving motivations behind the original creation of the Internet. See also *Anonymous file transfer protocol*.

Filing rules: The established principles used to arrange cards in a *card catalog* for library media centers that still maintain a card catalog.

Fill light: A form of supplementary illumination used to light the areas of a subject not adequately lighted by a *key light*. It is commonly used in photography. See also *Back light*.

Film: 1. A thin sheet or strip of transparent or translucent material with images or frames. 2. A *motion picture*. 3. To take a photograph of or make a motion picture of a subject. See also *Documentary film* and *Filmstrip*.

Filmloop: The ends of a *motion picture* film joined in a loop for continuous *projection*.

Filmstrip: A 16-mm or 35-mm strip of *film* containing still images with or without *text* to be used with a filmstrip projector and viewed *frame* by frame. A *cassette tape* can provide accompanying sound.

Filter: See *Blocking software*.

Filter software: See *Blocking software*.

Fine: A monetary penalty assessed for those patrons who do not return *library media center* material on the *date due*. Fine amounts vary, and some library media centers do not charge fines.

Firewall: A *network* security mechanism for a *local area network* connected to a larger network that prohibits outside *access* to the LAN.

FireWire: See *IEEE 1394*.

Fiscal year: A 12-month period (e.g., October 1–September 30 or July 1–June 30) for which money is appropriated and allocated and for which a *budget* for a *school district* is prepared.

Fixed asset: A durable capital asset such as a building, machinery, and furniture.

Fixed disk: See *Hard disk*.

Fixed field: Any *field* containing *data* of fixed field length and in fixed *format*. For example, the 043 field contains codes representing geographic data that are given in a form that the human eye can read elsewhere in the record: "no-us-ca" in the 043 field stands for "North America-United States-California." See also *Variable field*.

Fixed scheduling: A way to use a *library media center* where classes are scheduled for a specific day and time regardless of student need. Student *access* to the library media center is limited, *information literacy skills* are taught in isolation, and classes are often sent to the library media center without *cooperative planning* between teachers and the *library media specialist*. See also *Flexible scheduling*.

Flame: An angry, confrontational, or derogatory personal *message* sent over a computer *network*, often on an e-mail *listserv* or a *bulletin board system*. Many listserv administrators do not permit flaming and may remove the offender from the list.

Flatbed scanner: A type of *scanner* with a flat, glass surface that holds pages, books, or other thick objects for scanning. The scan head moves under the glass across the *page*.

Flexible scheduling: A type of *library media center* organization that permits classes and individual students to use the library media center as the need arises. Teachers and the *library media specialist* collaborate with *instruction*, *information literacy skills* are integrated into the *curriculum*, and students have more *open access* to the library media center. See also *Fixed scheduling*.

Floppy disk: A *magnetic disk* used for *secondary storage* of *data*. It is a removable device used in a *floppy disk drive*. There are two types—5.25-inch *disk* and 3.5-inch disk. However, the 3.5-inch disk is now more commonly used. See also *Backup*, *Hard disk*, and *Laser Servo-120*.

Floppy disk drive: A computer device that allows a *computer* to *read* and *write* information on a *floppy disk*. There are two sizes of floppy disk drives—a 3.5-inch drive and a 5.25-inch drive—and several densities that can handle a variety of floppy disks. See also *Density* and *Disk drive*.

Flowchart: A *chart* composed of symbols. The chart is used to designate each step of a process being evaluated or described.

Flyleaf: The blank sheet inserted at the beginning or the end of a *book*.

Focal length: In a *camera*, the distance from the focal point of the *lens* to the *image* when the lens is focused on infinity. The focal length determines the size of the image. The greater the focal length, the larger the size of the object. For example, a *telephoto lens* has a long focal length, and a *wide-angle lens* has a short focal length. Some inexpensive cameras have just one setting and cannot be focused. Other cameras may have a focal length of three feet to infinity. The focal length is measured in feet or meters, or both.

Folktale: A type of *traditional literature* that tells a *narrative* story with an oral tradition. All cultures have folktales. Folktales vary by type (such as a *pourquoi story* or a *beast tale*) and contain certain motifs (such as magical powers, trickery, and magical objects). Set in any time or place, they usually have animal or human characters. See also *Cumulative tale*, *Motif*, *Noodlehead story*, *Realistic story*, and *Wonder tale*.

Font: The size and style of print characters used on a *computer*. Each typeface, such as Times Roman or Arial, is available in normal weight, bold, italic, and bold italic. See also *Character*.

Footer: In *word processing*, *information* such as a *page* number that appears at the bottom of every page. It is the opposite of *header* or running head.

Footnote: A statement at the bottom of a *page* that contains explanatory *information* or is a *citation* for the source used.

Foreword: *Information* by the *author* or *editor* in the *preface* of a *book* explaining why the book was written.

Form feed: The automatic flow of paper through a *printer* until the printing is completed.

Formal bidding: 1. A process in which vendors submit sealed bids for certain items that have been advertised locally. The bids are publicly opened on a specified date. 2. State contract method in which vendors negotiate a contract for a specified time period with a state education department. Library media specialists need to be aware of the state *bid* law in terms of what types of materials need to be bid and the maximum expense needed to be bid; they also need to know the requirements of their *school system*. See also *Bidding* and *Informal bidding*.

Formal instruction: A systematic, planned approach to *teaching*. Teaching using a *lesson plan* is an example of formal *instruction*. See also *Informal instruction*.

Formal operations: The fourth stage in Piaget's theory of *cognitive development* that begins at approximately age 12. Beginning around this age, children have abstract thoughts. They can reason. They can remember several plots or subplots and see relationships among them. They can understand books with symbols and the meanings (themes) within a story. They can comprehend literary criticism. See also *Concrete operations*, *Preoperational period*, and *Sensory-motor period*.

Format: 1. The arrangement such as the shape, size, and general makeup of an item; for example, something that is printed. 2. The physical type of an item, such as a *book,* a *videotape*, a *filmstrip*, or a *compact disc*. 3. The physical arrangement of *data* on a *floppy disk*, a *hard disk,* or a *videodisc*. 4. The process of preparing a floppy disk to store *information*. 5. In a *document* of a *word processing* program, the format includes the margins, the *font* type and size, the alignment used for *text*, headers, footers, *page* numbering, and the way in which those numbers are displayed. 6. In MARC format, it is the compilation of codes used for identifying data for *computer* communication. Formats have been established for *bibliographic information*, authorities, holdings, and classification. See also *Machine-readable cataloging*.

Format integration: In the MARC *format*, the process by which individual formats for books, serials, maps, and other material forms, each developed separately, were brought together into one unified group of protocols called an *integrated format*. See also *Machine-readable cataloging*.

Formative evaluation: A type of ongoing *assessment* to improve current performance. See also *Evaluation* and *Summative evaluation*.

Formula budget: Used in library media centers to reflect such elements as the variation in student population, losses of materials through weeding, and attrition by date as well as the inflation rate for replacing materials. A formula *budget* may be used for specific areas such as a *maintenance budget* or an *equipment budget*.

Fragmentation: Occurs when a *file* is written over an entire *disk*. Different parts of a file are stored on vacant spaces on a disk. *Retrieval* time slows when the *read/write head* has to move over the entire disk. See also *Defragmentation*.

Frame: An individual picture in a *filmstrip, motion picture,* or *videodisc*, among others.

Frame rate: The number of *video* frames displayed each second. See also *Frame*.

Free verse: A type of *poetry* that does not rhyme.

Freedom to Read Foundation (FTRF): An organization that works closely with the *American Library Association* to promote First Amendment rights. For cases it accepts, FTRF supplies legal counsel for litigation involving libraries and librarians. See also *Censorship*.

Freedom to Read Statement: A *document* endorsed by the *American Library Association*, the Association of American Publishers, and other organizations to promote open *access* to ideas in books; to support the concept that publishers, librarians, and booksellers need to have books reflecting a diversity of views; and to oppose *censorship* efforts.

Freedom to View Statement: A *document* endorsed by the *American Library Association* that promotes freedom of *access* to *audiovisual* materials and that opposes *censorship* of these materials.

Free-floating subdivision: In *subject* authorities, a term that can be added to authorized terms as a *subdivision* without a specific listing or instruction. For example, the *Sears List of Subject Headings* has a list of subdivisions that can be added to the authorized subject headings. See also *Subject heading*.

Freenet: A community information server that provides *network* resources, services, and *Internet* access via ordinary telephone lines.

Freeware: See *Public domain software*.

Frequency: 1. The interval of time between issues of a *serial* such as weekly, monthly, quarterly, or annually. 2. The rate of repetition in cycles per second (*Hertz*).

Frequency distribution: An arrangement of *test* scores, typically from the highest to the lowest, indicating the frequency of the occurrence of each score.

Frequently asked questions (FAQ): Files maintained at many *Internet* sites, especially newsgroups, that supply answers to common problems. FAQs are intended to bring novices up to speed without posting repetitive questions. See also *Newsgroup*.

Front projection: The reproduction of images onto the front of a *screen*. The audience faces the screen. See also *Projection* and *Rear projection*.

Front projection screen: A light-reflecting *screen* onto which an *image* is projected. This is the *projection* method used for large-screen viewing with a 16-mm projector, a *slide* projector, or an *overhead projector*.

Frontispiece: An *illustration* that faces or precedes the *title page*.

F-stop: The numerical description of the size of the *aperture* (*lens* opening) that determines the amount of light entering a *camera*.

FTP: See *File transfer protocol*.

FTRF: See *Freedom to Read Foundation*.

Full text: Complete *document*. For example, many *periodical* databases contain full text articles. See also *Abstract*.

Full-motion video: *Video* frames displayed at 30 frames per second. See also *Frame*.

Function keys: Special keys on a *keyboard* that elicit a specific action from a *computer* system.

Functional illiterate: An adult who cannot *read*, *write*, or compute sufficiently to function successfully in society. For example, the person may be unable to write a check or complete a job application. See also *Literacy*. ■

Galley proof: A proof from type on a galley before it is made up into pages. The name is derived from the galley or tray used to store the metal type after setting. Given to authors or editors to review for corrections before the *work* is prepared in *page* format for printing.

Game: An activity that has prescribed rules for the participants to follow to achieve a *goal*; it may be played for education or for entertainment. See also *Gaming*.

Gaming: Use of simulated situations called games as a *learning* technique to enable a student to develop *critical thinking skills* to attain a specific objective. See also *Game*.

Garbage: *Data* that are meaningless.

Garbage in/Garbage out (GIGO): Incorrect data *input* results in incorrect data *output*.

Gateway: A device that connects *computer* networks using different communications protocols (e.g., Ethernet and Token Ring). It performs the translation among protocols that permits them to communicate properly. See also *Network* and *Protocol*.

Gazeteer: A geographical *dictionary*, generally in one *volume*. Used to obtain *information* on place names such as a city, river, or mountain.

GB: See *Gigabyte*.

GED: See *Certificate of High School Equivalency*.

Gender bias: A stereotyping of male or female roles, or both. These stereotypical expectations of gender appear in *literature*, standardized tests, the classroom, and in the workplace.

General material designation (GMD): Part of the first *area of description* in *cataloging* naming the *media* group, such as *text* or *microform*, to which an item belongs. Using a GMD descriptor is optional for a *cataloger*.

Genre: A type of literary *work* identified by its design or purpose; for example, *historical fiction*, *poetry*, *fantasy*, or *realistic fiction*.

Geographical dictionary: See *Gazeteer*.

Gestalt learning: A type of *learning* that emphasizes exposure to the whole rather than to the separate parts. Understanding an entire process is superior to the study of individual parts. It is based on Gestalt psychology, which postulates that the brain tends to organize experience into patterned wholes or configurations. Gestalt is a German word for configuration. For example, *whole language instruction* would be preferred over the *phonics instruction* method in the *teaching* of *reading*.

GIF: See *Graphics interchange format*.

Gifted and talented: Outstanding students who are capable of high academic or creative ability, or both. They are traditionally the top 3 to 5 percent of the population.

Gigabyte (GB): One billion bytes of *data*. Used in reference to the *storage* or *transmission* of massive amounts of *information*. See also *Byte*.

GIGO: See *Garbage in/Garbage out*.

Glitch: A temporary or random *hardware* malfunction such as that caused by a power interruption. The *computer* may generate *garbage* or may *crash*. A *software* problem is called a *bug*.

Globe: Spherical representation of the earth, universe, or other celestial bodies such as the moon. A globe is a relatively accurate representation of the earth as opposed to a *map*, which contains distortion.

Glossary: A list of terms and definitions in alphabetical order.

GMD: See *General material designation*.

Goal: The end to be achieved. A goal is developed from establishing needs to be met. Performance, instructional, and behavioral *objectives* are derived from educational goals.

Goals 2000: Legislation passed in 1994 that created eight voluntary national goals for schools to attain in an effort to improve educational *standards*. Federal money is available to states that apply for it to assist in addressing these goals.

GODORT: See *Government Documents Round Table*.

Gopher: A widely used *menu* system to make materials available over the *Internet*. Gopher is a *client* and server type program that allows a single Gopher client to *access* information from any accessible Gopher server, creating a single Gopherspace of *information*.

Government document: A publication printed by the authority of a governmental body such as the U.S. Department of Education. See also *Document, Government Printing Office*, and *Superintendent of Documents*.

Government Documents Round Table (GODORT): A unit within the *American Library Association* that deals with issues related to government documents. See also *Government document*.

Government Printing Office (GPO): An agency that has the responsibility for publishing federal documents. It began operations in 1860. The Public Printer, who serves as the head of the agency, is appointed by the President with the approval of the Senate. The agency produces and obtains printed and electronic documents for Congress and agencies of the federal government. Most publications are currently contracted out to private firms for printing. See also *Government document* and *Superintendent of Documents*.

GPO: See *Government Printing Office*.

Grant: A gift of money for a specific purpose. Federal, state, and local government agencies as well as private organizations offer money to support educational projects. Typically, a *grant proposal* must be written to request the money.

Grant proposal: A written *document* submitted to an agency or organization with the request for a gift of money. Most proposals require the *title* of the project; an *abstract*; an introduction about the requesting *school* or *school system* and the problem; an outline of goals and *objectives*; a description of the activities and materials needed to accomplish the objectives; a set of *evaluation* techniques to determine if the objectives have been achieved; and a *budget*. See also *Grant*.

Graphical user interface (GUI): (Pronounced "gooey"). A computer *application* program or *utility* that allows the user to interact through icons, buttons, hot spots, menus, or other graphical objects rather than by typing in a *command*. Windows is graphical, and DOS is textual. GUI was first widely used on Apple and Macintosh computers. Netscape is an example of a GUI Web *browser*. See also *Micro-Soft Disk Operating System* and *Windows*.

Graphics: Picture images such as charts and photographs, or those created by a *computer*.

Graphics file: A *file* that contains only visual *data* such as *clip art* or illustrations. See also *American Standard Code for Information Interchange file*, *Binary file,* and *Text file.*

Graphics interchange format (GIF): A *file format* that enables the creation and use of high-quality graphic images within and across networks. *Graphics* are compressed and transmitted on the *Internet.* See also *Compression* and *Joint Photographic Experts Group.*

Gratis: Without charge or free. Publishers often give materials gratis to the *library media center.*

Grolier Foundation Award: An award given by the *American Library Association* to a public or school librarian who has contributed to the stimulation and guidance of *reading* for children and young adults.

Groupware: *Software* programs used on a *network* to organize the work of users collaborating on a project. The software makes collaborative *writing* easier because each group member can make comments or change the *text.* Electronic schedulers and newsletters are other examples.

GUI: See *Graphical user interface.*

Guided practice: Practical experience gained by a library media student working under the supervision of an experienced *library media specialist* in a professional setting such as a resource center or *library media center.* Synonymous with internship and practicum.

Gutter: The area formed by the left margins on the pages of a *manuscript.* The gutter leaves room for *binding* the *work.* ∎

Hacker: 1. A *computer* enthusiast knowledgeable about computers and computer *software*. 2. A computer enthusiast who illegally breaks into a computer system.

Haiku: A Japanese form of *poetry* that contains three lines of seventeen syllables. The first and third lines each contain five syllables, and the second line contains seven syllables. Much of haiku poetry deals with nature.

Handbook: A *ready-reference* resource for a specific field of knowledge. An example is *The Handbook of School Psychology*. The term is often used synonymously with *manual*.

Hand-held device: A small, lightweight device that is compact enough to be easily operated while held in the hand. A calculator, a *cellular phone*, a *computer*, a pager, a *personal digital assistant*, a *smart phone*, and a *video camera* are some examples.

Hand-held scanner: A type of *scanner* that is moved across an image being scanned by hand. A hand-held scanner can be used in a *library media center* to scan a *barcode* for *circulation*, *inventory*, and other purposes.

Hanging indention: A type of *indention* for a *catalog* record when the *title* is the *main entry*. The title line is entered at the first indention, and the other lines of *information* begin at the second indention.

Hans Christian Andersen Award: An international award presented every two years to a living *author* and to a living *illustrator* whose total body of works has made an outstanding contribution to *children's literature*. The award was established in 1956 by the *International Board on Books for Young People*.

Hard bound: See *Hardback*.

Hard copy: A printed *copy* of computer-stored *data*.

Hard cover: See *Hardback*.

Hard disk: A rigid, nonremovable *disk* installed on a *computer*. It provides higher *storage* capacity and faster *retrieval* of *data* than a *floppy disk*. See also *Hard drive*.

Hard drive: The mechanism that can *read* and *write* information to a *hard disk*. The terms hard drive and hard disk are often used synonymously. See also *Disk drive*.

Hardback: A *book* that is bound or cased in boards. The boards may be covered with cloth or paper. Hard cover and hard bound are synonymous terms. See also *Binding*.

Hardware: 1. *Audiovisual* equipment used for the *projection* or playing of audiovisual materials. Examples include a *filmstrip* projector and a *cassette tape* recorder. 2. Computer components such as a *computer*, a *printer*, a *monitor*, and a *keyboard*. See also *Audiovisual hardware*.

Hazelwood School District v. *Kuhlmeier*: A 1988 Supreme Court case related to the free speech issue in the First Amendment. A *principal* in Hazelwood, Missouri, deleted two pages of a student *newspaper* that was produced as part of a high *school* journalism class because he considered the articles to be inappropriate. The court held that school officials may make decisions to further the school's educational mission. The court did not treat the case as a violation of the First Amendment rights of free speech. It treated the case as a challenge to a public school's power to control its *curriculum*. Because the newspaper was part of the school's curriculum, it was not a public forum in which students were free to express their views.

HD disk: See *High-density disk*.

HDTV: See *High-definition television*.

Head: A magnet used to play, *record*, or erase a signal on a magnetic *medium* such as a *cassette tape* or *videotape*.

Header: 1. A part of an *electronic mail* message that contains the addresses of the sender and the receiver, the subject of the *message*, and other technical *information*. 2. *Data* stored at the beginning of a *file* with information such as the name, the last update, and the contents, for example. 3. In *word processing*, it is the information at the top of the *page* (such as the *title*) that is repeated on every page of a *document*. The term is synonymous with running head, and the opposite is *footer*.

Heading: 1. The *topic* or *subject* content. 2. The term at the top of a *catalog* record that provides an *access point*. A heading may be a *subject heading*, a *title*, or a *corporate body*, among others. See also *Entry*.

Headphone: An electroacoustic receiver that is attached to a headband. The headphone is held to the ears by placing the headband over the head. It permits private listening to various *audio* sources such as a CD-ROM player or a radio.

Help: A feature of computer *software* systems in which the user can request instructional *information*. Information and assistance are provided for each function as needed.

Hertz (Hz): A unit of *frequency* of electrical vibrations or the number of cycles per second; one Hz is equal to one cycle per second.

Heterogeneous grouping: The technique of assigning students with different abilities to the same group or class. See also *Detracking* and *Homogeneous grouping*.

Hierarchy-of-needs theory: A theory of *motivation* espoused by Abraham Maslow. Humans have certain needs as expressed on a hierarchy from low to high. The needs to be satisfied are (1) physiological, (2) safety, (3) social, (4) esteem, and (5) self-actualization.

High-definition television (HDTV): A system for high-resolution color *television*.

High-density disk (HD disk): A *floppy disk* that has more *memory* capability than a double-density disk. Bits of *data* are more closely packed together, which increases memory *storage* capability. A 3.5-inch *disk* holds 1.44 MB of data, and a 5.25-inch disk holds 1.2 MB of data.

Higher order thinking skills: Mental processes, such as analyzing, comparing, and evaluating, that are used instead of memorization to allow students to develop complex reasoning skills. See also *Critical thinking skills*.

High-speed shutter: A *video camera* and *camcorder* feature that permits detail enhancement of fast-moving objects.

Historical fiction: A type of *literature* in which realistic stories are set in the past. Fact and *fiction* are blended. Actual events and people may be used, or the events and characters may be fictionalized.

Historical research: A type of *research* that describes and explains events of the past. Primary and secondary sources are analyzed to reach conclusions. See also *Primary source* and *Secondary source*.

Hit: An item retrieved from a *database* by a *search strategy*. A successful hit occurs when a correct item of *information* is retrieved through a database *search*. Match is a synonymous term. See also *Hit list*.

Hit list: A list of matches or results obtained from a *search* of a *database*. See also *Hit*.

Hold: A request by a user that an item currently checked out of the *library media center* be reserved for that user when it is returned. See also *Reserve*.

Holdings: See *Collection*.

Holistic learning: An educational theory that emphasizes the complete experience of *learning* and the ways in which the individual elements of the learning experience are interrelated. *Whole language instruction* is a *teaching* method that reflects this theory.

Home page: The initial starting *page* on the *World Wide Web*. The home page may contain introductory material and hyperlinks to related sites. See also *Hyperlink*.

Homogeneous grouping: The technique of assigning students with similar abilities to the same group or class. See also *Heterogeneous grouping* and *Tracking*.

Homonym: One of two or more words that have the same sound and often the same spelling but differ in meaning. For example, a *pool* of water and the game of *pool*. Other examples are *stationary/stationery* and *complement/compliment*. See also *Antonym* and *Synonym*.

Horizontal scrolling: A method of displaying *text* on a *computer* screen. Text is scrolled either right or left on the *screen*. When scrolled left, the text disappears on the left side of the screen. When scrolled right, the text disappears on the right side of the screen. See also *Scroll* and *Vertical scrolling*.

Host computer: The "home" *computer* or computer system that serves remotely connected users.

Host system: A larger *computer* system to which a smaller computer system is linked.

Hot link: A connection between two files so that when *information* in one *file* is updated, related information in the other file is updated as well.

Hot spot: *Screen* display that appears on a Web *browser* or a *hypermedia* application as highlighted or colored *text*, an *icon*, a *button*, or another object linked to further *information* anywhere on the *World Wide Web*.

Hotlist: A list of sites that can be saved by *browser* software. The hotlist enables users to *access* their favorite sites without retyping the URL. See also *Uniform Resource Locator*.

HTML: See *HyperText Markup Language*.

HTTP: See *HyperText Transport Protocol*.

Hub: 1. A regional *computer* server that ties local member computers into a larger *wide area network*. 2. A wiring device that contains several ports to connect computers. See also *Port*.

Hugo Awards: Awards given annually by the World Science Fiction Convention for *science fiction* excellence in categories such as *fiction* and *nonfiction*. The popularity of the *work* is the major criterion. It is named for writer Hugo H. Gernsback, who developed modern science fiction.

Hyperbole: The use of exaggeration for effect. Ridiculous situations such as those found in the rhyme "The Old Woman Who Lived in a Shoe" are examples of hyperbole.

Hyperlink: Words, phrases, or images that are underlined, highlighted, or colored differently. When clicked with the *mouse*, they display another *document*. A hyperlink provides a connection between one document and another.

Hypermedia: A form of *multimedia* (combined *audio*, *image*, *text*, *graphics*, and *video*) that is interactive or navigable. The user can choose designated hot spots that *link* to *information* of interest rather than having to follow a linear or sequential presentation of information. This process is controlled by *hypertext*, which uses the *hardware* and *software* of a *computer* system to integrate and link the information stored in multiple types of *media*. These applications require additional hardware such as *videodisc*, *compact disc* players, and high-resolution color monitors. See also *Hot spot*.

Hypertext: Displayed *text* on a computer *screen* that provides direct, *interactive* links or pathways to other related *resources* when activated by pointing and clicking with a *mouse* or by some other *command*. The *information* is linked in a non-sequential or non-traditional manner. Most applications require large random access memories (RAM) and *hard disk* drives. Web browsers display hypertext as hot spots that facilitate browsing on the *World Wide Web*. See also *Browser*, *Hot spot*, and *Hypermedia*.

HyperText Markup Language (HTML): Coding *language* used to create *hypertext* documents to be posted on the *World Wide Web*. HTML code consists of embedded tags that specify how a block of *text* should appear or that specify how a *word* is linked to another *file* on the *Internet*. HTML documents are viewed with a *browser* such as Netscape. See also *Tag*.

HyperText Transport Protocol (HTTP): The *protocol* for moving *hypertext* across the *Internet*; the most important protocol used on the *World Wide Web*. HTTP is the standard for the exchange of *information* on the World Wide Web. The abbreviation *http* indicates the beginning of a *Web site* address.

Hypothesis: A tentative statement or unproved theory asserting a relationship between certain facts. In *research*, the statement is tested and is either verified or rejected.

Hz: See *Hertz*. ∎

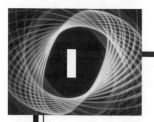

IASL: See *International Association of School Librarianship*.

IBBY: See *International Board on Books for Young People*.

Icon: A computer *screen* image that activates a *computer* operation by user *command*. Such commands are typically executed by placing a *mouse* cursor on the icon and clicking on it. For example, icons are found on a *desktop* screen and on *Internet* sites.

ICONnect: A *technology* initiative of the *American Association of School Librarians* that is designed to get students, library media specialists, and teachers connected to *learning* using the *Internet*. The ICONnect *Web site* is (http://www.ala.org /ICONN). See also *KidsConnect*.

IDEA: See *Individuals with Disabilities Education Act*.

IEEE 1394: A high-speed connection or *port* for hooking consumer electronic devices to a *computer*. It allows desktop computers to play streaming *audio* and *video*. See also *Desktop computer*.

IEP: See *Individualized Education Program*.

IFLA: See *International Federation of Library Associations and Institutions*.

IFRT: See *Intellectual Freedom Round Table*.

ILL: See *Interlibrary loan*.

Illustration: A drawing, *map*, photograph, or any other representation designed to clarify the *text* or to decorate the publication. An *illustrator* may use different types of *media* to create an illustration.

Illustrator: An artist who uses the visual elements of line, color, shape, and texture through such *media* as ink, woodcuts, oils, watercolors, acrylics, collage, or photography to create a visual effect that complements and enhances a story. See also *Illustration*.

ILS: See *Integrated learning system* and *Integrated Library System*.

Image: A graphic that contains *text* and *graphics*, a *picture*, or one *frame* of *film* or *video*

Image capture: The process of digitizing a *picture*. Although this term can be used with all image-digitizing processing, it is most often used to refer to *video* digitizing of single images. See also *Digitize*.

Imagery: Refers to the sensory images in a *poem* or story of sight, sound, touch, smell, or taste. Children respond to sensory images because they explore life through their senses.

Imaging device: The part of the *video camera* or *camcorder* that converts light into an electrical signal.

Impedance: The resistance of an electronic device to the flow of a signal toward it. For example, a *microphone* is rated for impedance.

Implied Boolean operators: The characters + and - that are used to expand or narrow a *search*. The + acts as the Boolean operator AND, and the - acts as the Boolean operator NOT. See also *Boolean operators*.

Import: To transfer a *file* from one *program* into a different program. If the *format* of the file being imported is not compatible with the program into which it is being imported, a conversion process is necessary. For example, library media specialists import *catalog* records from the publisher's or jobber's *disk* into their automated systems. See also *Export*.

Imprint: The publication *information* printed on the *title page* of a *book*. This information appears in the *publication and distribution area* in a *catalog* record.

In print: A *book* available for purchase from a *publisher* or *vendor*. See also *Out of print*.

Inclusion: The placement of disabled/special-needs children into a regular education classroom. This practice is sometimes referred to as mainstreaming, but inclusion is the more current term.

Incremental budget: Used to reflect large increases, generally over a three- to five-year period. For example, if a *library media center* needs increased funding to meet *accreditation standards*, this type of *budget* would be useful. Typically, a certain percentage increase would be given to the amount in a previous budget. The increments would be used over a stated time period to correct the deficiencies.

Incunabula: Books printed in the fifteenth century from moveable type.

Indention: A specific number of spaces from the left edge of a *catalog* card used for the typing of the various elements in a catalog *record*. See also *Hanging indention*.

Independent study: Self-directed *learning* by a student in which assignments are completed according to a previously agreed-upon plan that does not require constant supervision by a *teacher*.

Index: 1. A list of terms in a *book* along with the corresponding *page* number so that specific *information* can be located easily. The index is usually placed at the end of the book. 2. An analysis of the contents of a *document* or a group of documents. Access points, usually subjects and names, are given to ensure successful *information retrieval* by the user. For example, *Readers' Guide to Periodical Literature* is a *periodical index*. The *New York Times Index* is a *newspaper* index. Indexes can be printed, placed on a CD-ROM, and located *online*. See also *Access point*, *Cumulative index*, *Keyword index*, and *Relative index*.

Indicator: In the MARC *format* fields, a special value that instructs the *computer* to manipulate *data* in a particular way. For example, in the 245 *field*, the first indicator value controls making an *added entry* for *title proper*, and the second indicator controls indexing of title proper. See also *Content designators* and *Machine-readable cataloging*.

Indirect cost: An expense that is not readily identified with a specific *program* or activity. Utilities and rent are examples. Also referred to as overhead cost. See also *Direct cost*.

Indirect entry: An *access point*—often a geographic or *corporate body* name—in which the desired name is not the first part of the *heading*. For example, the desired name is BOSTON, but the indirect entry heading is MASSACHUSETTS—BOSTON. See also *Direct entry*.

Individualized Education Program (IEP): Written educational plans for students who have special needs as defined in the *Individuals with Disabilities Education Act* of 1991, which is an amendment to the *Education for All Handicapped Children*

Act of 1975. These documents include an *assessment* of the student's current educational level, goals and *objectives*, services to be provided with projected time frames, and an *evaluation* process.

Individualized instruction: A type of *teaching* based on the distinctive *learning* needs of each student. See also *Instruction*.

Individuals with Disabilities Education Act (IDEA): Public Law 101-476, a 1991 amendment to the *Education for All Handicapped Children Act*, that guarantees education for those eligible children or young people with disabilities. The act defines the specific learning disabilities covered. See also *Individualized Education Program*.

Inductive reasoning: The logical process of making a conclusion as a result of examining particular facts of evidence. Conclusions are drawn by reasoning from the specific to the general; for example, because it is snowing, it must be cold. It is the opposite of *deductive reasoning*.

Informal bidding: A less formal method of *bidding*. Generally, the *bid* is not advertised. A *vendor* may be asked over the telephone for a quote on the needed items. See also *Formal bidding*.

Informal instruction: *Teaching* that is not planned but that occurs spontaneously when a student asks for assistance. Recommending a good *book* or helping to locate materials are examples. See also *Formal instruction* and *Instruction*.

Information: 1. Facts or data. 2. Knowledge obtained from investigation, study, or *instruction*. 3. All ideas and facts that have been communicated in any *format*. 4. Any *data* that can be stored and retrieved in *machine-readable* form; the summarization of data.

Information access skills: See *Information literacy skills*.

Information literacy: The ability to locate, evaluate, understand, and use *information* effectively.

Information literacy process models: Taxonomies developed to assist teachers and library media specialists in *teaching* students that *research* is not product oriented; it is process oriented. Well-known models include *Big Six*, *Information Seeking Process Model*, *REACTS taxonomy,* and *Research taxonomy*. See also *Taxonomy*.

Information literacy skills: The capability to *access*, understand, and use *information*. A good library media *program* uses successful *teaching* and *learning* strategies as well as activities with information literacy skills to develop lifelong learners. This more current term replaces the terms information access skills and library skills.

Information Power: National professional guidelines for library media programs and for library media specialists published by the *American Association of School Librarians*, a division of the *American Library Association*, and the *Association of Educational Communications and Technology*. *Information Power: Guidelines for School Library Media Programs* was published in 1988. *Information Power: Building Partnerships for Learning* was published in 1998. See also *Roles of library media specialists*.

Information retrieval: The ability to locate *information*. The information may be in the form of an *abstract*, a *citation*, or *full text*.

Information Seeking Process Model: A process *model* derived from how people actually seek *information*. Library media specialists understand the process and the problems involved in trying to locate information in a *library media center* and can develop professional skills to assist the user. This model is described in *Teaching the Library Research Process*, 2nd edition, 1994, by Carol Collier Kuhlthau. See also *Information literacy process models*.

Information skills: See *Information literacy skills*.

Information specialist: A role of the school *library media specialist* as delineated in *Information Power* in which the library media specialist acquires and evaluates all formats of *resources* and models strategies for locating, using, and evaluating *information*. See also *Roles of library media specialists*.

Information superhighway: A *telecommunications* infrastructure envisioned in the United States for government, industry, education, and homes. A link to all these databases will take years to achieve. Although this term has been applied to the *Internet*, it is not the original concept. See also *Database* and *Infrastructure*.

Information utility network: See *Network*.

Informational book: A type of *literature* that contains factual, *nonfiction* material.

Infrastructure: The system of electronic pathways by which a *computer* is interconnected with other computers through local, regional, national, and global networks. The national highway system of interstate and state highways, secondary roads, and city streets is a transportation infrastructure. The various networks that make up the *Internet* constitute an *information* infrastructure. See also *Information superhighway*.

Initialize: To prepare *hardware* or *software* for use.

Ink cartridge: A *cartridge* that contains the ink used in an *ink jet printer*.

Ink jet printer: A nonimpact *printer* that forms characters by spraying ink onto paper. The *image* produced is similar to that created by a *laser printer* but is of lower quality.

Input: 1. To enter *information* into a *computer*. 2. The information that is entered into the computer. See also *Keyboard*, *Mouse*, *Output*, and *Scanner*.

Inquiry learning: See *Discovery learning*.

In-service: Programs designed to improve instructional practices. Typically, several days during a school year are designated for *professional development* programs.

Instruction: The *objectives*, skills, and activities involved in *teaching*. Some examples of instruction used in schools are *competency-based instruction*, *computer-assisted instruction*, *formal instruction*, *individualized instruction*, *informal instruction*, *integrated instruction*, *phonics instruction*, *programmed instruction*, *thematic instruction*, *Web-based instruction*, and *whole language instruction*. See also *Learning*.

Instructional consultant: See *Instructional partner*.

Instructional design: Systematic *planning* of *instruction*. Many models exist that present a formal approach to the design, implementation, and *evaluation* of instruction. A systematic plan for instruction results in more effective instruction than an unplanned approach.

Instructional development: See *Instructional design*.

Instructional module: See *Unit study*.

Instructional objective: See *Performance objective*.

Instructional partner: A role of the school *library media specialist* (as delineated in *Information Power*) in which the library media specialist works with those in the *school* community, such as the teachers, to design effective *instruction* related to the *curriculum* and *learning* outcomes. Typically, all formats of materials are used in this approach. This term replaces the former term of instructional consultant, which was used in the 1988 *Information Power* and revised to instructional partner in the 1998 revision. See also *Roles of library media specialists*.

Instructional technology: The *hardware* and *software* used in schools that enable students and teachers to meet the instructional goals of the *curriculum*. See also *Technology*.

Instructional television: The use of broadcast and *cable television* programming and *videotape* programs to enable students and teachers to meet the instructional goals of the *curriculum*. See also *Broadcast television*.

Integrated format: In the MARC *format*, the unified set of protocols applicable to all types of *library* materials now in use for encoding *bibliographic* data. See also *Format integration* and *Machine-readable cataloging*.

Integrated instruction: A process of incorporating topics and a variety of instructional strategies and skills into every content area of the *curriculum*. This process includes the integration of *information literacy skills* into the classroom curriculum. This method is considered by many educators to be a more effective approach than *teaching* topics and skills in isolation. See also *Instruction*.

Integrated learning system (ILS): An integrated and centralized *network* of computer *hardware* and instructional *software*. *Workstation* sites typically function as *client* nodes on a server that provides a full *menu* of prepackaged software ranging from curricular content to *teacher* management tools for record keeping, grading, and other instruction-related administrative tasks. See also *Integrated instruction* and *Instructional technology*.

Integrated Library System (ILS): 1. The term for a *network* package that includes the *hardware* for the network, the network *operating system*, applications programs, and management *software*. One company is responsible for packaging and selling the entire system. However, there may be some drawbacks. The system is sometimes expensive, all the needed applications may not be available, and adding other applications may be a problem. 2. The term for a software package that has different *application* programs, such as a *program* for *acquisition*, a program for *circulation*, and a program for a *catalog*, that are connected to each other. This connection allows *data* to be accessed and exchanged among the application programs. The data are stored in a single *file* that can be accessed by the different application software programs. See also *Automation*.

Integrated Services Digital Network (ISDN): A *telecommunications* service provided by several telephone companies in the United States and in other countries. Because this service offers a relatively high *bandwidth*, it is being promoted as an integrated "catch-all" capable of transmitting a full range of voice, *data*, and visual *information*. See also *Telecommunications*.

Integrated shelving: The shelving together of all formats of material in a *library media center*. The result is that all materials on a certain *topic*—such as books, films, and videos—will be located together on the shelf. A drawback is the wide variety of sizes involved in shelving the varying formats. See also *Format*.

Integrated software: *Software* that contains several applications in one *program*. *Word processing*, a *database management system*, and a *spreadsheet* are typical applications included in one software package. Library media centers use software packages with integrated modules for *circulation*, *online* catalogs, and *inventory*, among other tasks. These various applications are contained and integrated into one software program.

Intellectual freedom: The freedom of inquiry and expression as established in the First Amendment to the U.S. Constitution. See also *Censorship*, *Intellectual Freedom Round Table*, *Leroy C. Merritt Humanitarian Fund*, and *Office for Intellectual Freedom*.

Intellectual Freedom Round Table (IFRT): A unit of the *American Library Association* that provides a forum for *intellectual freedom* issues and offers ALA members an opportunity to become involved in the defense of intellectual freedom. The round table's publication *IFRT Report* is published on an irregular basis. See also *Censorship*.

Intellectual property: A concept in *copyright* law that protects the works of authors, publishers, and copyright owners. The concept gives authors the legal right to their original expressions, which means that they own the works created by their intellect. Copyright laws balance the rights of authors with society's need for the free dissemination of ideas. See also *Face-to-face teaching exemption* and *Fair use*.

Intelligence quotient (IQ): An index of intelligence expressed as the ratio of *mental age* to *chronological age*. IQ is determined from a score on a standardized intelligence *test* as compared with those of others of the same age.

Intelligent terminal: A computer *terminal* that has more *memory* and greater *processing* abilities than a *smart terminal*. See also *Dumb terminal*.

Interactive: The process that permits the user to communicate or interact reciprocally with a *computer*. Data *input* will elicit a response. Computer games and instructional *software* are interactive.

Interactive cable television: A developing *technology* to be used with *high-definition television* in which computers and *television* are combined into a single *interactive* format. Interactive video and data services is a synonymous term. See also *Cable television*.

Interactive media: Any type of *media* format, such as videodiscs, that permits the user to communicate reciprocally with a *computer*. The user can enter instructions and answer or ask questions, for example.

Interactive system: A *computer* system that permits users to *input* an entry to receive a response. The user communicates with the system.

Interactive video: Connecting a *computer* and a *videodisc* player so that a user can locate desired *information* on the videodisc.

Interactive video and data services (IVDS): See *Interactive cable television*.

Interface: The connection or *link* between two *hardware* devices. For example, signals are sent from the *computer* to the *printer* instructing the printer to print the *data*. See also *Parallel interface*, *Serial interface*, and *User interface*.

Interlibrary loan (ILL): The *loan* of an item in one library's *collection* to another *library* on request. Photocopies of requested items may also be provided. A fee for this transaction may or may not be charged. See also *Document delivery*.

Internal memory: Nonvolatile *memory* in the *central processing unit* of a *computer*. See also *Read-only memory*.

International Association of School Librarianship (IASL): Founded in 1971 with headquarters in Seattle, Washington, the group promotes the development of school library media centers and media center programs; it also encourages professional preparation for school library media specialists. Publications include *IASL Newsletter*, a quarterly, and the semiannual *journal School Libraries Worldwide*. An annual convention is held.

International Board on Books for Young People (IBBY): Founded in 1953 with headquarters in Basel, Switzerland, membership includes institutions and organizations in 60 countries interested in *literature* for children and young adults. The group fosters international goodwill through literature. There is a biennial meeting, and the organization awards the *Hans Christian Andersen Award*.

International Federation of Library Associations and Institutions (IFLA): Founded in 1927 with headquarters in The Hague, Netherlands, membership includes libraries and institutions around the world. The group promotes international cooperation, *research*, and discussion in all types of *library* activities. IFLA holds annual conventions.

International Reading Association (IRA): Founded in 1956 with headquarters in Newark, Delaware, membership includes teachers, administrators, psychologists, librarians, and parents, among others, who seek to promote *literacy* and raise the quality of *reading* instruction. Many awards are presented such as the *Arbuthnot Award* and the IRA *Children's Choices Book Awards*. Publications include the *Journal of Adolescent & Adult Literacy*, eight times a year; *Reading Research Quarterly*; and *The Reading Teacher*, eight times a year.

International Society for Technology in Education (ISTE): A group founded in 1989 with headquarters in Eugene, Oregon. Its members include teachers, administrators, *curriculum* coordinators, *computer* coordinators, and others seeking to use *technology* in innovative ways to improve education. Publications include *Journal of Research on Computing in Education*, quarterly, and *Learning and Leading with Technology*, eight times a year. ISTE holds annual conventions.

International Standard Bibliographic Description (ISBD): An international standard suggested by IFLA for describing materials. The standard mandates the sources for the descriptive *information*, the elements of description, the order in which the descriptive elements must appear, and the punctuation to identify the descriptive elements. See also *Area of description*, *Descriptive cataloging*, and *International Federation of Library Associations and Institutions*.

International Standard Book Number (ISBN): An internationally accepted unique identifier for each *book* issued by publishers participating in the *program*. This ten-digit number consisting of four parts separated by hyphens is typically located on the *verso* of the *title page*.

International Standard Serial Number (ISSN): An internationally accepted unique identifier for each *serial* issued by publishers participating in the *program*.

International Standards Organization (ISO): A nonprofit organization founded in 1946 and located in Geneva, Switzerland. The membership of ISO represents numerous nations, and the organization aims to advance *technology* and science by setting *standards*. The U.S. representative is the *American National Standards Institute*.

Internet: A worldwide *network* of *computer* networks linked together. *Electronic mail*, listservs, file transfer, and newsgroups are examples of communications services accessed on the system. See also *File transfer protocol*, *Listserv*, and *Newsgroup*.

Internet directory: A *search* site on the *World Wide Web* that is hierarchical in structure. It starts with a broad category and then subdivides into more specific areas. The items listed in a *directory* have been identified as items about the *topic*. Searching an *Internet* directory would be similar to using *subject* headings. Internet directories store a smaller number of sites than search engines. Examples are World Wide Web Yellow Pages and Yahoo!, which is both a directory and a *search engine*; however, Yahoo! is more like a directory with a search engine component. See also *Metasearch engine*.

Internet Service Provider (ISP): A commercial service that provides *Internet* access to subscribers for a fee. Such service is available in many areas, and Internet *access* is now being sold by an increasing number of traditional telephone companies.

Internship: See *Guided practice*.

Interpersonal skills: Using appropriate body *language* and verbal and written techniques to communicate effectively.

Interpretations of the *Library Bill of Rights*: Policy statements by the *American Library Association* that are generally issued when questions arise about how the *Library Bill of Rights* should be applied in specific cases. They clarify the application of the *Library Bill of Rights* to specific *library* practices.

Intranet: An in-house *network* that is available only to users within an organization.

Introduction: The part of the *preliminary pages* at the front of a *book* preceding the *text* that indicates the *subject* of the book and the treatment of that subject in the book.

Inventory: The process of checking the material on the shelves against the *shelflist* to identify items that are missing in a *library media center*.

Invoice: Paperwork from a *vendor* documenting such *information* as the type, quantity, and price of the materials delivered.

IQ: See *Intelligence quotient*.

IRA: See *International Reading Association*.

Iris: The mechanism that controls the lens *aperture* in a *camera*.

ISBD: See *International Standard Bibliographic Description*.

ISBN: See *International Standard Book Number*.

ISDN: See *Integrated Services Digital Network*.

Island Trees: See *Board of Education, Island Trees (New York) Union Free School District 26 v. Pico*.

ISO: See *International Standards Organization*.

ISP: See *Internet Service Provider*.

ISSN: See *International Standard Serial Number*.

Issue: A single uniquely numbered or dated part of a *serial* title such as a *periodical* or *newspaper*. See also *Issue date* and *Issue number*.

Issue date: The specific date, month, period (spring, summer, fall, winter), or year by which the publication date of a particular *issue* of a *serial* may be identified.

Issue number: The number assigned by the *publisher* to a separately issued part of a *serial* publication to distinguish it from other issues. See also *Issue*.

ISTE: See *International Society for Technology in Education*.

IVDS: See *Interactive video and data services*. ∎

Jack: A receptacle into which a plug from some type of equipment is inserted.

Java: A *programming language* for *World Wide Web* applications.

Jaz drive: A removable *disk drive* that holds up to 2 GB of *data*. This large *storage* capacity is ideal for *backup* storage.

Jewel box: The plastic container in which a *compact disc* is packaged. It cannot be used as a *caddy* to play the *disc*.

Job description: A written *document* that indicates the roles and responsibilities of a particular job. A job description should exist before an *evaluation* occurs.

Jobber: A wholesaler for *library* materials such as books, magazines, and videotapes. The advantages of using a jobber instead of individual publishers are (1) a discount that reduces the cost is given, (2) any problem with receipt of an item is handled by the jobber, and (3) only one *purchase order* is needed. A *magazine* jobber is often referred to as a *subscription agency*.

John Newbery Award: See *Newbery Award*.

Joint author: A writer who collaborates with one or more other writers to produce a *work*. See also *Author*.

Joint Photographic Experts Group (JPEG): A standard used to compress or reduce the size of *graphics*. JPEG is faster to transmit over the *Internet* than a GIF. See also *Compression* and *Graphics interchange format*.

Journal: A *periodical* containing more scholarly types of articles than are found in a *magazine*. A journal for educators would include professional articles related to education. See also *Electronic journal*, *Serial*, and *Subscription*.

103

Joystick: An *input* device that can be used in place of a *mouse* or *touch screen*. A joystick is often used with *computer* games to move objects on the *screen* in various directions.

JPEG: See *Joint Photographic Experts Group*.

Jukebox: A single *storage* device for several compact discs or for videodiscs. On request, an item is automatically moved from its location to a station for *reading* or *writing*, or both. See also *Compact disc-read only memory* and *Videodisc*.

Justification: The alignment of *text* evenly along the left margin, the right margin, or both margins. See also *Ragged*. ■

K: See *Kilobyte*.

Kbps: See *Kilobits per second*.

Key: One *button* or key on a *keyboard*.

Key light: The light used in *television* production to illuminate the subject. See also *Back light* and *Fill light*.

Keyboard: A group of keys arranged in a similar *format* as typewriter keys. When pressed, the keys serve as *input* devices for computers. The keys include alphabetic, numeric, and *function keys*. See also *Alphanumeric characters*, *Key*, and *Keypad*.

Keypad: A group of keys typically located to the right of the alphabetic keys on a *keyboard* that are arranged in a similar *format* as an adding machine or calculator. The keypad has numerical keys and mathematical operators. The keypad can be used to enter large amounts of numerical *data*. See also *Key*.

Keystone effect: The distortion of an *image* projected onto a *screen*. Usually, the image is wider at the top than at the bottom because the projector is not at a right angle to the screen. The word relates to the keystone, which is wide at the top of an arch

Keyword: 1. A significant *word* in a *title* or *subject heading*. 2. A searchable word such as a significant word in a title or subject heading.

Keyword index: An *index* in which significant words from titles and subject headings are access points. See also *Access point*, *Key-Word-in-Context index*, and *Key-Word-Out-of-Context index*.

Keyword search: Using a *word* or term contained within a *database* or directory of databases on which user searches may "key." A keyword *search* will locate and list records containing the desired word. See also *Boolean search*.

Key-Word-in-Context (KWIC) index: An *index* of *title* or *subject* words in which the titles are given in natural word order. For example, the title *Managing the Library Automation Project* would appear as:

Managing the Library	AUTOMATION	Project
Managing the	LIBRARY	Automation Project
	MANAGING	the Library Automation Project
Managing the Library Automation	PROJECT	

Key-Word-Out-of-Context (KWOC) index: An *index* of *title* or *subject* words in which the titles are given in indirect order, bringing the *keyword* to the filing position. For example, the title *Managing the Library Automation Project* would appear as:

AUTOMATION	Project, Managing the
LIBRARY	Automation Project, Managing the
MANAGING	the Library Automation Project
PROJECT	Managing the Library Automation

KidsConnect: A help and referral service for K-12 students on the *Internet* that is a component of *ICONnect*. The *goal* is to answer questions and to assist students to *access* and use Internet *information* effectively. Students can use *electronic mail* to contact KidsConnect and receive a response from a volunteer *library media specialist* within two school days. The *Web site* is (http://www.ala.org/ICONN/kidsconn.html), and the e-mail address is (AskKC@ala.org).

Kilobits per second (Kbps): A measurement of data *transmission* speed in thousands of *bits per second*, usually in reference to a *wide area network* or dial-up connection to a remote *computer*. See also *Bit*.

Kilobyte (K): A unit of measurement indicating 1,024 bytes. Typically used to indicate computer *memory* or *disk* capacity. See also *Byte*.

Kinesthetic learner: Refers to a type of learner who learns primarily by touching, manipulating, and moving. Manipulatives, models, *role-play*, and physical activity, among others, are useful to this type of learner. See also *Learning style* and *Manipulative*.

Kit: A *collection* of materials involving more than one type of *medium*. A kit is usually on a specific *topic* and might contain a *filmstrip*, a *videotape*, and a *book* on that topic. Although the materials are designed to be used as a unit, the *media* may be used independently.

KWIC index: See *Key-Word-in-Context index*.

KWOC index: See *Key-Word-Out-of-Context index*. ■

Labeling: 1. Classifying a person as a member of a category (retarded, deprived, rebel) based on a particular characteristic and assuming that he or she possesses all the attributes associated with a stereotype of that category. 2. The practice of describing specific *library* materials by placing a prejudicial label on them or by separating them from the remainder of the *collection*.

Lag time: The period of delay between data *input* and *data* display.

LAMA: See *Library Administration and Management Association*.

Lamination: The process of covering books or any visual with two or more clear plastic sheets to protect them from wear and tear and to enhance appearance.

LAN: See *Local area network*.

Lance Study: See *Colorado Study*.

Landscape: A horizontal arrangement of a printed *page* or visual *image*, such as in an advertisement or on a computer *screen*, in which the width is greater than the height. The opposite vertical arrangement is *portrait*.

Language: 1. Words, their pronunciation, and the methods of combining words that are used and understood by a community. 2. A system used for communication. 3. The machine language used and understood by the *central processing unit* of a *computer*; it is written in *binary code*.

Laptop computer: A portable *computer* that is small enough and light enough to be used on a person's lap. It can be plugged into an electrical outlet, or it can operate on batteries.

Large print: Any type size larger than 16-point; used to print material for the visually impaired or for the beginning reader.

Laser: See *Light Amplification by Stimulated Emission of Radiation*.

Laser beam: A light source used to create and *read* information on a *compact disc* and a *videodisc*. See also *Light Amplification by Stimulated Emission of Radiation*.

Laser printer: The highest quality, nonimpact *printer*, a high-resolution printer that uses a light beam to create *text* and *graphics*.

Laser Servo-120 (LS-120): A high-capacity *floppy disk* technology that provides 120 megabytes (MB) of data *storage* capacity on a 3.5-inch *disk*. The disk holds more than 80 times as much *data* as the standard 3.5-inch 1.44-MB disk. The LS-120 disk requires an LS-120 *disk drive*. See also *Laser Servo-120 disk drive* and *Megabyte*.

Laser Servo-120 disk drive: A drive that reads and writes an LS-120 (120-MB) *disk* as well as the standard 3.5-inch 1.44-MB disk. See also *Laser Servo-120*.

Laserdisc: See *Videodisc*.

Laura Ingalls Wilder Award: An award to an *author* or *illustrator* whose books published in the United States have made a substantial and lasting contribution to *children's literature*. The award, which began in 1954, is given by the *Association for Library Service to Children*, a division of the *American Library Association*. Originally, this medal was given every five years, but since 1983 it has been given every three years.

Lavaliere microphone: A small *microphone* worn around the neck or possibly attached to an individual's clothing to amplify sound.

LC: See *Library of Congress*.

LCC: See *Library of Congress Classification*.

LCCN: See *Library of Congress Control Number*.

LCD panel: See *Liquid crystal display panel*.

LCD projector: See *Liquid crystal display projector*.

LCSH: See *Library of Congress Subject Headings*.

LEA: See *Local education agency*.

Leader: 1. A blank portion of *film* or tape used at the beginning to protect the first few sections or to assist with threading into equipment such as a *filmstrip* projector or a *microfilm* machine. 2. In a MARC record, the leader is the top line of *information* about the record that allows the computer *program* to process it. See also *Machine-readable cataloging record*.

Leadership: The exercise of authority in directing the work of others. The authority may be formal, which is based on a person's rank or office. The authority may be informal, which is based on the willingness of others to follow an individual because of his or her special qualities that they admire and respect. The most effective leader is able to employ both types of authority.

Leaf: A single sheet of paper equaling two pages; one per side.

Learner characteristics: Traits that indicate the different methods by which *learning* occurs. Various tests measure learner characteristics. Once they are identified, appropriate *teaching* activities and materials can be used to achieve more effective learning.

Learner outcomes: The knowledge, attitude, and skill acquired by a student as a result of a *learning* experience.

Learning: The process of acquiring knowledge, skills, and behavior through experience, education, *instruction*, and training, among others. Some types of learning are *active learning*, *authentic learning*, *brain-based learning*, *cooperative learning*, *discovery learning*, *distance learning*, *expository learning*, *gestalt learning*, *holistic learning*, *resource-based learning*, and *rote learning*. See also *Teaching*.

Learning center: A specific area in a *library media center* or a classroom where a variety of materials are placed to be used by students without direct interaction with the *library media specialist* or classroom *teacher* unless assistance is needed.

Learning disorder: Any type of physical or psychological disability that interferes with a student's ability to learn.

Learning style: The way in which a person receives and processes new *information*. Individuals can be auditory, visual, or kinesthetic learners or some combination of these. An educational objective is to recognize and to teach to these various learning styles to increase student achievement. See also *Auditory learner*, *Kinesthetic learner*, and *Visual learner*.

Legend: 1. The explanation of the symbols used on a *map*. 2. A story with an oral tradition that deals with human heroes rather than the gods and goddesses in mythology; examples are King Arthur and Robin Hood. See also *Epic* and *Traditional literature*.

Lens: A curved piece of glass or plastic used in a *camera*, a *camcorder*, or an *opaque projector*, for example, to collect light and to magnify an image.

Leroy C. Merritt Humanitarian Fund: A fund that contributes to the support of librarians who are (1) denied employment rights or are discriminated against on the basis of sex, sexual preference, race, color, creed, or national origin or (2) threatened with loss of employment or fired because of their stand for *intellectual freedom*.

Lesson plan: A written plan for a lesson to be taught during a single class period. A lesson plan typically includes goals, *objectives*, *resources*, activities, and methods of *evaluation*. Instructional modules with predesigned lesson plans, including those for *computer* use, are available for purchase in many different disciplines. See also *Goal*, *Module*, and *Unit study*.

Letter-by-letter filing: The arrangement of entries by the letters in which the space between the words is ignored. For example, *New York* is treated as *Newyork* and follows *Newark*. See also *Word-by-word filing*.

Levels of description: Describes the three types of *descriptive cataloging* based on the amount of *bibliographic information* used for a *bibliographic record*. First Level contains minimal *information*, Second Level is considered the standardized level, and Third Level is the most detailed.

Lexicon: A *dictionary*.

Library: A *collection* of materials organized to provide physical, *bibliographic*, and intellectual *access* to a specific group. For example, academic libraries, public libraries, school library media centers, and special libraries serve a specified clientele. A library may be staffed with professional librarians or paraprofessionals, or both, who are trained to provide services and programs for the library clientele. See also *Library media center*, *Library media specialist*, *Paraprofessional*, and *Virtual library*.

Library Administration and Management Association (LAMA): A division of the *American Library Association* that seeks to improve administration in all types of libraries. Aspects such as public relations, buildings, personnel, and financial *management* are emphasized. Publications include the quarterly *Library Administration and Management*.

Library aide: Typically refers to a student who assists in the *library media center* as a *volunteer* or for course credit. The aide performs duties assigned and supervised by the *library media specialist*.

Library and Information Technology Association (LITA): A division of the *American Library Association* that deals with dissemination of *information* in library *automation*, *video* and cable communications, and *telecommunications*. Publications include the quarterly *Information Technology and Libraries* and the *LITA Newsletter*.

Library Bill of Rights: The philosophy of the *American Library Association* that affirms libraries as a source for all types of *information* and that espouses freedom of *access* to materials and services for all. Most schools or school systems adopt this policy for inclusion in their selection policies. See also *Interpretations of the Library Bill of Rights* and *Selection policy*.

Library binding: A type of *binding* used for *library* materials to provide durability because of heavy use (as opposed to the binding on trade books). See also *Trade book*.

Library clerk: A person, typically with a high school education, who is employed in a *library media center* and performs primarily clerical duties as assigned by the *library media specialist*. See also *Paraprofessional*.

Library instruction: See *Bibliographic instruction*.

Library Instruction Round Table (LIRT): A unit of the *American Library Association* that provides a forum for discussing *information*, problems, and *research* related to *instruction* in the use of libraries; publishes the quarterly *Library Instruction Round Table News*.

Library media center: An area in a *school* that contains varied formats of materials and equipment with programs and services provided by a *library media specialist* and additional staff as needed and as funds are available. It functions as a *learning* laboratory for students. This is the more current term for school library.

Library media coordinator: The professional with the administrative authority and responsibility for developing and implementing a *program* of *library* service for a district, county, region, or state. The coordinator supplies *leadership* in all aspects of the library media program with major opportunities and responsibility to effect change.

Library media information skills: See *Information literacy skills*.

Library media personnel: Personnel needed for the effective *management* of a *library media center*. The requirements for personnel differ according to student and staff enrollment and *program* mission and goals. The heart of the program is the *library media specialist* who has many roles in the program. Support staff, such as clerks and technicians when available, perform nonprofessional tasks so that the library media specialist can perform professional roles. Program effectiveness depends on the attitudes, competencies, and interpersonal skills of all library media personnel. See also *Professional librarian*, *Nonprofessionals*, and *Roles of library media specialists*.

Library media specialist: The professional administrator of a *library media center* who has the appropriate degree and meets the requirements for state *certification*. Most states require a master's degree although some states require only a bachelor's degree. The degree *program* offers specialized training in the *selection*, organization, and use of *media* and in *instructional design*. State certification as a library media specialist often depends not only on the degree but also on a required period of employment (such as one or two years) as a *teacher*. School library media specialist is a synonymous term. Library media specialist replaces the term school librarian.

Library media technical assistant: A person employed in a *library media center* with technical training and typically some college education. These technical skills are used to perform duties assigned by the *library media specialist*. Also called library technician. See also *Paraprofessional*.

Library network: A type of *library* cooperative that results in centralized development of library programs and services such as *cataloging*, *interlibrary loan*, and *computer* services. A central office and staff are sometimes used to implement and maintain the *network* programs. Also called a consortium.

Library of Congress (LC): Designated as the *library* of the U.S. Congress, it functions as a national library. It provides many services to the nation's libraries such as services to the blind and physically handicapped and original *cataloging* information with *catalog* cards or MARC records. See also *Machine-readable cataloging record*.

Library of Congress Classification (LCC): A *classification system* used with large collections such as those in academic and some public libraries. Knowledge is divided into 21 main classes that can also be subdivided. Alphabetical characters and Arabic numerals are used to create a *mixed notation*.

Library of Congress Control Number (LCCN): A unique number assigned by the *Library of Congress* to each *catalog* record it creates and by which its customers order *cataloging* on cards or in MARC *format*. Before the advent of computerized cataloging products, the *acronym* stood for Library of Congress Card Number. See also *Machine-readable cataloging*.

Library of Congress Subject Headings (LCSH): A *subject* authority produced by the *Library of Congress* and used to locate recognized subject headings. The authority is used in conjunction with the *Library of Congress Classification* system. See also *Subject heading*.

Library Power: A *program* begun in 1988 by the DeWitt Wallace-*Reader's Digest* Fund to make a $40 million investment over ten years to revitalize library media centers across the United States. From 1988 through 1998, Library Power operated in 19 communities, affected almost 700 public elementary and middle schools, and affected more than 400,000 students in the United States. Funding, assistance, and *assessment* were used to improve library media centers which helped to improve *teaching* and *learning* in the schools.

Library science: The study of libraries and their role in society and the procedures by which *information* is selected, acquired, organized, and used to meet the needs of *library* users.

Library security system: See *Security system*.

Library skills: See *Information literacy skills*.

Library technician: See *Library media technical assistant*.

License: A legal agreement that indicates how a software *program* can be used. Frequently used types of licenses are *multi-user license*, *network license*, *single-user license*, and *site license*. See also *Copyright*.

Light Amplification by Stimulated Emission of Radiation (Laser): A device that creates uniform light that can be focused precisely. It is used in many applications such as communications, printing, and disk *storage*. See also *Laser beam*.

Light pen: An *input* device resembling a pen that is connected to a *computer*. It can *read* optical characters such as a *barcode*. Used to *charge* and *discharge* materials and for *inventory*.

Limerick: A five-line *poem* in which the first, second, and fifth lines rhyme and the third and fourth lines rhyme. Popularized by Edward Lear in the nineteenth century, most limericks are humorous. See also *Poetry*.

Limited edition: An *edition* that has only a certain number of copies printed.

Line-item budget: A budgeting system that is a list of items and services. It does not provide for *program* accountability. See also *Budget*.

Link: 1. To establish a connection between two files in such a way that a change in *data* in one *file* is reflected in a change of data in the second file. 2. A *keyword* or graphic on the *World Wide Web* that will allow a user to connect to another location.

Liquid crystal display (LCD) panel: A device connected to a *computer* and placed on top of an *overhead projector* to permit the display of computer images on a large *screen*. See also *Liquid crystal display projector*.

Liquid crystal display (LCD) projector: A device containing an LCD panel and a light source in one unit, which projects *computer* images onto a large *screen*. See also *Liquid crystal display panel*.

LIRT: See *Library Instruction Round Table*.

List price: The price of items as advertised by a *publisher*.

Listening guidance: See *Reading, viewing, listening guidance*.

Listening skills: Skills for communicating with others that combine hearing, evaluating, understanding, and responding. Constructive listening involves attention, interpretation, selection, and acceptance or rejection of ideas. Students' listening abilities are a vital part of their total *language* development, and students must be directed toward selectivity and evaluation of that which is heard.

Listening station: An independent or small group area in a *library media center* or classroom that is equipped with *hardware* and *software* in a variety of *media* formats for students to use as a part of their instructional *program*.

Listserv: A type of *software* used to manage a mailing list. It allows special interest groups or professional associations to provide a distributed *electronic mail* membership list on the *Internet*. All members of a listserv can post messages to or receive messages from other members on the *mail list*. The software allows messages to be sent to all list members simultaneously. It also allows the list administrator to control and manage the list by performing certain operations automatically. See also *Message*.

LITA: See *Library and Information Technology Association*.

Literacy: The state of being able to *read* and *write* at a level expected by one's culture. See also *Functional illiterate*, *Media literacy*, and *Visual literacy*.

Literary elements: Used by authors in *writing* a story. Some literary elements include *characterization*, *plot*, *point of view*, *setting*, *style* of writing, and *theme*.

Literature: 1. Writings in prose or verse. These writings have an excellence in form, and they express ideas of a permanent or universal interest. 2. The body of works written or produced on a *subject*, or in a field of inquiry, or in a particular *language*, country, or period. See also *Children's literature* and *Young adult literature*.

Literature search: A systematic and comprehensive *search* for *information* on a *subject*.

LM_NET: A *listserv* on the *Internet* whose subscribers are predominately school library media specialists. To subscribe, send the *command*:

SUBSCRIBE LM_NET Firstname Lastname to:

LISTSERV@LISTSERV.SYR.EDU

Loan: A recorded transaction in which an item is charged (checked out) to a user for a stated time period. See also *Charge* and *Renew*.

Local area network (LAN): Cabling and other equipment such as bridges and interface cards that support high-speed *transmission* of *data* among computers within a building or among several buildings. Most LANs are interconnected or networked by means of a *file server*. An exception is a *peer-to-peer network*. See also *Firewall*, *Network architecture*, and *Networking operating system*.

Local education agency (LEA): A term applied to a local agency that operates public schools such as a *school district*.

Log in: See *Log on*.

Log off: To disconnect from, to quit, or to end a *computer* session. Synonymous with log out.

Log on: To initiate, to connect, or to gain *access* to a *computer* session. Synonymous with log in.

Log out: See *Log off*.

Long-range budget plan: A *budget* planned three to five years in advance. It enables the *library media specialist* to focus on and plan for long-range goals.

Long-range planning: A plan of future goals and the manner in which they may be achieved. A three- to five-year plan indicating priorities and timetables for achievement is ideal. This type of *planning* is very helpful for *collection development* purposes. See also *Goal* and *Short-range planning*.

Loop: A *programming* technique in which a sequence of instructions is repeated for a specified number of times until a condition is fulfilled.

Loop tape: A *cartridge* of tape, such as a *videotape* or *audiotape*, that has the ends joined together to allow continuous playing.

Loose-leaf publication: A *serial* publication whose pages are inserted into a binder. The publication is updated by replacing old pages with new pages according to the publisher's instructions.

LPT1: For a *microcomputer*, the term for the first *parallel port*, typically used for the main *printer*.

LPT2: For a *microcomputer*, the term for the second *parallel port*, typically used for a second *printer*.

LS-120: See *Laser Servo-120*.

Lump-sum budget: A budgeting system that does not provide for accountability. A lump sum may be allocated for library media purchases if individual costs or needs are not known. See also *Budget*.

Lyrical poetry: A type of *poetry* that has musical and emotional qualities. It "sings" its way into the mind of the reader. The term is derived from the word *lyric*, which is derived from the *word lyre*. This type of poetry, which originated in ancient Greece, was originally sung to the accompaniment of a lyre. ■

M: See *Mega-*.

Machine code: See *Machine language*.

Machine language: The most basic *programming* language that can be recognized and processed by a *computer* without further interpretation. The term is also used as a synonym for machine code.

Machine readable: *Data* in a form that can be *read*, sensed, or directly interpreted by a *computer* or other electromechanical device.

Machine-readable cataloging (MARC): A group of identifying codes used to communicate *bibliographic* data. The MARC standardized *format* was developed in the 1960s for storing library *catalog* records in *machine-readable* form. *Data*, such as *subject*, publication date, or *language*, can be extracted from MARC records and used for *collection* analysis. See also *Bibliographic information*, *Machine-readable cataloging record*, and *United States Machine-Readable Cataloging*.

Machine-readable cataloging record (MARC record): A variable length *bibliographic record* that conforms to the national standard for communicating and storing *cataloging* data in a computerized *format*. The MARC format can accommodate long or short cataloging records and is used by the *Library of Congress*, by most automated *library* systems, and by bibliographic utilities. See also *Bibliographic utility* and *Machine-readable cataloging*.

Magazine: Regular publication containing miscellaneous articles, stories, and poems by various contributors. Most magazines are published weekly or monthly. See also *Periodical*, *Serial*, and *Subscription*.

Magazine jobber: See *Jobber* and *Subscription agency*.

Magnet school: A type of *alternative school* that offers a *curriculum* and resources to attract all types of students in the community. Typically, these schools offer an emphasis in a certain area such as the arts or sciences.

Magnetic disk: Direct access *storage* on a circular plate coated on one or both sides with a magnetic film. The *data* are stored in *binary code* in concentric *tracks* on the magnetic surfaces of the *disk*. Data are retrieved from magnetic disks by means of a *disk drive*.

Magnetic tape: A tape that can store *binary code* data on reels or in cartridges. The tape is coated with magnetic material on which *data* can be recorded in microscopic magnetic domains by magnetizing and demagnetizing particles on the surface of the tape. A *cartridge* tape drive is often used in microcomputer-based automated library systems to *backup* data from the *hard drive*.

Mail list: A mailing list system that permits users to send *electronic mail* to one address, and from that address the *message* is then sent to all the other list subscribers. See also *Listserv*.

Mailbox: A *file* for storing *electronic mail* (e-mail). An area in *memory* or on a *storage* device where e-mail is automatically placed. Mail can then be copied, filed, deleted, or saved.

Main entry: The first and most important descriptive *access point* assigned to a *catalog* record by which the item can be retrieved or uniformly identified. The main entry may include the *tracings* for all other entries for that *record*. See also *Access point*, *Added entry*, *Author entry*, *Corporate entry*, *Subject entry*, and *Title entry*.

Main memory: The internal *memory* that is directly accessible to the *central processing unit*. Main memory in a *computer* is called *random access memory* (RAM).

Mainframe: A very large *computer* with an internal *memory* unit capable of controlling other computer systems. These computers are used primarily by large companies and academic libraries. They are increasingly being replaced by powerful *desktop computer* systems connected through a *local area network* (LAN). See also *Supercomputers*.

Mainstream: See *Inclusion*.

Maintenance budget: A type of *budget* that maintains the same level of expenditures from year to year. It is a simple budget to use when no changes are planned. This type of budget is not often used or recommended for use.

Management: 1. The process of coordinating the resources of an organization toward the accomplishment of established goals. 2. The persons in an organization who have the responsibility for executing the process of management.

Manipulative: A type of *learning* material used to help students understand abstract ideas by using concrete objects. An abacus is an example of a math manipulative.

Manual: 1. To perform a function by hand or with physical effort as opposed to automatically. 2. A compact *book* or *handbook* with instructions or *documentation* for doing, using, making, or performing something.

Manuscript: A *document* that is handwritten or typescript. Librarians and archivists distinguish between manuscripts and official documents that are regarded as *archives*.

Map: A representation, normally to scale, of the features of an area, usually on a flat surface. The area can be of Earth, a celestial body, or other areas that can be represented in this format. A relief map is one with raised surfaces to indicate land elevations. See also *Atlas* and *Globe*.

MARC: See *Machine-readable cataloging*.

MARC record: See *Machine-readable cataloging record*.

Margaret A. Edwards Award: See *Edwards Award*.

Maslow's theory: See *Hierarchy-of-needs theory*.

Mass storage: Devices such as discs or tapes that are used to store large quantities of *data*. An *online* backup system is capable of storing several hundred gigabytes. See also *Gigabyte* and *Storage*.

Master teacher: An effective and proficient *teacher* who has considerable experience and, in most cases, an advanced level of training. Because of these characteristics and qualifications, this teacher is recognized as one who is capable of providing guidance to student teachers, interns, and other teachers.

Mastery: Competency achieved in a skill or body of knowledge.

Mastery teaching: The process of organizing *instruction* to ensure that students master each part of a *subject* before continuing to the next.

Match: See *Hit*.

Material specific details: The third *area of description* on a *catalog* record. Used only for cartographic material, printed music, *computer* files, and serials.

Materials review committee: A committee appointed to review *library* materials that are challenged or questioned as to their suitability for inclusion in the *collection* of a *library media center*. The committee reads or views the *challenged material* and applies established criteria to determine their suitability.

Matte: A frame or border for a *chart*, *picture*, or poster.

May Hill Arbuthnot Award: See *Arbuthnot Award*.

May Hill Arbuthnot Honor Lecture: See *Arbuthnot Honor Lecture*.

MB: See *Megabyte*.

Mbps: See *Megabits per second*.

Mean: A measure of *central tendency* that is the arithmetic average. The mean is equal to the sum of all the scores divided by the total number of scores. See also *Median* and *Mode*.

Measurement: The process of obtaining quantitative descriptions of a student's characteristics or performance such as *test* scores.

Media: 1. Types of *information* sources or any type of media used as a means of communication or to transmit information, or both. Examples are books, compact discs, motion pictures, newspapers, *television*, and videotapes. 2. Types of material such as woodcuts, oils, acrylics, collages, and photographs used to create illustrations in children's books to illustrate the *text*. The term media is plural; *medium* is singular. See also *Illustration*.

Media center: See *Library media center*.

Media committee: See *Advisory committee*.

Media literacy: Possessing efficient, accurate, and effective skills and strategies for accessing, evaluating, and using ideas and *information*. See also *Literacy*.

Media production: The process of producing materials for instructional and entertainment purposes.

Media Programs: District and School: National guidelines and *standards* developed jointly in 1975 by the *American Association of School Librarians* and the *Association for Educational Communication and Technology*. These standards reflected the influence of a systems approach to *media* services, and programs were designed to respond to *objectives* of both district and schools. Because of these standards, the role of the media program changed from support service to an integral role in a school's instructional *program*. These guidelines have been superseded by *Information Power: Building Partnerships for Learning*, which was published in 1998.

Media specialist: See *Library media specialist*.

Mediagraphy: A list of books and other formats of materials such as videotapes or compact discs on a particular *topic*. This term is used rather than *bibliography*, which generally is a list of books and periodicals only, to reflect a variety of formats. See also *Webliography*.

Median: A measure of *central tendency*, the middle score in a distribution of scores that has been arranged in order of magnitude (i.e., high to low or low to high). The median is the score above and below which all the scores fall. In the following distribution of numbers, 85 is the median number: 100, 95, 90, 85, 80, 75, 70. See also *Mean* and *Mode*.

Medium: 1. A type of *information* source or any type of medium used as a means of communication or to transmit information, or both. Examples are a *book*, a *compact disc*, a *motion picture*, a *television*, or a *videotape*. 2. A type of material such as a woodcut, oil, acrylic, collage, or photograph used to create illustrations in children's books to illustrate the *text*. The term medium is singular; *media* is plural. See also *Illustration*.

Mega- (M): A prefix indicating a multiple of one million. For example, 8 MB ("B" stands for bytes) equals 8,000,000 (eight million) bytes. 8 M bits equals 8,000,000 bits. The symbol for mega is M. See also *Bit* and *Byte*.

Megabits per second (Mbps): A measurement of *transmission* speed that operates at 1 to 10 million bits per second or higher. This measurement is usually in reference to a *local area network* (LAN). See also *Bit*.

Megabyte (MB): A unit of measurement used to describe an amount of *memory* and *disk* capacity on a computer *hard drive*. Each MB consists of roughly one million bytes of *storage*. See also *Byte*.

Megahertz (MHz): A unit of measurement used to indicate how fast a computer's *central processing unit* can compute. This measurement refers to its *operating speed* or clock speed. The higher the number, the faster the CPU operates. MHz refers to one million cycles per second.

Memoirs: A record of the events in a person's life written or recorded from his or her personal observation.

Memory: The capability of a computer system to retain *information*. The electronic *storage* area in a *computer* where the microchip processes information. Memory is measured in megabytes and gigabytes and consists of RAM and ROM. RAM is volatile memory, and the information is lost when the *terminal* is turned off or fails. ROM is nonvolatile memory and is saved when the terminal is turned off. See also *Chip*, *Main memory*, *Random access memory*, and *Read-only memory*.

Memory chip: A *chip* on which *data* are stored as electrical charges. See also *Memory*.

Mending: Minor restoration of a *book* that does not involve replacing any part of it. Gluing loose pages or taping a torn *spine* are examples of mending. See also *Rebinding*.

Mental age: A score on a *test* of mental ability expressed in terms of *chronological age*; that age for which an individual's score is average. For example, if a student whose mental ability test score is equal to the average score earned by children who are nine and one-half years old, the student has a mental age of 9.5. See also *Intelligence quotient*.

Mental retardation: Subaverage intellectual development resulting in impairments or deficits in adaptive behavior and manifested during the developmental period.

Mentoring: Guidance, *information*, and encouragement offered by a more experienced person or professional.

Menu: A list of options that the *computer* displays to the user from which selections may be chosen. Selections can be made with a *mouse*, a *stylus*, or the *keyboard*. Menus range from very simple *text* lists that occupy the entire *screen* to pull-down or pop-up menus that appear from a menu bar or *icon*.

Merge: To join or consolidate; a term often used when two serials join to become one title. See also *Serial*.

Merit pay: A salary increase given to *school* personnel for excellent job performance.

Message: *Information* to be communicated or transmitted, or both.

Meta-analysis: A statistical technique that allows researchers to combine and evaluate *data* from *research* studies. This type of analysis permits the reporting of overall quantitative findings.

Metacognition: Refers to one's knowledge about one's own cognitive processes and to a learner's knowledge about his or her learning characteristics, such as strengths, weaknesses, and preferences. A good student is aware of the state of his or her mind and the degree of his or her own understanding. Good students may say that they do not understand because they monitor their understanding. Poor students do not monitor their understanding and do not know whether they understand or not. The issue for educators is to make students aware of the difference between what they do know and what they do not know.

Metadata: 1. Descriptive *information* used to describe or analyze *data*. This term describes how, when, and by whom a particular set of data was collected and how it was formatted. Examples are data dictionaries, repositories, files, or any *database* that holds information about the structure or characteristics of other databases. 2. An encoded description of an information package. Examples are a Dublin Core record and an AACR2R *record* encoded with MARC. Metadata are designed to provide an intermediate level for making choices about the information packages a user wishes to *search* or view without having to search large amounts of *full text* that may be irrelevant.

Metaphor: A figure of speech in which one object is compared to a different object by speaking of one as if it were the other. An example is "all the world's a stage." See also *Simile*.

Metasearch engine: A *search* site that consolidates several search engines under one umbrella so that a *World Wide Web* user does not have to go from one *search engine* to another to locate *information*. See also *Internet directory*.

Metatag: A special HTML *tag* that provides *information* about a *Web page*. Metatags do not affect how the *page* is displayed but provide information such as who created the page, the frequency with which it is updated, what the page is about, and which keywords represent the page content. Many search engines use this information when building their indices. Metatags help with a *keyword search* when Web pages do not have much *text*. See also *Search engine*.

Methodology: In general, a coherent set of methods with a defined, structured approach used in carrying out a complex activity. A typical process involves analysis, design, *evaluation*, development, installation, and maintenance. This term is most frequently used in describing system design methodology or *programming* methodology, or both. Those who develop *multimedia* and *hypermedia* applications should follow a methodology to ensure product usability and viability. See also *Research methodology* and *Teaching methodology*.

MHz: See *Megahertz*.

Michael L. Printz Award: An award given annually by the *Young Adult Library Services Association*, a division of the *American Library Association*, to the *author* of a young adult *book* published during the preceding year. The award is based solely on literary quality. The award, which was established in 2000, is named for Michael Printz, who was a high school librarian from Topeka, Kansas. Printz was known for discovering and promoting books for young adults. *Booklist* sponsors the award.

Microbrowser: A *World Wide Web* browser designed for small display screens such as those found on a *smart phone* and other hand-held *wireless* devices. The *browser* has a small *file* size that accommodates the low *memory* constraints of a *hand-held device*. See also *Wireless Application Protocol*.

Microcard: A three-by-five-inch opaque *microform* on which micro-images are affixed in rows and columns. The reverse side of the card may contain additional micro-images or *bibliographic* data that are legible to the human eye. A microcard is used to facilitate the *storage* of books, newspapers, and records, among others, and requires special magnification devices for *reading*.

Microchip: See *Central processing unit*, *Microprocessor*, and *Chip*.

Microcomputer: A general purpose or personal *computer* that uses a *microprocessor* as its central control or *central processing unit*. This type of computer can operate alone or in conjunction with other personal computers in a *local area network*. These types of computers range from inexpensive machines with limited *memory* and *floppy disk* storage to machines with powerful processors, large-capacity disk *storage*, and high-resolution color *graphics* systems.

Microcomputer Library Interchange Format (MicroLIF): A standard established in 1987 by *library* vendors to allow for the exchange of *machine-readable cataloging* (MARC) records in microcomputer-based automated systems. In 1991, this standard became known as the *United States Machine-Readable Cataloging/MicroLIF protocol* for its conformity with the *Library of Congress* U.S. MARC. See also *United States Machine-Readable Cataloging*.

Microfiche: A flat sheet of *film* about the size and shape of a filing card that contains multiple micro-images in a grid pattern of rows and columns. A microfiche can only be used with a magnification device such as with a microfiche reader. See also *Microform*.

Microfilm: Fine-grain film containing, or capable of containing, a sequence of microphotographs that are greatly reduced in size. A microfilm machine is needed to use this type of film. See also *Microform*.

Microform: A generic term for any *storage* medium that contains images too small to be *read* without magnification on special machines. Microform formats include *microcard*, *microfiche*, *microfilm*, and *ultrafiche*. See also *Computer output microform*.

MicroLIF: See *Microcomputer Library Interchange Format*.

Micro/minicassette: One of several types of audiocassettes that are much smaller than the compact *cassette*. These cassettes are mainly used for dictation and for taking notes. See also *Audiocassette*.

Microphone: An *audio* component that converts sound waves into electrical energy to amplify sound such as the human voice or music. Types of microphones include *bidirectional microphone*, *condenser microphone*, *lavaliere microphone*, *omnidirectional microphone*, *shotgun microphone*, *surface-mount microphone*, and *unidirectional microphone*. See also *Pickup pattern*.

Microprocessor: The *central processing unit* (CPU) chips that operate a *microcomputer*. The CPU is a preprogrammed control device that is often called the "brain" of the *computer*. It is also known as a microchip. Each generation of chips is exponentially faster in speed of execution and has increased width of *data* paths on the *chip*.

MicroSoft-Disk Operating System (MS-DOS): A term more commonly known as DOS, which is an *acronym* for Disk Operating System. This was one of the first major operating systems with a set of programs and instructions controlling and permitting interaction among a *computer*, *software* programs, and disks.

Microwave: A high-frequency electromagnetic wave capable of carrying *data*, radio, and *television* signals. Microwave signals can be transmitted from an antenna to another point or can be diffused to several sites at once. The microwave usually has a wavelength from 1 millimeter to 30 centimeters.

MIDI: See *Musical Instrument Digital Interface*.

Mildred L. Batchelder Award: See *Batchelder Award*.

Mixed notation: A *notation* that combines two or more kinds of symbols such as numbers and letters. The *Library of Congress Classification* system is an example.

Mixed responsibility: An item created by various individuals making different contributions to a *work*, such as a *book* that has an *author*, an *editor*, and an *illustrator*.

Mnemonics: Techniques used to aid and develop memory abilities. Examples are the use of songs, rhymes, pictures, or acronyms to help remember facts, people, events, or *information*.

Mobile library: See *Bookmobile*.

Mockup: A representation of a process or device that can be modified for analysis or training to emphasize a particular part or function. A mockup often has movable, *manipulative* parts.

Mode: 1. An operating condition or method; a way of doing something. 2. A measure of *central tendency*. In a distribution of numbers, the item that occurs most frequently. For example, in the following distribution of ten *test* scores, 90 is the mode: 100, 98, 95, 90, 90, 90, 88, 85, 82, 80. See also *Mean* and *Median*.

Model: 1. A three-dimensional representation of a real object reproduced in the original size or to scale. 2. An instructional strategy or educational *program* that usually incorporates new procedures or techniques for accomplishing stated teaching *objectives*. A *teaching* model commonly serves as a basis for the development of other programs. An example of an instructional model is the *Big Six*. See also *Information literacy process models*.

Modeling: 1. An instructional technique by which someone demonstrates how to perform a skill or task or how to solve a problem. *Learning* is achieved by observing the models of desired behaviors and imitating the models. 2. *Software* that can replicate real-life situations. See also *Model*.

Modem: See *MOdulator-DEModulator*.

Modifying search results: The process of changing an initial *search* expression to obtain more relevant results. This can involve adding keywords, subtracting keywords, or narrowing the results by *field*, for example. See also *Keyword*.

MOdulator-DEModulator (Modem): A device used to connect remotely located computers and terminals for *transmission* of *data*. It converts the *digital* computer signals into *analog* signals that can be transmitted through a telephone line while simultaneously converting analog data to digital signals that can be read by a *computer*. A modem can be internal or external. See also *Baud rate* and *Bits per second*.

Module: A major *program* segment or package in an integrated automated *library* system. A module is designed to perform one function in a multifunction system. For example, a system may consist of a *circulation* module, a *cataloging* module, and an *online catalog* module. The term is also often used interchangeably with the term *software*.

Monitor: A video *screen* or display device used with a *computer*. Types of monitors include EGA, VGA, SVGA, and others. A video monitor accepts a *video* signal and does not have a tuner. See also *Multiscan* and *Pixel*.

Monochrome: A *video* picture that consists of different saturations of a single-color foreground displayed against a black background.

Monograph: An item published or produced in one part or in a finite number of separate parts. Usually a systematic and complete study of a particular *subject*.

Monologue: 1. A long speech. 2. A *poem* in the form of a soliloquy. 3. A play or skit for only one actor.

Mother Goose: See *Nursery rhymes*.

Motherboard: See *Circuit board*.

Motif: The smallest part of a tale that can exist independently. Motifs can be seen in the recurring parade of characters in folktales such as the wicked stepmother or the clever trickster. See also *Folktale*.

Motion picture: A transparent *film* bearing a sequence of pictures that create the illusion of movement when projected at the proper speed. Can operate with or without sound.

Motivation: An inner drive that prompts or moves an individual to set and achieve goals, dreams, and desires that may be intrinsic or extrinsic. Intrinsic goals dominate when the behavior itself is satisfying. Extrinsic goals result in subsequent rewards or avoidance of subsequent punishment. Motivation to engage in certain tasks may arise spontaneously from within an individual or may be fostered and encouraged by a *teacher*, coach, parent, employer, or other person who is aware of and concerned with the individual's goals, abilities, interests, and desires.

Mounting: See *Dry mounting* and *Wet mounting*.

Mouse: An *input* device that allows a *computer* user to choose *menu* and *icon* options to perform tasks. The user clicks the mouse to execute the *command* or to choose an option.

Moving Picture Experts Group (MPEG): (Pronounced em-peg). This is a group within the *International Standards Organization*, and the term also refers to the *standards* for *digital video* compression that the group developed. MPEG-1 is used in CD-ROMs and video CDs; it provides a video resolution of 352 by 240 at 30 frames per second. MPEG-2 is a newer standard that provides a resolution of 720 by 480 and 1280 by 720 at 60 frames per second. It is a full-screen *video* standard with full CD-quality *audio*. MPEG is used in DVD-video and can compress a two-hour video into a few gigabytes. See also *Digital versatile disc-video*.

Moving Picture Experts Group Audio Layer 3 (MPEG Audio Layer 3): MP3, the shortened version of the term, is a system used to compress the *digital* codes of *compact disc* songs into files that can be easily posted to the *Internet* or transferred via *electronic mail*. Illegal copies of popular recordings are currently being made in this manner; their free availability on the Internet has created concern in the recording industry.

MP3: See *Moving Picture Experts Group Audio Layer 3*.

MPEG: See *Moving Picture Experts Group*.

MPEG Audio Layer 3: See *Moving Picture Experts Group Audio Layer 3*.

MS-DOS: See *MicroSoft-Disk Operating System*.

Multichannel: Using or having several channels, such as a multichannel *cassette tape* recorder.

Multicultural education: *School* programs and *curriculum* that help students understand and appreciate cultural and ethnic diversity.

Multicultural literature: A type of *literature* about racial or ethnic minority groups that are different both culturally and socially from the Anglo-Saxon, white majority in the United States.

Multiculturalism: The state or quality of being multicultural; blending many cultures.

Multimedia: A combination of *text*, image, sound, animation, *video*, or any other common *medium* in a computer-driven operation. This combination is often called *hypermedia*. Computer-driven devices such as *compact disc* players often enable multimedia *computer* operations, as do advanced, high-capacity *Internet* interfaces such as Netscape and Microsoft Internet Explorer.

Multimedia kit: See *Kit*.

Multiple intelligences: A theory first described in 1983 by Howard Gardner, professor of education at Harvard University, in his book *Frames of Mind*. Dr. Gardner suggests that intelligence is not just a single general capacity possessed by all individuals to a greater or lesser extent but is rather "an ability or set of abilities." The theory suggests that all individuals possess all of the intelligences, but in varying degrees of strength and skill. This theory also proposes that there are different pathways of *learning* or ways of knowing, more commonly known as types of "smart." Gardner's most current *research* indicates nine distinct forms of intelligence—Visual/Spatial, Verbal/Linguistic, Mathematical/Logical, Bodily/Kinesthetic, Musical/Rhythmic, Intrapersonal, Interpersonal, Naturalist, and Existentialist. He speculates that there may be more yet to be identified. This theory describes a broader view of cognitive functioning, broadens ideas of what it means to be intelligent, and has many implications and applications for education.

Multiprocessing: Refers to more than one *microprocessor* executing different programs simultaneously. A *computer* system can contain more than one microprocessor, and multiprocessing can occur within that system.

Multiscan: A process by which a type of *monitor* automatically adjusts to the signal frequency of the *video* display board to which it is connected. Multiscan monitors can display images based on a variety of *graphics* display systems.

Multitasking: A *computer* or automated *library* system capable of performing two or more tasks simultaneously. Each open task is assigned a portion of the *screen* called a *window*. A user can run a large *database* sort in one window and switch to *word processing* in another window.

Multitype library network: A cooperative *network* with several types of libraries sharing *resources* with each other. It commonly includes public, academic, and special libraries along with, in some cases, school library media centers. An example is the Library Management Network of north Alabama libraries, which was organized in 1983 and currently has 26 members including public libraries, academic libraries, and some high school library media centers. This consortium is a nonprofit organization with a shared computer *database* of the materials held in the participating libraries. Members use the network for *automation*; *cataloging*; *circulation* management; *resource sharing*; Internet *access* for homes, schools, and businesses; *electronic mail* between member sites; and *listserv* access to the *Internet* for local, national, and global communication. This type of network provides an invaluable service to rural libraries and homes as they benefit from "libraries without walls." Shared *planning* for the future is a key to the success of a consortium. See also *Networking* and *Virtual library*.

Multiuser license: A *license*, usually for a specific number, that permits *software* to be installed on multiple machines and used at the same time by multiple users.

Musical Instrument Digital Interface (MIDI): A specification developed as a *hardware* standard for synthesizers. A *synthesizer* is a musical instrument or device that generates sounds electronically. The MIDI specification allows computers to control musical instruments by using a MIDI *interface* and *software*. MIDI contains *information* about the sound, and MIDI files provide the instructions on how to produce the music. The computer interprets the MIDI instructions, and music is produced using sounds embedded in the *sound card* or sound module. The MIDI standard enables files to be interchanged among MIDI synthesizers, sound cards, and sound modules. MIDI software allows a user to "edit an orchestra" by changing the parameters of both the instruments and the notes. However, MIDI *technology* is not appropriate for human voices or narration, and the results of MIDI files may sound different when played back through different synthesizers and sound cards. In addition, musical talent is recommended for creating or editing this type of music. For those who are less musically talented, MIDI files can be obtained via the *Internet*, a *compact disc*, or a *bulletin board system*.

Myth: Mythology; a *legend* or story of unknown origin that expresses a people's religious beliefs or attempts to account for something in nature. A type of *traditional literature* that attempts to explain through symbolism the outlines of existence and attempts to make the realities of life more acceptable by explaining them as part of a sacred order in the universe. This type of *literature* is created by and appeals to the imagination. ■

Nanosecond: The speed at which many computers get and execute instructions. One nanosecond equals one thousandth of one millionth of one second.

Narrative: Discourse, description, *poetry*, or *storytelling*.

Narrative poetry: Story poems and ballads with rapid action, refrains, repetition, and a certain rhythm. Examples are "A Visit from St. Nicholas" by Clement Clarke Moore and "Paul Revere's Ride" by Henry Wadsworth Longfellow. See also *Poetry*.

Narrowband: A *telecommunications* channel that carries lower *frequency* signals. This includes telephone frequencies of approximately 3,000 Hz and radio subcarrier signals of about 15,000 Hz. See also *Broadband* and *Hertz*.

Narrower term (NT): A type of *cross-reference* that directs a searcher from a *broader term* to a more specific topic or *related term*. For example, under the *subject heading* for Birds there may be a cross-reference or *see reference* to the *heading* Robins.

National Book Awards: Awards given annually to U.S. authors whose books have contributed most significantly to human awareness, national culture, and the spirit of excellence. These awards were established in 1950 and are awarded by the National Book Foundation.

National Coalition Against Censorship (NCAC): Founded in 1974 with headquarters in New York, New York, this is a group of more than 40 national nonprofit organizations. All the participating organizations, which include literary, artistic, educational, professional, and civil liberties groups, seek to promote First Amendment rights and to oppose *censorship*.

National Commission on Libraries and Information Science (NCLIS): A federal agency in the executive branch of government. Its purpose is to advise the President and Congress on the status of libraries in the United States. The agency produces reports about the status of libraries and has sponsored two White House Conferences on Library and Information Services, one in 1979 and the other in 1991. See also *White House Conference on Library and Information Services*.

National Council for Accreditation of Teacher Education (NCATE): Founded in 1954, this voluntary accrediting body evaluates and accredits education programs at colleges and universities that prepare K-12 personnel such as teachers, principals, and library media specialists. It is located in Washington, D.C. See also *Accreditation*.

National Council for the Social Studies (NCSS): The largest association in the United States devoted solely to social studies education. Founded in 1921, NCSS serves as an advocate for and supporter of social studies in the education field. The association functions as an umbrella organization for elementary, secondary, and college teachers of social studies topics. The mission of NCSS is to provide leadership, service, and support for all social studies educators. It is located in Washington, D.C.

National Council of Teachers of English (NCTE): Founded in 1911 with headquarters in Urbana, Illinois, this organization works to improve classroom *instruction* in English *language* and *literature* at all school levels. The organization publishes numerous publications including *College English*, eight times a year; *English Education*, quarterly; *English Journal*, eight times a year; and *English Leadership Quarterly*. NCTE holds annual conventions.

National Council of Teachers of Mathematics (NCTM): Founded in 1920 with headquarters in Reston, Virginia, this organization seeks to improve the *teaching* of mathematics at all school levels. NCTM publishes several publications including *Mathematics Teacher* and *Mathematics Teaching in the Middle School* and holds annual conventions.

National Education Association (NEA): An organization founded in 1857 with headquarters in Washington, D.C. Its purpose is to advance the cause of public education in the United States. Every state has an affiliate chapter. The organization initiated *Read Across America*. The Web site is (http://www.nea.org).

National Information Center for Educational Media (NICEM): Founded in 1958 and located in Albuquerque, New Mexico, NICEM's purpose is to *catalog* and *store* in computerized form *information* on *audiovisual* materials such as films, filmstrips, audiotapes, videotapes, recordings, and transparencies for dissemination to schools, universities, or libraries. Its *database* contains more than 500,000 items.

National Information Standards Organization (NISO): A unit of the *American National Standards Institute* (ANSI). NISO developed the *Z39.50* protocol for the *network* retrieval of *bibliographic* data.

National library: A *library* that serves a nation and is maintained by the government, collecting and preserving the *literature* of the country. It is usually the country's largest *depository library*. See also *Library of Congress*.

National Library Week: Sponsored by the *American Library Association*, a week in April is designated to celebrate the contributions of all types of libraries and librarians. See also *School Library Media Month*.

National Public Radio (NPR): A loose affiliation of *frequency* modulation (fm) radio stations located principally on American college and university campuses. The member stations generate live *network* programs. Other programs are shared on a syndicated basis. NPR is funded from federal monies, grants, and donations.

National School Library Media Program of the Year Award: An award presented each year by the *American Association of School Librarians*, a division of the *American Library Association*, and currently sponsored by Follett Library Resources. This award emphasizes the importance of the school library media *program* as an integral part of the instructional process and encourages the development of library media programs that are the result of the collaborative efforts of those responsible for student *learning*.

NCAC: See *National Coalition Against Censorship*.

NCATE: See *National Council for Accreditation of Teacher Education*.

NCLIS: See *National Commission on Libraries and Information Science*.

NCSS: See *National Council for the Social Studies*.

NCTE: See *National Council of Teachers of English*.

NCTM: See *National Council of Teachers of Mathematics*.

NEA. See *National Education Association*.

Nebula Awards: Awards given annually by the Science Fiction Writers of America for various categories of works such as a novel or a short story. The major criterion is excellence of *science fiction* writing based on the artistic use of such *literary elements* as *plot*, *theme*, and *setting*, among others.

Needs assessment: A process that includes the gathering and analyzing of *information* used to identify needs. As an example, the *library media specialist* who gathers *circulation*, *collection*, equipment, *inventory*, *program*, and service information to project needs for the *library media center* is performing a needs assessment. A second example is the process by which educators determine what topics should be included in the *curriculum*. See also *Assessment*.

Needs hierarchy theory: See *Hierarchy-of-needs theory*.

Nested Boolean logic: The use of parentheses in *Boolean search* expressions to embed a logical operation within another logical operation to indicate the order (syntax) in which the logical operators or commands are to be executed by a *computer*. For example, the nested expression ((rivers OR lakes) AND canoeing) NOT camping will first find *resources* that contain rivers or lakes and the term canoeing but not resources about camping. See also *Boolean logic* and *Boolean operators*.

Netiquette: Standards of courtesy and consideration to which computer *network* users are expected to adhere. Some of these conventions can be found in written form. Others include a growing unwritten code of commonly accepted practices among *Internet* users.

Network: 1. An interconnected or interrelated group or system. For example, the *Educational Resources Information Center* (ERIC) is a network. 2. An interconnected community of electronic communication devices, such as computers, through which a wide variety of *information* can be exchanged and shared. Many of the more recent networks are *interactive*, which means that any connected device can send and receive information. A *local area network* (LAN) is often used to connect computers to share *bibliographic* data and materials in an automated *library* system. See also *Network architecture* and *Wide area network*.

Network architecture: The method of data *access* in a *local area network*. *Ethernet*, *Token ring*, and *Fiber distributed data interface* are three types of interfaces that transmit *data* in a LAN. Most interfaces are internal cards either built into the machine or added to each *computer* on the *network*.

Network interface card: The *interface* card that is inserted into a *computer* motherboard *slot* to make it a LAN *workstation*. The card governs the LAN standard or how *data* are sent through the *local area network* (LAN).

Network license: A *copyright* agreement that permits legal use of *software* on a specific *network* such as Novell or Windows NT. See also *License*.

Network operating system (NOS): The *software* that enhances a basic *operating system* by adding *network* features that include special functions for connecting computers and devices into a *local area network* (LAN).

Networking: 1. A term commonly used to refer to the discourse and sharing of *information* among people with common interests or needs. 2. Connecting terminals to provide *access* and to share information and *resources*. For libraries, this includes sharing materials through *interlibrary loan*, telefacsimile exchange, or other cooperative arrangements such as a *multitype library network*.

New Members Round Table (NMRT): A unit of the *American Library Association* that helps those new to the *library* profession and those who have been ALA members for less than ten years to become involved with ALA and the profession.

New Realism: A type of *literature* that deals with serious coming-of-age stories for young adults. Also called problem novel.

Newbery Award: An annual award presented by the *Association for Library Service to Children*, a division of the *American Library Association*, to the *author* of the most distinguished contribution to *children's literature* published in the United States in the preceding year. The award, which was established in 1922, was named for John Newbery, the first English *publisher* of children's books.

Newbie: A slang term for a new and usually inexperienced *network* user, especially a green *listserv* or *newsgroup* member. Often used as a self-deprecating term.

Newsgroup: An electronic *bulletin board system* accessible through the *Internet* that consists of discussion forums on thousands of topics. Newsgroup users can *read*, post, and reply to messages. Usenet is an example of a newsgroup. See also *Message*.

Newspaper: A publication issued periodically, usually daily or weekly, which contains the most recent news in addition to editorials, advertising, and features.

NICEM: See *National Information Center for Educational Media*.

NISO: See *National Information Standards Organization*.

NMRT: See *New Members Round Table*.

Nobel Prize in Literature: A notable award with prize money given to individuals with achievements in the field of *literature*. The award was established by Alfred B. Nobel and is awarded by the Nobel Foundation.

Node: A connection of a *hardware* device to a *local area network*. In a *network* system, a connection point that can create, receive, or repeat a *message*. Computers, printers, CD-ROM towers, and other hardware devices can be nodes.

Noise: 1. Any signal that occurs in an electronic or communication system and is extraneous to the signal being propagated. 2. Interruption to the *digital* transmission of *data*. 3. Poor quality in a *video* picture, such as graininess or snowiness.

Nonbook material: Materials or *resources* other than books that are available in print or nonprint format. Examples include periodicals, videorecordings, sound recordings, maps, and globes.

Nonfiction: *Writing* that deals with real people and events; factual material that is not a creation of an author's imagination. See also *Fiction*.

Nonprint materials: See *Audiovisual software*.

Nonprofessionals: Library media personnel or volunteers who work in supportive positions in a *library media center* but do not meet the *certification* requirements for a professional *library media specialist*. These include paraprofessionals, technicians, adult or student aides, and parent or student volunteers. See also *Paraprofessional*.

Noodlehead story: A type of *folktale* that is humorous or absurd. Children enjoy the story because they know it couldn't possibly have happened. "How the Peasant Helped His Horse" and "Hans in Luck" are two examples.

Norm-referenced assessment: Generally, a *standardized test* that measures a student's performance in comparison to scores of other students tested. The *test* has *norms* that were obtained in its standardization. The test scores are meaningful in their comparison to the norms. Scores are often reported in percentiles or grade-level equivalencies. Most nationally standardized achievement tests are norm-referenced. See also *Achievement test*, *Assessment*, and *Criterion-referenced assessment*.

Norms: *Data* used to describe the performance of *test* takers in a norm group. Norms represent average or typical performance and are not to be interpreted as *standards*.

NOS: See *Network operating system*.

Notation: A system of symbols, primarily numbers or letters (or both), used to represent subjects and a classification scheme of classes, subclasses, divisions, and subdivisions of classes. The *Dewey Decimal Classification* system uses only numbers and is a pure notation. The *Library of Congress Classification* system, which uses letters and numbers, is a *mixed notation*.

Notebook computer: A lightweight *computer* that typically weighs less than six pounds and is small enough to fit easily in a briefcase. The principal differences between notebook computers and personal computers are the light, nonbulky display screens that use flat-panel technologies, the quality of the notebook display screens, and the purchase price. A notebook computer can cost twice as much as a *desktop computer*.

Notes: The seventh *area of description* on a *catalog* record reserved for descriptive *information* that cannot be included in the preceding areas. Each note is usually recorded in a separate paragraph. This area more fully describes a *work* and its contents, such as a *book* containing an *index*.

NPR: See *National Public Radio*.

NT: See *Narrower term*.

Nursery rhymes: Rhymes that were easily remembered and passed on by *word* of mouth for generations. They are, for the most part, skillfully composed, exuberant or dramatic, and lead naturally into modern nonsense verse and *narrative poetry*. When nursery rhymes first achieved permanency of print, they became known as Mother Goose. The name Mother Goose was first associated with the eight folktales recorded by Charles Perrault. The popularity of the eight tales helped to establish more firmly the nonsense name Mother Goose. Many of the rhymes are nonsense jingles, but many others reveal interesting bits of history, old customs, manners, and beliefs. The first American edition of Mother Goose was probably a pirated reprint of an early Newbery *edition* published in about 1785 by Isaiah Thomas. Many fine editions are available today. See also *Folktale*. ∎

Objectives: Short, precise statements of specific activities, behaviors, or skills to be acquired and described in terms that can be quantified and measured. A *performance objective* constitutes a plan of action for achieving an instructional *goal*. An *enabling objective* is one that performs as subparts of performance objectives to achieve a desired skill or behavior.

Object-of-expenditure budget: A popular type of *budget* in which related expenditures are often grouped in categories. For example, furniture and equipment may be in one category; books may be in another category.

OCLC: See *OCLC Online Computer Library Center, Inc.*

OCLC Online Computer Library Center, Inc. (OCLC): A *bibliographic network* that provides *cataloging*, *resource sharing*, and reference services. The headquarters, which was formerly known as the Ohio College Library Center, is in Dublin, Ohio. OCLC has the largest membership of all the bibliographic utilities. Approximately two million records are added annually. See also *Bibliographic utility*.

OCR: See *Optical character recognition*.

Office for Intellectual Freedom (OIF): A unit of the *American Library Association* that implements policies concerning *intellectual freedom* as addressed in the *Library Bill of Rights*. Education of librarians and the public about intellectual freedom as it relates to libraries is one of OIF's goals.

Offline: Not connected or not in direct communication with a *computer*. A term used to indicate time spent preparing *information* to *upload* to a remote system or to *read* information downloaded from a remote system. *Data* stored on magnetic tapes must be loaded into *online* storage to be available to the computer.

OIF: See *Office for Intellectual Freedom*.

Omni catalog: A *catalog* in which records of all formats are found and the records for all books and *software* are interfiled.

Omnidirectional microphone: A microphone *pickup pattern* that is equally sensitive in all directions. See also *Microphone*.

Online: Connected or having direct *access* to the *information* stored in a *computer* via a modem or other *telecommunications* devices. Having interactive communication with a computer. See also *Offline*.

Online catalog: The distribution of *cataloging* information by *online* computer *transmission*. A computerized *catalog* that replaces the traditional *card catalog* and allows for more *search* options than are available in the card catalog, such as *keyword* searching. See also *Online public access catalog*.

Online Computer Library Center (OCLC): See *OCLC Online Computer Library Center, Inc.*

Online database: An information *collection* that shares a common characteristic such as *subject* discipline or type. These collections are published electronically by public or private *database* producers and made available for *interactive* searching and *information retrieval*. Online databases are accessed via *telecommunications* or *wide area network* links to remote *online* host services. Commercial vendors such as Dialog offer *access* to numerous databases. A charge is incurred by either the *library* or the individual using each database.

Online library catalog: See *Online catalog*.

Online public access catalog (OPAC): A computer-based *catalog* that can be accessed via *computer* terminals in a *library media center*. See also *Online catalog*.

Online retrieval: Using a *computer* to directly *access* collections of stored *data* and *information*.

Online searching: Using a computer *terminal* and a *keyboard* to seek *information* or *data* from one or more sources such as databases or the *Internet*. *Subject* terms, keywords, or *author* names can be used to *access* information. See also *Keyword*, *Search strategy*, and *Wild card*.

Online service: *Information* stored in a *computer* that can be searched electronically by means of a computer *terminal* connected by modem to a telephone line. An example is an *online* reference service to databases such as ERIC, Dialog, BRS, etc. See also *MOdulator-DEModulator*.

Onomatopoeia: A poetic term for the words in a verse suggestive of the sounds to which they refer. For example, the word *buzz* refers to and also sounds like the sound a bee makes, and "Clickety clack, the sound of the track" sounds as if it is a train.

On-order file: An acquisitions *file* containing copies of order slips or purchase orders for items ordered but not yet received. See also *Purchase order*.

OP: See *Out of print*.

OPAC: See *Online public access catalog*.

Opaque projector: A machine with a mirror and *lens* that can project and enlarge the *image* of a drawing, book *page*, or other opaque object onto a *screen*.

Open access: A type of *library media center* organization that offers maximum *access* to a library media center's facilities, *resources*, and staff. Access at point of need is crucial to the *information* and *learning* needs of students. See also *Flexible scheduling*.

Open entry: 1. A catalog *entry* for a *serial* or set that has not completed publication. 2. A part of the *descriptive cataloging* not completed at the time of *cataloging*.

Open shelves: See *Open stack*.

Open stack: Direct *access* to the shelves of a *library media center*. See also *Closed stack*.

Operating speed: The speed at which the *central processing unit* of a *computer* is able to process *information*. Also referred to as clock speed.

Operating system: A type of *software* that serves as a controller to manage all the operations of a *computer*. DOS and *Windows* are examples. See also *MicroSoft-Disk Operating System* and *Platform*.

Optical character recognition (OCR): The process of *reading* printed characters with a light-sensitive scanning device that converts them into electrical signals to be sent to a *computer*. *Software* designed to convert *text* on paper into *digital* format.

Optical disc: A plastic *disc* that can be read using a low-power laser that assigns binary values to small areas on the disc. *Data* are written by heating the small areas with a high-power laser. Optical discs use magneto-optical or phase-change methods, which make them rewritable. See also *Light amplification by stimulated emission of radiation*.

Optical scanner: A scanning device that can sense or *read* information such as pictures, *text*, and barcodes via reflected light. The *information* is converted into *machine-readable* data that can be processed by a *computer*. See also *Scanner*.

Oral history: An aural record or the transcript of an aural record that is usually the result of a planned interview. This record includes historical documentation of times, places, and events. The spoken recollections of the participant are recorded on a magnetic *medium* such as an *audiocassette*.

Orange book: The *format* standard for *write once read many* (WORM) compact discs. See also *Compact disc*.

Orbus Pictus Award: An award presented by the *National Council of Teachers of English* for the outstanding *nonfiction* book of the previous year.

Order number: The number of a *purchase order* when it is placed with a supplier. This number identifies all the items on a particular order, which facilitates record keeping when the items are received.

Orientation: The process of orienting patrons to a *library* facility and its *collection*, *resources*, equipment, and *policies and procedures*.

Original cataloging: The process of creating a *catalog* record for the first time. Various *cataloging* tools are used to create the *record* without prepared *copy* supplied by a *vendor*.

Original footage: See *Raw footage*.

Other physical details: *Data* relating to the physical properties of a item being cataloged other than its extent, dimensions, and *accompanying materials*. For example, data for a *book* include illustrations, and data for a computer *file* include the presence of sound and color, among others.

Out of print (OP): A designation indicating that a *book* cannot be purchased from the *publisher* because the book is no longer *in print*.

Out of stock: Items not available from a *publisher* at the present time. The publisher usually places the items on *back order* and notifies the person placing the order.

Outcome-based education: A controversial education reform movement of the public schools during the 1990s, once called competency- or performance-based education. It is contrasted with traditional *teaching* methodologies in that it specifies "outcomes" that will determine the design of *assessment* methods and the *curriculum*. Many people define the term differently, and there are strong divisions about how the outcomes would affect student *learning* and behavior. Programs described as outcome-based have often been very different from one another. Whether someone is for or against this philosophy depends on what he or she believes those outcomes should be and what schools would be like if they were more outcome-based. Those in favor of outcome-based education state that the *goal* is to produce students who are able to demonstrate and apply the knowledge and skills needed for success in life. This process shifts the focus from what teachers have taught to what students have learned. Some of the common points of divergence are whether the outcomes are state mandates or guidelines, how the outcomes are assessed, who assesses them, and the sanctions for failing to meet the goals. Those in opposition charge that the outcomes identified by some states have been ambiguous, vague, and difficult to measure. They further claim that outcome-based education usurps local control and argue that the movement is really a *methodology* that will lead to lower expectations of students and a "dumbing down" of the education system.

Outcomes: See *Student outcomes*.

Outline: To indicate the different parts or principal features of a *book*, article, *manual*, or *computer* program.

Outliner: A feature of *presentation software* that allows a user to type an *outline* and create an automatic bullet *slide* from the outline.

Output: The transfer of *data* from a computer's internal *memory* to a *peripheral device* such as a *printer* or *monitor* for display. This process supplies the results of the computer's operations to the user. See also *Input*.

Outsourcing: The practice of contracting with an external organization for various tasks or services that were once provided internally.

Overdue: *Library* material returned past the *date due*. See also *Fine*.

Overdue notice: A notice sent to a *borrower* as a reminder to return *overdue* materials.

Overhead cost: See *Indirect cost*.

Overhead projector: A type of equipment used for projecting images of transparent material onto a *screen*. This equipment enables the operator to face the audience and to present material without turning off the lights. An overhead projector can also be used with an LCD panel to project computer *text* and *graphics*. See also *Liquid crystal display projector* and *Transparency*.

Overhead transparency: See *Transparency*.

Overlay: 1. Material placed over other material to add to or alter the *information* or display. 2. A section of code that is loaded into the *memory* of a *computer* during the execution of a *program*, overwriting what was previously there.

Over-the-shoulder shot: A *video* composition technique in which the shoulder and part of the back of the head of an interview participant, observer, or worker is included in the shot. ∎

Page: 1. To scroll through a *document*. 2. In a *book*, one side of a *leaf* or sheet of paper. 3. In *word processing* and *presentation software* programs, an on-screen representation of a printed page of *text* or *graphics*. See also *Home page* and *Web page*.

Pagination: 1. A system of numbers or letters indicating the order of the pages in a *book*. 2. The part of the *physical description area* that indicates the number of pages or leaves in a book. 3. An option included in a *word processing* program that permits the assignment of *page* numbers.

Palmtop computer: A *computer* small enough to hold in one hand but with limited capabilities. It permits the use of scaled-down versions of common applications.

Pamphlet: A small printed *work* on a *topic* of current interest. Many libraries use these materials to maintain *information* on current topics. Pamphlets are independent publications bound in paper covers.

Pan: Horizontal movement of a *camera*.

Paperback: A *book* that has been bound in some type of paper. See also *Binding*.

Paradigm: 1. A pattern, *model*, or example. A popular term used in the late 1980s and early 1990s in the phrase "paradigm shift." 2. A pattern or model of the *methodology* and environment in which systems and *software* are developed and operated.

Parallel interface: A multiline channel/device that allows *data* to be transmitted along parallel wires. The *interface* consists of the wires, their connectors, and the parallel ports into which each of the devices is connected. It is faster than a *serial interface* because several bits, and often one or more bytes, are transmitted concurrently. See also *Bit*, *Byte*, and *Parallel port*.

Parallel port: A *parallel interface* that allows external peripheral devices, such as printers, to be connected to a *computer*. The *port* is capable of transmitting eight bits, or one *byte*, simultaneously. It is often unidirectional and can only send *information* out to a device, not back to the computer. Most personal computers have a parallel port and one or more serial ports. See also *Peripheral device*, *Serial port*, and *Universal Serial Bus*.

Parallel title: The main *title* of an item written in another script or *language*.

Paraprofessional: A person who has some level of training or proficiency in *library* operations but who has not completed formal training for the profession. See also *Library clerk* and *Library media technical assistant*.

Parody: A type of *literature* that changes another author's work to make it humorous. These stories or books are used as a way to reintroduce *traditional literature* in a humorous or different light. *The Stinky Cheese Man* by Jon Scieszka is an example.

Partitions: Sections of the *storage* area of a *hard disk* created for organizational purposes such as to increase efficiency. These partitions are created when the hard disk is prepared and before the *disk* is formatted.

Password: A secret word or code known only to the user that allows a user to *access* a *program*, *file*, or *database*. Often, passwords must be entered to *log on* to an automated *library* or *electronic mail* system. These codes help to protect the system from curious or malicious patrons.

Paste: To insert *text* or *graphics* that have been *cut* from one *document* into another location in the same document or into another document. See also *Cut and paste*.

Patch cord: An electrical wire used to connect two types of sound equipment. Electrical impulses are transferred between the two units to make a recording. As an example, a cord is used to connect a tape recorder and record player.

Patron: An individual who is a regular *library* user or a library supporter.

PBS: See *Public Broadcast System*.

PC: See *Microcomputer*.

PDA: See *Personal digital assistant*.

Pedagogy: The art or science of *teaching*.

Peer coaching: A process in which a *teacher* visits another teacher's class to observe *instruction*. The visiting teacher offers feedback for the improvement of *teaching*. See also *Coaching*.

Peer tutoring: An instructional method used in schools whereby a student is used to tutor one or more other students. This method has been effectively used to integrate students with disabilities in regular classrooms. Older students can also effectively tutor younger students.

Peer-to-peer network: A *local area network* (LAN) without a central *file server* in which all computers in the *network* have equal *access* to the files on all other workstations.

Percentile: Any of the 99 points along the scale of *test* score values that divide a distribution into 100 groups of equal frequency.

Percentile rank: The percentage of individuals examined in a specified group who fall at or below a given score on a *standardized test*.

Performance appraisal: A process by which the performance of *school* staff can be evaluated. Various procedures for appraisals are predetermined by administrators and staff. Appraisals can include such methods as formal and informal observations, planning and closure conferences, portfolio preparation, and peer collaboration, among others. See also *Evaluation*.

Performance assessment: *Assessment* based on *resource-based learning*. *Learning* is assessed by observing student demonstrations of ability, knowledge, or competencies. Student portfolios and other assessment techniques are used to measure outcomes or competencies. See also *Competency-based instruction*.

Performance budget: A *budget* that is basically a *program* budget in which emphasis is placed on quantitative measurement of *library* functions and the development of standard costs. This type of budget groups anticipated expenditures according to activities to be carried out and establishes cost *standards* for each set of activities. The emphasis is on efficiency of operations and control of quantity rather than on quality of service.

Performance objective: An *objective* derived from an instructional *goal* that states or describes what a student should be able to do as a result of *instruction*. In other words, it is the performance the student should exhibit after the instruction has occurred. The objective should use action verbs to measure the performance; for example, list, recite, sing, or throw. See also *Enabling objective* and *Objectives*.

Performance-based instruction: See *Competency-based instruction* and *Resource-based learning*.

Periodical: A publication that appears regularly in a *series* and at certain intervals, such as a *magazine* or *newspaper*. Each *issue* typically contains a mixture of articles, stories, reviews, or other writings by several different contributors. See also *Journal*, *Serial*, *Subscription*, and *Subscription agency*.

Periodical index: An *index* used to *search* for *information* on a particular *subject* in articles from magazines and journals. See also *Journal*, *Magazine*, and *Periodical*.

Peripheral device: A component or *hardware* device such as a *monitor*, *printer*, and modem that is connected to a *computer* through a *port* that allows *information* to be transferred to and from a *microprocessor*. See also *MOdulator-DEModulator*.

Permanent loan: An agreement between a library *patron* and the *library* whereby the patron can keep an item permanently unless another patron requests it later.

Person against nature: A type of *plot* conflict in which a person clashes with nature. For example, *Julie of the Wolves* by Jean Craighead George depicts a protagonist struggling with the elements in Alaska.

Person against person: A type of *plot* conflict in which two characters, either human or animal, are in conflict with each other. For example, *Jacob Have I Loved* by Katherine Paterson deals with a sister who is jealous of her twin sister.

Person against self: A type of *plot* conflict in which a character deals with fears and personal problems. Problems with the death of a parent, jealousy of a new baby, or anxiety on the first day of school are examples of this type of plot conflict.

Person against society: A type of *plot* conflict in which a person is at odds with some group in society. For example, *Blubber* by Judy Blume deals with the conflict between an overweight child and her peer group.

Personal computer: See *Microcomputer*.

Personal digital assistant (PDA): A *hand-held device* that has computing, telephone, fax, and networking features. Many of these devices use a *stylus* to tap selections on menus. Some use handwriting recognition, and some use *voice recognition*. See also *Menu*.

Personification: Gives human qualities to inanimate objects. For example, a *poem* stating that "the wind hides" uses personification. See also *Anthropomorphism*.

Phonics instruction: A method used to teach *reading* by associating letters and combinations of letters with their appropriate speech sounds. See also *Instruction*.

Phonograph record: A sound *disc* made of vinyl plastic that uses a needle to reproduce sound from grooves pressed into the surface. See also *Record*.

Photocopy: To *copy* a *document* or printed materials using a machine that photographs and develops images of an original.

Physical description area: *Information* on a *catalog* record used to give the physical form of a *work*. Examples include *pagination*, dimensions, and illustrative matter. A work's physical description appears in the fifth *area of description* on a catalog *record*.

Pickup pattern: A description of the directionality of a *microphone*. The two most prominent microphone pickup patterns are omnidirectional and unidirectional. See also *Omnidirectional microphone* and *Unidirectional microphone*.

Pico: See *Board of Education, Island Trees (New York) Union Free School District 26 v. Pico*.

Picture: A two-dimensional work of art on an opaque material such as an art print, photograph, or *study print*.

Picture book: A *book* for young children in which the illustrations are often the dominant feature with little or no *text* in some cases. This type of book gives children opportunities for self-discovery experiences and for sharing in listening as the book is read aloud. Easy-to-read books are a type of picture book designed for the beginning reader. They often use controlled vocabulary. See also *Alphabet book*, *Concept book*, *Counting book*, *Illustration*, *Toy book*, and *Wordless book*.

Pin-feed forms: *Printer* forms that have perforations along the edges so that they can be used in a printer that moves the paper through by means of a conveyor system with protrusions.

Pin-feed printer: A type of *printer* that uses a conveyor system with protrusions to move *pin-feed forms* with perforated edges through the printer. This type of printer is capable of accepting only one width of paper, as opposed to an adjustable *tractor-feed printer*.

Pixel: 1. The smallest element of a bit-mapped visual display, or a scanned *image*, that can be distinguished by a *computer*. 2. A single dot or point of an image on a *monitor*. The more pixels, the better the *resolution*. Pixel is a contraction of the words *picture element*. See also *Bitmap*.

PLA: See *Public Library Association*.

Plagiarism: An expression, idea, or *plot* taken from another person's *work* and used as one's own without giving proper credit for the *language*, thoughts, or ideas of the original creator.

Plain old telephone service (POTS): The standard telephone service that most homes use. The main distinctions between POTS and non-POTS are speed and *bandwidth*.

Planning: A decision-making process that leads to implementation by developing the means to accomplish a desired end. Initial planning produces an action plan of steps and activities with the formulation and review of goals, *objectives*, programs, budgets, and *policies and procedures*. Continuous planning results in ongoing decision making. See also *Budget*, *Goal*, *Long-range planning*, *Short-range planning*, and *Strategic planning*.

Planning, Programming, Budgeting System (PPBS): A type of budgeting technique that involves establishing goals, analyzing costs, and allocating expenditures according to a program *evaluation* that is based on goals and measurements of the education products. See also *Budget*.

Plate: An illustrative *leaf* that is not an integral part of the *text* of a *work* and is not included in the *pagination* of the text. Frequently, the plate is printed on paper that is different from that used for the text.

Platen: 1. The roller or backing on a *printer* against which the paper rests as the print head strikes it to form a *character*. 2. Used on an *opaque projector* to lower or accept materials for *projection*.

Platform: *Hardware* or *software* architecture that refers to a particular *computer* family. This term also refers to an *operating system*. Some operating systems and types of hardware are commonly used together. Windows and IBM-compatible computers and DOS and Apple computers are examples.

Plot: A series of actions in a *book* that moves in related sequence to a logical outcome; what happens in the story. A good plot includes enough action, excitement, suspense, or conflict to develop interest in the story. There are four types of plot conflicts: *person against nature*, *person against self*, *person against person*, and *person against society*. A story can contain one or more of these plot conflicts. See also *Literary elements*.

Plotter: An *output* device for graphing *data* with an automated pen. *Information* is translated from a *computer* into a pictorial or graphical form on a type of paper. The two types are drum and flatbed plotters.

Plug-and-play: The ability of a *computer* system to automatically configure expansion boards and other devices connected to a computer without having to set jumpers, *DIP switches*, and interrupts.

PO: See *Purchase order*.

Poem: An arrangement of words in verse that often leaves a lingering image after being read. The *language* of a poem can articulate *theme*, *characterization*, and feelings. See also *Poetry*.

Poetry: There is an elusiveness about this term that defies precise definition, for it is not so much what it means but the feelings it conveys. It is words in verse written by poets, but, more importantly, it is the description of experiences that captures the essence of objects, thoughts, or feelings, and is therefore deemed an important vehicle of communication. However, poetry expresses more than ordinary *language*. It communicates experiences by appealing to a reader's thoughts and feelings. It has the power to evoke strong emotional responses and rich sensory images that invite a reader to participate in an experience that happens only when the *poem* and the reader connect. A certain amount of ambiguity is characteristic of poetry because more is hidden than is expressed in words. *Ballad*, *concrete poetry*, *free verse*, *haiku*, *limerick*, *lyrical poetry*, and *narrative poetry* are examples of types of poetry.

Point of view: A literary element that describes who is telling the story. The first-person point of view tells the story from one character's perspective. The third-person point of view gives readers a broad overview of all the characters. This is the omniscient or "all knowing" point of view. The consistency of point of view encourages readers to believe in a story. See also *Literary elements*.

Point to Point Protocol (PPP): A *telecommunications* protocol that allows standard telephone lines to be used for full, graphic navigation of the *Internet*. PPP connections provide for TCP/IP to run over a standard telephone line and require high-speed modems. See also *Protocol* and *Transmission Control Protocol/Internet Protocol*.

Pointing device: A device that allows a *computer* user to control the location of a *cursor* on the *monitor* (e.g., a *mouse*).

Policies and procedures: Plans or guidelines that delineate acceptable practices and actions for a wide range of activities such as *collection development*, *circulation*, and *inventory*. See also *Policies and procedures manual*.

Policies and procedures manual: A compilation of adopted *policies and procedures* designed to ensure consistency and effectiveness in the operation of a *library media center*.

Port: An input/output connection or channel through which a *peripheral device* can communicate with a *computer*.

Portfolio: 1. A container for holding paintings, drawings, loose papers, unbound pages of a *book*, or other similar materials. 2. A systematic collection of a student's work, records of observations, and *test* results used to assess student progress. See also *Assessment* and *Evaluation*.

Portfolio assessment: An *evaluation* of a student's abilities based on a systematic collection of the student's work, records of observation, and *test* results. See also *Assessment* and *Portfolio*.

Portrait: A vertical arrangement of a printed *page* or visual *image*, such as an advertisement or a computer *screen*, in which the height is greater than the width. *Landscape* is the term for the opposite arrangement.

Post: 1. A *message* sent or contributed to a *newsgroup*, *online* discussion group, or a mailing list. 2. To publish *information* on the *Internet*.

Postproduction: The phase of *media production* that includes all activity after the *raw footage* has been shot.

POTS: See *Plain old telephone service*.

Pourquoi story: A type of *folktale* that explains certain animal traits or characteristics or customs of people. "Why Monkeys Live in Trees" is an example. Pourquoi is a French word meaning why.

Power spike: See *Power surge*.

Power supply: The component that supplies power to a computer system, usually a standard electrical outlet. A power supply is rated in watts capacity. A minimum power supply of 200 watts is recommended for *computer* use.

Power surge: An increase in the amount of electricity going to a *computer*. Also commonly called a spike. See also *Surge protector*.

PPBS: See *Planning, Programming, Budgeting System*.

PPP: See *Point to Point Protocol*.

PR: See *Public relations*.

Practicum: See *Guided practice*.

Pragmatics: The study of the use of *language* in social situations. This emphasizes functional language use rather than the mechanics of language and communication.

Prebound: A term used for books that have been bound in a heavy-duty reinforced *binding* rather than in a trade or publisher's binding.

Preface: The section of a *book* that introduces and states the origin, purpose, and scope of the book. The preface appears after the *title page*.

Preliminaries: The pages of a *book* that begin with the cover and end with the *verso* of the *title page*. This includes the cover title, the binder's title, half title page, any added title pages, and the *spine*.

Preliminary pages: The pages found at the beginning of a *book* such as the *contents page*, the *introduction*, and the *foreword*.

Preoperational period: The second stage in Piaget's theory of *cognitive development* that covers approximately the two- to seven-year-old age period. The child's thinking is self-centered (egocentric) and based on his or her own immediate perception and experience. Children are not selfish; they just cannot assume another person's point of view. Because of the egocentricism, children at this stage like stories in which they can identify with the main character and stories in which the *plot* or *theme* resembles their own actions and feelings. Some children cannot hold an *image* in their mind, which is why they like constant repetition in stories that they are told or that they read. See also *Concrete operations*, *Formal operations*, and *Sensory-motor period*.

Preprocessing: An option provided by a *publisher*, a *jobber*, or a *producer* whereby materials are made ready for *circulation* before they are shipped to a *library*. A recent option includes prepared *cataloging* data for use with automated catalogs.

Pre-reading skills: The skills or abilities needed for *reading*, including left-right discrimination and letter recognition.

Prescriptive: Defines words in a *dictionary* and sets standards of usage and acceptability. See also *Descriptive*.

Prescriptive teaching: A process by which instructional methods are designed to assist individual students in developing needed skills or abilities. Clearly defined goals, *objectives*, and strategies are predetermined before instruction begins. *The library media specialist* is a vital component in the *planning* and implementation of this method of *instruction*.

Presentation software: Software tools for producing professional-looking programs to be used in speeches and sales promotions, for example. Presentations can be enhanced with *graphics*, notes, *clip art*, slides, *outline* pages, and handouts. This type of *software* enables the presenter to become an independent producer of high-quality programs. See also *Outliner*.

Preservation: The process of changing the state of *library* material to protect the contents and keep them safe. An example is microfilming of newspapers. See also *Microform*.

Preview: Inspect, evaluate, or survey; to view or display materials such as books and videotapes before purchasing.

Primary source: A *document* based on firsthand knowledge, such as a diary, a *journal*, or an eyewitness account. Materials that have not been interpreted by other individuals. See also *Secondary source*.

Primary storage: A computer's *internal memory* (RAM). See also *Random access memory* and *Secondary storage*.

Prime mark: A mark placed at the end of a basic *classification number* and after each complete expansion of the number. The mark indicates where the classification number can be shortened without any loss of meaning in the remaining classification number.

Principal: The chief administrator of a *school* who manages the total *program* of the school. This person normally reports to the *superintendent of schools.*

Print resources: All *resources* available in print *format* including books, periodicals, newspapers, pamphlets, booklets, and brochures.

Print server: A *computer* on a *local area network* that is used to *sort* and send printing requests and to control one or more shared printers.

Printer: 1. The *output* device that is used to produce a *hard copy* of *information* from a *computer*. Some types of printers are *dot matrix printer*, *inkjet printer*, *laser printer*, *pin-feed printer*, and *tractor-feed printer*. 2. A person or firm that prints books. See also *Book*.

Print-screen key: A *key* that is used to print *text* as it appears on a computer *monitor*.

Printz Award: See *Michael L. Printz Award*.

Priority purchase: See *Wish file*.

Problem novel: See *New Realism*.

Problem solving: Instructional strategies used to involve the learner in the solving of various problems. These strategies do not simply impart accumulated knowledge. See also *Instruction*.

Procedures manual: See *Policies and procedures manual*.

Processing: 1. The process of preparing an item for use in a *library media center*. 2. The manipulation of *data* by the *central processing unit* of a *computer*.

Processing center: A central office or resource center that processes and distributes the materials of more than one *library media center* and often coordinates the *acquisition* of *hardware* and *resources*.

Producer: A person or agency responsible for the administration, production, and commercial promotion of a play, *motion picture, television, video*, or *machine-readable* data *file*.

Production: 1. The design and creation of all types of *media* such as *audio, video*, photographic, *computer* programs, or combinations of these types. 2. A phase of *media production* that includes recording the scenes of the program on *videotape*. This is also called shooting *raw footage*.

Professional collection: A *collection* of journals, books, and other materials used primarily by teachers and administrators for professional and instructional enhancement.

Professional development: Opportunities and experiences such as conferences and seminars that enable teachers and administrators to build knowledge and skills for improved *instruction*. See also *Staff development*.

Professional librarian: A person who has completed a university or equivalent qualifications in *library science*, library media, or *information* management, and is employed in a professional position, such as a school *library media specialist*. See also *Non-professionals*.

Program: 1. A sequence of instructions that enables a *computer* to solve a problem or perform certain tasks. 2. An event planned by the library media staff to provide *information*, entertainment, and *reading* motivation or to introduce patrons to the materials and services of the *library media center*. 3. A plan or system, such as a library media program or a *school* instructional program, that is developed and implemented. See also *Code* and *Programming*.

Program administrator: A role of the school *library media specialist* as delineated in *Information Power* in which the library media specialist works with the *school* to define policies of the library media *program* and shows proficiency in staff management, budgets, equipment, and facilities. See also *Roles of library media specialists*.

Programmed instruction: A method of presenting instructional materials printed in small bits or frames. Each bit or *frame* includes an item of *information*, a sentence to be completed, and the correct answer. See also *Instruction*.

Programming: 1. Developing programs and activities such as those planned and implemented by a *library media specialist*. 2. Designing, *writing*, and testing *program* instructions. See also *Programming language*.

Programming language: A special *language* in which *computer* programs are written. Examples are FORTRAN, BASIC, and COBOL. Computer languages have progressed from basic machine code to high-level languages such as C, HyperTalk, and Lingo. See also *Programming*.

Projection: 1. A way to represent the three-dimensional earth on a two-dimensional *map*; however, distortion is always a problem with maps. A *globe* is the only relatively accurate representation of the earth. 2. The process of projecting or producing images on a *screen*. The two main types of projection are *front projection* and *rear projection*.

Projection lens: A convex *lens* or system of lenses that recreates an enlarged *image* of a *film* or object on the *screen*. These lenses are used with all types of projectors such as an *overhead projector*, an *opaque projector*, and a *slide* projector.

Prompt: A symbol, letter, or *message* on a computer *screen* that indicates to a user that the *computer* is ready to accept instructions, *data*, *information*, or a request. An example is the C prompt, which appears on the screen as C> when using DOS.

Proposal: See *Grant proposal*.

Protocol: Documents and procedures that enable consistency and courtesy in using a *computer* system. It ensures that users follow prescribed formats or sequences of activities. Protocols can describe low-level details of machine interfaces or high-level exchanges between programs. See also *Hypertext Transport Protocol, Point to Point Protocol, Serial Line Internet Protocol/Point to Point Protocol, Transmission Control Protocol/Internet Protocol,* and *Uniform Resource Locator*.

Proximity operators: Indicators that use words or special punctuations to narrow searches and increase the accuracy of a *keyword search*. These allow a *computer* user to specify how close the desired terms must be to each other to *retrieve* a *record*. The operators SAME, ADJACENT, NEAR, and WITHIN are examples. The operator SAME requires that two words occur in the same *field*. The record is not retrieved if none of its fields has both terms. The operator ADJACENT retrieves records in which the terms appear next to each other in the order entered in the *search*. The operator NEAR retrieves records in which both terms appear next to each other but in any order. The operator WITHIN retrieves records in which the terms appear within a certain number of words of each other. See also *Proximity search*.

Proximity search: A search feature that allows a *computer* user to *search* for words that are near each other in a *document* and to specify the closeness of the keywords within the document. For example, the user can specify that the keywords must be less than ten words apart and located in the same paragraph. See also *Keyword* and *Proximity operators*.

Pseudonym: A fictitious or assumed name used by an *author* to conceal his or her identity.

Psychomotor domain: One of the three domains included in *Bloom's taxonomy*. This domain, unlike the *cognitive domain* and the *affective domain*, deals primarily with physical or motor skills and coordination. A psychomotor *test* is used to measure gross and fine motor skills. Instructional *objectives* and activities or tasks typically have cognitive/affective elements, but the focus for objectives and activities in this domain should be on motor skill development. The suggested areas for use are *reading readiness*, speech development, handwriting, *manipulative* skills, and physical education.

Public access catalog: See *Online public access catalog*.

Public Broadcast System (PBS): An agency that manages the public television *network* and coordinates the operations of *public television* stations and develops national programming. PBS is an agency of the Corporation for Public Broadcasting.

Public domain software: *Computer* software that is made available for public use entirely free of charge. Much public domain *software* is available for downloading from sites on the *Internet*. Freeware is a synonymous term. See also *Shareware*.

Public Law 94-142: See *Education for All Handicapped Children Act*.

Public Law 101-476: See *Individuals with Disabilities Education Act*.

Public library: A publicly funded *library* that provides library services to all the people in a community or city.

Public Library Association (PLA): A division of the *American Library Association* that represents public librarians. It advocates *research*, *continuing education*, *standards*, and legislation for public libraries. It publishes *Public Libraries* bimonthly.

Public relations (PR): Activities, programs, and marketing techniques designed to promote public understanding of the policies, procedures, programs, and services of a *library*.

Public television: A form of *broadcast television* that is noncommercial and available to the public; features chiefly cultural, educational, and discovery type programs. See also *Cable television* and *Public Broadcast System*.

Publication and distribution area: The area of a *catalog* description used to record *information* about the place, name, and date of publishing or distributing an item. This is the fourth *area of description* on a catalog *record*.

Publisher: The person, group, or *corporate body* responsible for preparing and issuing printed materials and *information* packages.

Pulitzer Prize: Various prizes given annually for distinguished works in American *literature*, drama, journalism, and music. The prize was established in 1917 by Joseph Pulitzer, a *newspaper* publisher, as an incentive for excellence. They are awarded by the Pulitzer Prize Board.

Pull-out program: A special education *program* in which students with disabilities leave regular classrooms and attend special classes or resource rooms for *instruction* during part or all of the school day.

Pura Belpre Award: See *Belpre Award*.

Purchase order (PO): An order placed with a supplier that indicates an intent to purchase the items included on the order form. See also *Encumbrance*. ■

Qualitative assessment: A process that uses observations and other methods that do not focus on providing numerical *data*. Facts and claims are usually presented in *narrative* instead of numerical format. See also *Assessment* and *Quantitative assessment*.

Qualitative research: A broad category of *research* that seeks to describe the way things are in a particular context. It can describe persons and events in a scientific manner without a numerical analysis of *data*. Library and information science research increasingly uses qualitative analyses such as observation, content analysis, and categorization. An example of this type of research might be an interview with illiterate individuals to determine how their lives were affected by their lack of *literacy*. See also *Quantitative research*.

Quantitative assessment: A process of *assessment* that focuses on the use of numerical quantities or values. Facts and claims are usually represented by numbers. See also *Qualitative assessment*.

Quantitative research: A broad category of *research* in which the *data* can be analyzed numerically. It is expressible in terms of quantity; that is, a definite amount or number. An example might be a comparison of two methods of *teaching* reading to first-graders. The scores of both groups are compared and analyzed. See also *Qualitative research*.

Quatrain: A *poem*, unit, or stanza of four lines of verse, which usually rhyme alternately. The four-line verse has an AABB, ABAB, ABBA, or ABCD rhyming pattern. It is the most common stanzaic form of verse, which means that the lines are of the same length and meter and are therefore isometric. An example is the heroic quatrain or heroic verse, the form in which *epic* poetry is usually written. The English form is also called the elegiac stanza. A well-known example of this verse is Gray's "Elegy Written in a Country Churchyard." See also *Poetry*.

Questioning: A *teaching* method designed by teachers and library media specialists to extend student thinking and assess prior student knowledge. This instructional technique encourages *critical thinking skills*, divergent thinking, and *higher order thinking skills*. See also *Instruction*.

Queue: 1. A group of people, items, or messages arranged in priority order or in a line. 2. A list of items, such as *library* materials, that are waiting for processing. 3. A holding area or *buffer* for storing *output* data until a *printer* is ready to print the *information*. ■

Ragged: *Text* that is not aligned evenly with a margin. See also *Justification*.

RAM: See *Random access memory*.

Randolph Caldecott Award: See *Caldecott Award*.

Random access memory (RAM): A computer's internal *memory* chips used to *store* the *data* and *program* instructions with which the *computer* is currently working. Random access means that the time needed to *read* or *write* data is not dependent on its location within the memory. RAM is the most widely used memory technology for computing. However, all data entered in RAM are destroyed or erased when the computer is turned off or fails. For this reason, it is known as volatile memory. See also *Read-only memory*.

Raw footage: The unedited *audio* and *video* recorded during the *production* process; the footage from which a program is constructed. The term is synonymous with original footage.

Raw score: 1. The basic score obtained from scoring a *test* according to the test maker's directions. 2. The number of questions answered correctly.

REACTS taxonomy: A *model* of *teaching* a reaction to *research* and *information literacy skills* that emphasizes *critical thinking skills*. The six levels in the model that create the *acronym* are Recalling, Explaining, Analyzing, Challenging, Transforming, and Synthesizing. The six levels of the REACTS taxonomy and the six levels of the *research taxonomy* are correlated. For example, level one of the REACTS taxonomy is recalling, which correlates to level one in the research taxonomy, which is factfinding. The *taxonomy* is discussed in *Brainstorms and Blueprints: Teaching Library Research as a Thinking Process* by Barbara Stripling and Judy Pitts, which was published in 1988 by Libraries Unlimited. See also *Information literacy process models*.

Read: 1. The process of obtaining meaning from print. 2. The act of retrieving *data* or *program* instructions from computer *memory* or a *storage* device such as a *compact disc* or a *floppy disk*. See also *Reading*.

Read Across America: An annual promotion held on March 2, the birthday of Dr. Seuss, to promote *reading*. The event is a project of the *National Education Association* and is supported by other organizations, including the *American Library Association* and the *International Reading Association*.

Read the shelves: A process for examining the items on shelves to ensure that they are all located in the proper *call number* sequence.

Readiness skills: The basic skills deemed necessary before academics can be mastered. This includes attending skills, knowledge of letter names, and the ability to follow directions. See also *Listening skills* and *Reading readiness*.

Reading: 1. Retrieving *data* from a *peripheral device* such as a *disk* and placing the data into the *random access memory* of a *computer*. 2. A transactive process in which a reader determines meaning to comprehend or create an interpretation. The reading process involves a series of stages during which readers construct interpretations—known as comprehension—as they *read* and respond to the *text*. See also *Phonics instruction* and *Whole language instruction*.

Reading ability: A complex negotiation between the *text* and the reader that is shaped by many factors, including the reader's intellect, knowledge about a *topic*, the purpose for *reading*, cultural background, *language*, previous experiences, and the reader's expectations about reading.

Reading guidance: See *Reading, viewing, listening guidance*.

Reading readiness: The process of exposing young children to a variety of *reading* materials, particularly books, that encourage aesthetic responses stemming from personal engagement with the story. Some activities that involve such aesthetic experiences are reliving, comparing, imaging, and relating. See also *Read*, *Readiness skills*, and *Reading ability*.

Reading, viewing, listening guidance: Guidance offered by library staff members to *library* patrons in the *selection* and use of print and nonprint materials.

Read-only access: A *file* status that permits *information* to be *read* but not changed.

Read-only memory (ROM): The portion of a computer's internal *memory* that is permanently programmed during manufacturing. ROM data can be *read* but cannot be erased or changed. These *data* remain after the *computer* is turned off. For this reason, it is referred to as nonvolatile memory. See also *Random access memory*.

Read/write head: The magnetic device that travels back and forth across the surface of a *disk* or tape. It can *read* and *write* data on a disk or a tape.

Ready reference: Readily available reference sources that contain *information* for questions requiring short, factual answers. An example is a one-volume *encyclopedia* or a subject *dictionary*.

Ready reference question: A question requiring a short factual answer that can be answered from readily available sources such as enyclopedias or almanacs. See also *Directional question* and *Research question*.

Real time: The processing of *data* by a *computer* as quickly as data are *input*.

Realia: Real three-dimensional objects such as models, specimens, and artifacts as contrasted with replicas. See also *Model*.

Realism: Thoughts and actions based on realities. When pertaining to art and *literature*, realism portrays life as it really is. See also *New Realism* and *Realistic fiction*.

Realistic fiction: Stories or plots that are usually set in the con temporary world. The characters and settings are believable and also completely realistic in the present-day world. The authors primarily rely on relevant subjects and everyday occurrences or extreme *realism* to create stories that are convincingly true to life. The concern is with externals; how things look rather than how things are. The *author* commonly begins with a problem rather than a *plot* or *character*. See also *New Realism*.

Realistic story: A type of *folktale* that tells a story that could have happened. "Who Will Wash the Pot?," a Russian folktale based on the life of a married couple, is an example.

Rear projection: A method of reverse image *projection* that projects from behind a specially coated translucent *screen*. The audience faces the opposite of the screen. See also *Front projection*.

Rear projection screen: A translucent *screen* onto which a reverse *image* is projected from a *slide* projector or *filmstrip* projector while the viewers sit facing the opposite side of the screen. This type of screen is frequently used in the carrels of a *library media center*. See also *Carrel* and *Projection*.

Reasoning: The process of thinking from which conclusions can be drawn from facts. See also *Deductive reasoning* and *Inductive reasoning*.

Rebinding: The process of repairing worn books by trimming, resewing, cleaning, and replacing the covers and spines. See also *Mending*.

Reboot: To restart a *computer*. See also *Boot, Cold boot*, and *Warm boot*.

Reciprocal borrowing: The exchange of borrowing privileges between two or more cooperating libraries.

RECON: See *Retrospective conversion*.

Reconsideration of materials: A series of actions used to respond to a *library* user's complaint about certain library materials. The complainant completes a reconsideration of materials form. The process should be included in a *selection policy*.

Record: 1. A *document*. 2. A sound recording made on a vinyl *disc*. 3. *Data* relating to a document in a *database* or *catalog*. 4. A *collection* of related items treated as one complete unit of information, such as a *bibliographic citation*. 5. To preserve *information*. 6. To reproduce *audio* or *video*, or both, using *magnetic tape* or discs. See also *Bibliographic record, Machine-readable cataloging record, Phonograph record,* and *Sound recordings*.

Recto: The right-hand *page* of a *book*, usually bearing an odd number; the side of a *leaf* intended to be *read* first. The reverse of *verso*.

Red Book: *Standards* for creating CD-audio discs. See also *Compact disc-digital audio*.

Reference and User Services Association (RUSA): A division of the *American Library Association* that seeks to stimulate and support reference in all types of libraries. It publishes *RUSA Update*, quarterly, and *Reference and User Services Quarterly* (formerly *RQ*).

Reference book: An important source of *information* used to answer questions or *research* a *topic*. A *work* intended to be used for referral and research rather than for general *reading* interest.

Reference collection: A noncirculating *collection* of selected materials used for locating *information* and shelved together for easy *access*. These materials are usually not for *loan* outside a *library*.

Reference interview: The face-to-face exchange between *library* personnel and a person searching for *information* to clarify a reference inquiry.

Reference materials: Selected materials intended to assist users seeking *information*. Examples are encyclopedias, dictionaries, and almanacs. These materials are usually housed in the reference area of the *library media center*.

Reference strategy: The process of locating *information* and answers to reference questions in the most efficient and speedy manner.

Related term (RT): A *cross-reference* from a *subject heading* specific to another *heading* and related *subject* matter. For example, under the subject heading for Pets there may be a cross- reference or *see reference* to the heading Domestic animals. See also *Broader term* and *Narrower term*.

Relative index: An alphabetical list of all the topics and synonyms in a classification scheme, which brings together aspects of subjects from the disciplines used in classification. The *index* shows the relation of the topics to all the disciplines with which they are associated. See also *Classification system* and *Synonym*.

Reliability: The extent to which a *test* is consistent and dependable over a period of time in measuring what it is designed to measure. The attribute of consistency in measurement. See also *Validity*.

Remainder list: 1. A list of items issued by a *publisher* or bookseller to be sold at or below cost. 2. A list of duplicate or unwanted materials circulated to other libraries before their disposal.

Remediation: A process designed to teach students to overcome deficiencies through training and education.

Remote control: The control of various types of equipment such as a *computer*, a *slide* projector, or a *television* from a distance, usually with a wired or wireless device.

Renew: To extend the amount of time for which an item is on *loan* or checked out from a *library media center*. See also *Charge*.

Repeater: A *hardware* device used on a *network* that is needed at regular intervals to extend the length of network cabling by amplifying and sending along the messages traveling through the network. See also *Message*.

Report: The process of compiling and presenting *information* that results from the collection and *evaluation* of various *data* regarding an entity such as a *library media center*. Student information, financial updates, and monthly or annual reports are some examples. These reports provide useful documentation for *planning* and supply important information for *school* personnel and the public.

Reprint: A new printing of material that has been published before by resetting the original typeface or by photographic methods. The time interval between the first printing and the reprinting may be a day, weeks, months, or hundreds of years.

Reproduce: The process of copying by hand, photography, or recording onto a *videotape* or a *cassette tape*. Synonymous term for duplicate.

Request for proposal (RFP): A *document* used to publicize or solicit proposals from consultants, vendors, or other groups. A set of specifications that describes what services are requested or needed; the format for bids or proposals; and the guidelines, timelines, and other requirements to be followed.

Research: 1. A careful, systematic study and intensive investigation in some field of knowledge, usually through *hypothesis* and experiment, to discover and establish new knowledge, facts, theories, principles, or laws. 2. In general, any careful study or investigation that seeks to increase one's knowledge of a *topic* or given situation. The purpose of library research is to provide *data* to support decisions about day-to-day library operations, to guide the design of information systems, or to build models that explain certain aspects of information dissemination. A specialized area of library and information research is the statistical study of *bibliographic information*. Library and information science research increasingly uses qualitative analyses such as observation, content analysis, and categorization. 3. Methods used in a *library* or *library media center* that enable students and staff to *access* and use *information* located in a variety of sources such as reference books, periodicals, the *Internet*, and *online* databases. See also *Action research*, *Descriptive research*, *Experimental research*, *Historical research*, *Qualitative research*, *Quantitative research*, and *Research methodology*.

Research Libraries Group (RLG): A consortium of major universities and research institutions in the United States. The members collaborate on programs and projects. See also *Research Libraries Information Network*.

Research Libraries Information Network (RLIN): The automated information *network* of the *Research Libraries Group*. The network combines databases and *computer* systems to serve the materials-processing requirements of RLG members and other nonmember institutions.

Research methodology: The application of the scientific method using *research* techniques (e.g., surveys, experiments, and participant observations) for collecting and organizing *data*. Once the data are analyzed, conclusions can be drawn resulting in the accumulation of knowledge.

Research question: A question that usually requires detailed *information* and extensive use of reference materials and sources of information. See also *Directional question* and *Ready reference question*.

Research taxonomy: A *model* of teaching *research* and *information literacy skills* that emphasizes *critical thinking skills*. The six levels in the model are Fact finding, Asking/Searching, Examining/Organizing, Evaluating/Deliberating, Integrating/Concluding, and Conceptualizing. The six levels of the research taxonomy and the six levels of the *REACTS taxonomy* are correlated. For example, level one of the research taxonomy is fact-finding, which correlates to level one in the REACTS taxonomy, which is recalling. The *taxonomy* is discussed in *Brainstorms and Blueprints: Teaching Library Research as a Thinking Process* by Barbara Stripling and Judy Pitts, which was published in 1988 by Libraries Unlimited. See also *Information literacy process models* and *Teaching*.

Reserve: 1. An item that has been returned and is being held at the request of a *borrower*. 2. Material held for a borrower, often in a special *collection* and loaned for short periods of time. See also *Hold*.

Reserve collection: A *collection* of materials being held for a specified group of users who normally use them in the *library media center*. The *teacher* decides on the materials to be placed on *reserve*, and the *library media specialist* makes them available for student use.

Reset keys: A *key* combination required to *reboot* a *computer* system. Control/Alt/Delete is an example.

Re-shelve: The process of returning books to their proper location on the shelves.

Resolution: The sharpness or clarity of a computer *screen* determined by the number of dots or pixels that can be displayed on a *computer* screen. Higher resolutions create brighter images. Displays with more pixels and lines have better resolution. A widely accepted term currently used is *dot pitch*. See also *Dots per inch* and *Pixel*.

Resource sharing: The sharing of materials between libraries with users of all participating libraries having *access* to the materials.

Resource-based learning: *Learning* that results from students working independently or in small groups using multiple *resources*. This type of learning requires that students are effective users of *information* in many formats such as books and periodicals as well as electronic resources such as *computer* databases and laser videodiscs. See also *Performance assessment*.

Resources: 1. The *information* materials available from a *library* that convey information, thoughts, or feelings. These materials may include books, periodicals, databases, pamphlets, reports, microforms, videocassettes, and recordings. 2. The means used to produce a *program* or activities including information, financial support, people, equipment, facilities, materials, and supplies. 3. Sources of information or expertise.

Response time: The time between the entry of a *command* or *search* request and the delivery of a response or results of the search. Response time is an important measurement of an automated *library* system.

Retrieval: The procedures involved in locating, displaying, and printing *data* that have been stored in a *computer* system.

Retrieve: To call up *data* that have been stored in a *computer* system.

Retrofit: To modify to include new or improved materials or parts in an existing piece of equipment or a structure; an add-on or accessory.

Retrospective conversion (RECON): The process of changing *information* from a printed form into a *machine-readable* format. This term often refers to changing *catalog* information from catalog cards to the MARC *format* for use on an automated system. See also *Machine-readable cataloging*.

Retrospective selection aids: Professional tools used to select materials that were published in previous years as distinct from *current selection aids*.

Review: 1. An *evaluation* of a literary *work*, *videotape*, concert, or play that is published in a *periodical* or *newspaper*. 2. A periodical devoted primarily to articles of criticism and appraisal, such as a literary review. See also *Book review*.

Revised edition: A new *edition* of a *work* with the main *text* changed and corrected.

RFP: See *Request for proposal.*

Rich text format (RTF): A type of formatted *text* that can be *read* by many different types of word processors.

Ring: A type of *network* topology in which data are transmitted in one circular direction among the workstations in a *local area network*. Each *workstation* is connected to those on either side of it. One or more file servers can be used. *Data* are transmitted through the ring before it reaches its destination. See also *Daisy-chained network*, *File server*, and *Topology.*

RLG: See *Research Libraries Group.*

RLIN: See *Research Libraries Information Network.*

Robert F. Sibert Award: See *Sibert Award.*

Role-play: An instructional method using a *simulation* in which the participants assume various roles. This method is often very useful in counseling and training situations.

Roles of library media specialists: The roles of library media specialists (as defined in *Information Power: Building Partnerships for Learning*) are *teacher, information specialist, instructional partner*, and *program administrator*.

ROM: See *Read-only memory.*

Rote learning: Memorization and repetition without always understanding or internalizing the *information* or its meaning. See also *Learning.*

Router: 1. A networked *computer* or similar device that stores *network* addresses and determines the path for routing *information* to and from the computers in a network. 2. A computer or *software* package that handles the traffic between two or more networks.

Routing slip: A list of users to whom new publications are to be circulated. Used most frequently with current issues of a *journal.*

RT: See *Related term.*

RTF: See *Rich text format.*

Rubrics: Criteria established to describe what must be included or completed to satisfy requirements for an assignment or project.

Rule of thirds: A *video* composition technique that draws an imaginary tic-tac-toe grid on the *screen*, and the important parts of the scene are placed along the lines and their intersections.

Run: *Computer* jargon for "execute."

Running head: See *Header*.

Running title: A *title* or abbreviated title that is repeated at the top or bottom of each *page* of a *work* or at the head of the *verso*.

RUSA: See *Reference and User Services Association*. ∎

SAT: See *Scholastic Aptitude Test* and *Stanford Achievement Test*.

Satellite: Active reflectors or electronic *transmission* vehicles that orbit the earth and receive signals from ground stations, amplify them, and retransmit them to ground stations in other parts of the world. Satellite communication allows *data*, *information*, and entertainment materials to be transmitted. See also *Satellite dish*.

Satellite dish: A receiver for *data*, *information*, and entertainment sent from *satellite* stations that orbit the earth.

Satellite library: An extension of a *library media center* at a different location such as a classroom or conference room.

Satire: A literary *work* in which follies or vices are held up to contempt and ridicule.

Save: The process of storing *data* in a computer's *memory*, on a *disk*, or on tape. See also *Delete* and *Storage*.

Scaffolding: An instructional technique that supports students to ensure their success. The term denotes the scaffolding that builders use around a building. The *teacher* shows the students how to successfully complete a task before they start. As the students become successful, the teacher withdraws assistance and gives them more responsibility. See also *Instruction*.

Scale: The proportion that a *map* or a *model*, among others, bears to what it represents. For example, a scale of one inch to one mile on a map.

Scan: 1. In *video*, a mode of playing or examining *information* in which the user is able to skip over several frames at a time in either forward or reverse. 2. A method of *reading* a printed *document* into a *computer*. 3. To *search* a computer *file*.

Scanner: A hardware *peripheral device* that converts images on paper to electronic impulses that a *computer* can *read*. Some common types of scanners are *barcode scanner, flatbed scanner, hand-held scanner, optical scanner,* and *sheet-fed scanner*.

Schedules: The classes and divisions of a *classification system* arranged in a systematic order. The ten main classes of the *Dewey Decimal Classification* system that are in numerical order are an example.

Schemata: A term used by *Piaget* and other psychologists with reference to the conceptual structures used to interpret *information* presented to the senses by the external world or to think out or model aspects of the real world in the mind. When a person encounters a new object or situation, it is matched against the existing schemata and treated accordingly. The schemata are changed if the results are inappropriate or additional ones are developed. More sophisticated and differentiated schemata are developed as a child encounters more new experiences and as the cognitive powers develop. The singular is schema.

Scholastic Aptitude Test (SAT): A *standardized test* sponsored by the College Board and administered by the Educational Testing Service. The *test* is commonly required for college admissions. See also *Scholastic aptitude tests*.

Scholastic aptitude tests: Tests that measure the cognitive skills necessary for successful *learning* in schools. These tests are also used to predict the ability of a person to learn the kinds of *information* and skills to be mastered in *school*. An example is the *Scholastic Aptitude Test* (SAT). The abilities measured by these types of tests are similar to those measured by general intelligence tests.

School: A physical plant of one or more buildings where students are provided educational opportunities.

School board: See *Board of education*.

School district: The geographical area served by a public *school system*.

School librarian: See *Library media specialist*.

School library: See *Library media center*.

School Library Bill of Rights: A *document* adopted by the *American Association of School Librarians* concerning *intellectual freedom* and *access* to *information*. AASL withdrew the document in 1976. See also *Library Bill of Rights*.

School library media center: See *Library media center*.

School library media coordinator: See *Library media coordinator*.

School Library Media Month: A special emphasis designed to promote the *library media center*. The observance is sponsored by the *American Association of School Librarians*, a division of the *American Library Association*. It coincides with the one week in April designated for *National Library Week* and has the same theme.

School library media personnel: See *Library media personnel*.

School library media specialist: See *Library media specialist*.

School partnerships: 1. Joint efforts between schools and businesses to meet the financial, physical, and volunteer needs of students and the staff. 2. Joint efforts between school library media specialists and teachers or principals to facilitate instructional programs and provide students *access* to *hardware* and *resources*.

School reform: Any proposed changes in *school* policies, operations, *curriculum*, or *instruction*. School reform has been and continues to be an ongoing issue in education.

School system: All the public schools created to serve a legally defined *school district*. The system is typically controlled by a *board of education* (school board) and administered by a *superintendent of schools*.

Science fiction: A novel, short story, or play that combines science, adventure, and *fantasy* and deals with life in the future, life in other galaxies, or with exploration of other fantastic situations.

Scope and sequence: An educational term used to denote the subject matter and *learning* experiences that are provided for students.

Scope note: A notation in the *Dewey Decimal Classification* system or the *Library of Congress Classification* system that explains the meaning, limitations, or qualifications of a classification *notation*; a notation in the *Sears List of Subject Headings* or the *Library of Congress Subject Headings* that explains the meaning, limitations, or qualifications of a *subject heading*.

Screen: 1. A type of surface used for the *projection* of images such as those from a *film*, a *filmstrip*, a *slide*, or a *television*. The two basic types used for *front projection* are wall-mounted screens and standing screens that are mounted on tripods or detachable legs. Screens are also available for *rear projection*. 2. The surface of a *cathode ray tube* on which *computer* information is displayed. See also *Front projection screen*, *Monitor*, and *Rear projection screen*.

Screen capture: See *Capture*.

Screen resolution: See *Resolution*.

Screen saver: A *program* that takes over a display *screen* after a specified period of time if there are no *mouse* or *keyboard* movements. The screen saver fills the screen with images or *animation* that the user chooses in advance. Its purpose is to prevent a *monitor* from being etched or "burned" by an *image* displayed for a prolonged period of time. By moving a mouse or pressing a *key*, the original screen image is restored.

Screening: A process in which students are tested or examined to identify high-risk students with special needs who should have further assessments and additional assistance.

Script: 1. The *manuscript* of a play, screenplay, or *television* production. 2. A series of commands written in a *language* embedded in a *hypermedia* program.

Script font: A computer *font* that resembles handwriting.

Scroll: Horizontal or vertical movements of *text* or images on a computer *screen* display. See also *Horizontal scrolling* and *Vertical scrolling*.

SCSI: See *Small computer system interface*.

SCSI card: See *Small computer system interface (SCSI) card*.

Search: 1. The process of locating and retrieving *information* on a specific *topic*. For example, a computer *database* can be used to locate information on the planets. 2. The result or end product of locating and retrieving information on a specific topic.

Search engine: *Database* query *software* that executes searches in response to specific user commands. These commands are often expressed as *keyword* entries as they *search* for words contained in files or *file* directories. For example, *Veronica* is used for *Gopher* searches; AltaVista is used in *World Wide Web* browsing; and *Archie* is used to locate remote files at public FTP sites. See also *File transfer protocol*, *Internet directory*, and *Meta-search engine*.

Search skills: The skills necessary for locating, evaluating, and using *research* information.

Search strategy: An organized plan by which a user searches electronic *information* sources. This usually involves an *outline* of the *search* with terms to be used and the use of *Boolean operators* to increase search results. See also *Online searching* and *Wild card*.

Sears List of Subject Headings: A list of *subject* headings widely used in *cataloging* for school and small public libraries. It is modified to meet the needs of smaller collections but follows the *Library of Congress* form of headings. The list is generally used in conjunction with the *Dewey Decimal Classification* system. See also *Subject heading*.

Secondary source: Materials that other individuals have reported, analyzed, or interpreted. See also *Primary source*.

Secondary storage: External *storage* such as a *disk* or a tape. See also *Primary storage*.

Sector: Section of a *track* on a *disk*. When a disk is formatted, it is divided into sectors and tracks. Tracks are concentric circles around the disk, and a sector is a segment within each circle.

Security system: An electronic system placed at the exit to a *library media center* to detect items being removed from the *collection* that have not been properly checked out. Various systems are used, and most incorporate an electrically charged device that may be attached to or inserted in an item. If the device is not desensitized at the *circulation desk*, it will trigger an alarm when the item passes through the detection gate. See also *Desensitize* and *Sensitize*.

See also reference: An instruction or *cross-reference* that directs a reader or user from one term to other related terms.

See reference: An instruction or *cross-reference* that directs a reader or user from an unused term to one used in a *catalog* or reference *work*.

Selection: 1. The process of evaluating and deciding on items to purchase for a *library media center*. 2. The process used by a library *patron* for choosing books and other *resources* to borrow from a *library*.

Selection criteria: The criteria used by library media specialists for evaluating and selecting items to add to a *collection*. See also *Collection development* and *Selection policy*.

Selection policy: A policy developed by a *school* or a school board, or both, to guarantee students *access* to a broad range of ideas and materials. These include policies on *collection development* and procedures for the review of *resources* that are questioned or challenged as to suitability for a *library media center* or students. The policy provides for a timely and fair hearing for all concerned and ensures that proper procedures are applied. See also *Challenged material*, *Collection maintenance*, and *Selection criteria*.

Selection tools: Basic bibliographies and reviews from journals that aid in the *selection* of materials for a *library media center*. See also *Current selection aids* and *Retrospective selection aids*.

Semantics: The study of the meaning in *language* including context, intent, and the meaning attached to words and sentences.

Sensitize: To reverse the magnetic field on security tape placed in an item being returned to the *library media center* so the facility's alarm will activate if the item is later removed without being properly checked out. See also *Desensitize* and *Security system*.

Sensory-motor period: The first stage in Piaget's theory of *cognitive development* that covers birth to approximately 18 months of age. *Learning* takes place by sensory perception and motor activity. Children learn through their senses; they place objects in their mouths; they crawl. A child likes action rhymes such as "Pat-a-Cake" and tactile books such as the scratch and sniff books. See also *Concrete operations*, *Formal operations*, and *Preoperational period*.

Sequencing: The process of arranging ideas into logical order.

Serial: An item published indefinitely and issued in successive parts. Serials include periodicals, newspapers, reports, and bulletins, among others. See also *Periodical* and *Subscription agency*.

Serial interface: A *data* channel that transmits data bits in a serial fashion—one *bit* after another. *Digital* data are sent as serial transmissions over telephone lines; therefore, modems are connected to a *serial port*. See also *Interface*, *Parallel interface*, and *Transmission*.

Serial Line Internet Protocol/Point to Point Protocol (SLIP/PPP): A telecommunications *protocol* that allows standard telephone lines to be used for full, graphic navigation of the *Internet*. See also *Telecommunications*.

Serial port: A standard connection that allows a peripheral *serial interface* device such as a modem or *scanner* to be attached to a *computer*. See also *MOdulator-DEModulator*, *Parallel port*, *Peripheral device*, and *Universal Serial Bus*.

Series: A number of separate works, usually related in *subject* or form, with a *collective title* that identifies them as part of the group. Each *work* also has its own separate *title*. This is the sixth *area of description* on a *catalog* record.

Server: See *File server* and *Print server*.

Setting: The location of a story in time and place. This literary element helps readers share what the characters see, smell, hear, and touch. It also makes the characters' values, actions, and conflicts more understandable. The setting may create a mood, establish background, or supply symbolic meanings. Different types of *literature* have their own requirements as far as the setting is concerned. See also *Literary elements*.

Shared responsibility: An item created by more than one responsible party who share the same type of contribution in the creation of a *work* (e.g., a *book* with two equal authors).

Shareware: *Computer* software that is made available to users at no initial cost. Payment to the developer is expected at a later time if the *software* is adopted by the user. Shareware is available for downloading from the *Internet*. See also *Public domain software*.

Sheet-fed scanner: A type of *flatbed scanner* that automatically loads paper for scanning rather than a thick object such as a *book*. The paper is moved across a scan head that remains stationary. See also *Scanner*.

Shelf guide: A guide to show the sequence of call numbers in a set of shelves. See also *Call number*.

Shelflist: 1. A *record* of the items in a *library media center* placed in *call number* order (e.g., the order in which they are shelved). 2. *Information packages* can also be considered in the record of items that comprise a shelflist. A shelflist is used to *inventory* a library media center *collection*.

Shelve: Placing materials on the shelves of a *library media center* in the correct *call number* order.

Shelving: The shelves in a *library media center* upon which books and other items are placed.

Short-range planning: Adapting long-range goals into more specific short-term *objectives*. Specific objectives are developed for all areas of the library media *program* for a designated *planning* cycle, usually annual or biennial. The objectives are translated into an operational plan with performance objectives to be met each year. See also *Long-range planning* and *Performance objective*.

Shotgun microphone: A long *microphone* that is capable of picking up sound from a long distance. It is very useful for large or outdoor production sets.

Shrink wrap license: A *copyright* statement that takes effect when the purchaser opens the plastic shrink wrap to use a computer *program*. See also *License*.

Shutter: A projector or *camera* device that blocks the passage of light through the *aperture* while a photograph is taken or *film* is moved.

Sibert Award: An award presented annually by the *Association for Library Service to Children*, a division of the *American Library Association*, to the *author* of the most distinguished *informational book* for children published in the preceding year. The award, which began in 2001, is named in honor of Robert F. Sibert, the long-time president of Bound to Stay Bound Books, Inc., which sponsors the award.

Silicon chip: See *Chip*.

Simile: A figure of speech or a statement that describes one thing as being like another. It uses the words "as" or "like." An example is "hard as nails." See also *Metaphor*.

SIMM: See *Single in-line memory module*.

Simulation: A *learning* experience or type of software *program* that simulates a real-life, historic, physical, or biological situation. An example is an educational *game* that simulates the consequences of decisions made in the operation of a rocket.

Simulation game: A format for *instruction* that combines the elements of *simulation* such as *role-play* with the elements of a *game*, which usually has specific rules and in which players strive toward a *goal*. Many *software* vendors provide *computer* games such as golf, flying, and cards, among others.

Single in-line memory module (SIMM): A small printed *circuit board* containing *memory* chips. The board plugs into a socket on the motherboard or memory board to increase the RAM capacity. The boards can range from 30- to 72-pins connectors. See also *Memory chip* and *Random access memory*.

Single-lens reflex camera: A type of *camera* in which the *viewfinder* image is formed by the camera *lens* and reflected to a top-mounted viewing *screen* by a hinged mirror normally inclined behind the camera lens. During exposure of the *film*, the mirror flips up and allows light to pass through onto the film.

Single-user license: A *license* that permits a *software* item to be used by a single user.

Site license: A *copyright* agreement between the *software* producer and the user that allows a set number of copies to be used. A *local area network* needs a site *license* so that all users can *access* the *program*.

Site-based management: An approach to *school* governance that gives significant decision-making opportunities and experiences to local school personnel, parents, and community leaders.

Skimming: To *read*, study, or examine rapidly; to glance through to determine the *plot* or main ideas.

Slide: 1. A single *frame* of *film* or other transparent material projecting an *image* with the use of a slide projector or viewer. 2. An on-screen representation of an individual "*page*" created with a computer *presentation software* program such as Microsoft PowerPoint. These *computer* slides can include *text* or *graphics*. They can be printed or projected as black and white or color overhead transparencies. In addition, 35-mm slides can also be produced using a film service. See also *Slide* and *Transparency*.

SLIP/PPP: See *Serial Line Internet Protocol/Point to Point Protocol*.

Slot: A place on a computer *circuit board* enabling a user to add an internal device or additional *memory*.

Small computer system interface (SCSI): (Pronounced "scuzzy"). The standard for attaching *hardware* peripheral devices to a *computer*. These interfaces are useful for file servers and *multi-processing* systems. See also *File Server*, *Interface*, *Peripheral device*, and *Small computer system interface card*.

Small computer system interface (SCSI) card: An *interface* card that allows several *hardware* peripherals to be connected to the same system *slot* on a *computer*. See also *Peripheral device* and *Small computer system interface*.

Smart barcode: A *barcode* that is printed with book *title* and *call number* processed from a library media center's bibliographic *database*. These types of barcodes are applied to the matching items in the *collection*. They are preferred over dumb barcodes. See also *Dumb barcode*.

Smart phone: A *digital* cellular telephone that provides typical voice services as well as any combination of *electronic mail*, pager, *text* messaging, *voice recognition*, and *World Wide Web* access. See also *Cellular phone* and *Hand-held device*.

Smart terminal: A computer *workstation* on a *network* that can function as a *stand-alone* computer. It can function as an independent *computer* and is able to retrieve and process *data*. See also *Dumb terminal* and *Intelligent terminal*.

SMD: See *Specific material designation*.

Snail mail: A term used by some computer *network* users to describe the conventional national postal service.

Social Responsibilities Round Table (SRRT): A unit of the *American Library Association* that offers a forum for discussion and provides for exchange of *information* about social issues and problems. Its publications include *Counterpoise: For Social Responsibilities, Liberty and Dissent*, quarterly; and *SRRT Newsletter*.

Software: 1. A term commonly used for *audiovisual* materials such as filmstrips, slides, and videocassettes. 2. Programs written in a special *language* with a series of instructions to a *computer* or its peripherals that cause the computer to solve a problem or perform a task to achieve a specific set of results. A *program* provides a routine that the computer follows to provide the user with desired *data* or *information*. Software programs are used in many library media centers for *instruction*, management, *automation*, and *multimedia* applications, among others. See also *Module* and *Programming*.

SOLINET: See *Southeastern Library Network*.

Sort: To arrange *data* and records into a given sequence or a specific, logical order such as alphabetical sort, numeric sort, and date sort.

Sound card: An *expansion card* enabling a *computer* to produce higher quality sound than the built-in speaker. The card can also allow for recording or sampling of *audio* and using *software* for *voice recognition* or voice synthesis.

Sound recordings: Aural recordings such as phonograph records, cartridges, cassette tapes, phonodiscs, phonowire, and *magnetic tape*.

Southeastern Library Network (SOLINET): Founded in 1973 with headquarters in Atlanta, Georgia, SOLINET is a nonprofit regional *network* that offers services such as shared *cataloging* and *interlibrary loan*. This *bibliographic utility* is one of the nation's largest regional networks.

Spamming: The practice of using free public *network* facilities for promotion or commercial advertising. The same *message* can be sent to numerous newsgroups and individual users on the *Internet*.

Special library: A *library* that specializes in a limited *subject* area and is commonly maintained by an association, a government agency, or a corporation. Law libraries, hospital libraries, and prison libraries are examples.

Specific entry: A practice or principle observed in many library *subject* lists by which the most specific term available is used rather than a broader *heading*.

Specific material designation (SMD): A part of the fifth *area of description* on a *catalog* record that is a designation naming the physical description of an item or indicating the specific class or type of material to which an item belongs. Examples are *atlas*, score, and *filmstrip*. The SMD is required; the *general material designation* is optional.

Speech: The forming and sequencing of oral *language* sounds using breath and muscles during communication.

Speech and language disorder: An impaired ability to communicate effectively.

Speech synthesizer: A device that allows a *computer* to produce words and phrases as audible sounds.

Spider: A *computer* program that travels the *Internet* to locate *resources* such as Web documents, *Gopher* documents, and *file transfer protocol* (FTP) archives. It indexes the documents in a *database* and then searches using a *search engine* such as AltaVista or Excite. Each search engine uses a spider to build its database. A spider is also called a robot or a wanderer.

Spike: See *Power surge*.

Spine: The part of the cover of a *book* that conceals the bound edge that holds the front and back together. The book *title* and often the name of the *author* are located on the spine.

Splice: Joining two parts together, as in connecting two pieces of *film*.

Spreadsheet: A type of *computer* ledger *program* that performs mathematical calculations and graphing. The program includes rows, columns, and cells into which numeric values, formulas and labels, or *character* strings are placed. If the values of cells are changed, the calculated results change as well. See also *Cell*.

Sprocket: A roller in a *film* or *filmstrip* projector that has teeth along the edge designed to fit into the holes on the edge of the film. The roller pulls the film through a projector.

SRRT: See *Social Responsibilities Round Table*.

SSR: See *Sustained Silent Reading*.

Stack: A group of theme-related *hypermedia* cards used in a computer *program*.

Stacks: 1. Shelves used to house the *collection* in a *library media center*. 2. An area containing seldom-used *library* materials, usually accessible only to library personnel.

Staff development: Programs, *resources*, and seminars that contribute to the growth and development of staff members, including teachers, paraprofessionals, and clerks. See also *Paraprofessional*, *Professional development*, and *Teacher*.

Stand-alone: A single purpose, self-contained *computer* that is not connected to a *network*. A *dedicated* word processor is an example.

Standard deviation: A statistical measure that indicates how far *test* scores fall from the *mean* of a distribution.

Standard number: An *International Standard Book Number* (ISBN), *International Standard Serial Number* (ISSN), or any other internationally agreed-upon standard number that uniquely identifies an item. It appears in the eighth *area of description* on a *catalog* record.

Standard subdivision: A number from auxiliary Table 1 in the *Dewey Decimal Classification* system. It indicates the form of a *work* such as a *dictionary* or a history of a *topic*. The number can be added to a number from the main schedules without a specific instruction to do so.

Standardized test: 1. A *test* with specified content, procedures for administration and scoring that have been established as valid and reliable, and for which *norms* and standard procedures have been established. 2. A form of measurement that has been "normed" against a specific population. Standardization is obtained by administering the test to a given population and then calculating *mean*, *standard deviation*, and percentiles. Equivalent scores are then used for comparing individual scores to the norm group's performance. These types of *data* are useful for classifying students with special needs. See also *Criterion-referenced assessment* and *Norm-referenced assessment*.

Standards: 1. Accepted measurements of comparison for quantitative or qualitative values, or both, that serve to describe the criterion for the norm at a given time by a given group. Standards describe challenging and progressive goals toward which *school* personnel strive. 2. Expectations of a *library* or *library media center* expressed in a statement describing the required criteria. These standards are usually set at state, regional, or national levels to ensure quality control. An example is *Information Power: Building Partnerships for Learning*, which was published in 1998. 3. Set rules for *software* production, *format*, or *access*. 4. Criteria established by authority, customs, or general consent. These criteria govern behavior, *management*, and practices in many situations.

Standing order: An order placed with a *subscription agency* to ensure that all requested issues of *serial* titles will be received automatically. See also *Subscription*.

Stanford Achievement Test (SAT): A type of *test* used in many states to determine the levels of student achievement in various subject matter such as *reading* and mathematics. The test scores are used to compare students in one *school* with those in other schools, school systems, or states. The test scores are also analyzed to assess student performance and progress each year. See also *Standardized test*.

Star: A *network* topology in which a cable is used to connect several workstations directly to a central location or *file server* in a *local area network*. Because the computers are connected to a *hub* rather than to each other, any problems with cabling are easily located and corrected. See also *Topology*.

Star Schools: A *program* developed by and managed through the U.S. Department of Education to promote use of *distance learning* through *television* as a way to bring *school* programs to rural areas.

Statement of responsibility: A statement included in the first *area of description* naming the person or *corporate body* responsible for the overall creation of a *work*.

Statistic: Any parameter that can be determined based on the quantitative characteristics of the sample.

Stevana Case, et al. v. United School District No. 233, Johnson County, Kansas, et al.: A 1996 U.S. District Court decision involving the free speech issue in the First Amendment. Students and parents sued the Olathe, Kansas, *school district* for banning *Annie on My Mind*, a young adult novel about two high school girls who fall in love. The district court held that the *book* cannot be removed simply because the school board disagreed with the views expressed in the book. Much of the *language* was taken from the *Pico* case. Although the decision is only binding for that district, it is nevertheless one that other courts will review, and it may make it easier for library media specialists to fight future challenges. See also *Board of Education, Island Trees (New York) Union Free School District 26 v. Pico*.

Storage: 1. The semipermanent or permanent holding place for *digital* data. 2. The capability of a *computer* system to receive, *save*, and *store* information or digital *data*. Often referred to as the computer's *memory*. 3. The capability of CD-ROM, DVD, and *microform* to receive and store data. See also *Mass storage*.

Store: To place computer *information* in a *storage* device such as a CD-ROM, *disk*, or DVD. See also *Mass storage* and *Save*.

Story collection: A *collection* of books in a *library media center* that are written or produced in short story *format*.

Storyboard: A sequential, visual representation of the *information* that will be included in a computer *program*, *videotape*, or *slide* presentation.

Storytelling: The art of telling stories or recreating a story in a way that captivates the listeners; an art form used in schools and libraries for sharing *literature*, to make a point, or to preserve a cultural heritage. A storyteller captures and holds the listener's attention with wise choices of words, repetitions, actions, and even noises.

Strategic planning: A process for developing an organization's short- and long-range goals usually covering a three- to five-year period. The plan is updated at least once a year. See also *Planning*.

Streaming tape: Tape used in computer tape *backup* systems in which *data* are recorded in large continuous blocks. It is a cost- and time-efficient method of preserving data. However, specific blocks of data cannot be selected for restoration.

Student assistant: A type of *volunteer* in a school *library media center* who performs a variety of tasks as assigned by the school *library media specialist*. Student assistants at the secondary level are unpaid but may receive *school* credit.

Student evaluation: See *Assessment*, *Evaluation*, and *Performance assessment*.

Student outcomes: The intended results of *learning*. What students are expected to know and be able to do at the conclusion of an instructional activity or experience. See also *Instruction*.

Student-centered learning: A type of teaching *methodology* in which students are given the opportunity to decide what and how they will learn. Student needs are the basis for this type of *learning*. In addition, students are encouraged to take responsibility for their own learning and to be self-directed.

Study print: A *picture*, generally with *text*, that is used for *instruction*.

Style: The way a writer uses words and phrases. This involves the author's choice of words, the sentence patterns, the imagery used, and the rhythm of the sentences. Each *author* has his or her own individual style of *writing*. See also *Literary elements*.

Style manual: A *manual* containing a set of rules designed to ensure consistency of spelling, style, and abbreviations, among other elements, in *writing* and *research* projects. Examples are *Publication Manual of the American Psychological Association* (APA); *MLA Style Manual and Guide to Scholarly Publishing*, published by the Modern Language Association of America; or *A Manual for Writers of Term Papers, Theses, and Dissertations* (Turabian*)* by Kate L. Turabian. See also *Bibliographic citation*, *Dissertation*, and *Thesis*.

Stylus: A pen-shaped instrument used to "draw" images or point to menus. See also *Image*, *Menu*, and *Touch screen*.

Subdivision: An authorized term used to narrow a *subject heading* to make it more specific. See also *Free-floating subdivision*.

Subfield: A content-designated segment of a *field* in a *machine-readable cataloging* record containing a small segment of description or *information*.

Subfield code: A *character* in a MARC record that identifies a *subfield* and its *data*. *Machine-readable cataloging* subfield codes are preceded by a *delimiter* sign placed before the specific *information* that they identify. See also *Content designators* and *Machine-readable cataloging record*.

Subject: 1. A term describing content. 2. The main topics or ideas included in such items as books, databases, essays, and lectures. See also *Topic*.

Subject authority: A record of an acceptable *subject* term containing the term, the cross-references established with it, and the sources of the *information*. See also *Controlled vocabulary*.

Subject bibliography: A list of items that deals with a particular *topic*. See also *Bibliography*.

Subject entry: A *catalog* entry for a *work* under the *heading* for the *subject*. See also *Access point*, *Added entry*, and *Main entry*.

Subject heading: A *word* or phrase that describes a *subject* and provides subject *access* to a *catalog*. See also *Descriptor*, *Library of Congress Subject Headings*, and *Sears List of Subject Headings*.

Subject heading list: A list of terms and cross-references for indexing the items to be cataloged. Subject heading lists cover most of the branches of knowledge. Examples are the *Sears List of Subject Headings* and the *Library of Congress Subject Headings*.

Subject subdivision: A word or phase added to a *subject heading* that restricts or limits the *subject* to a more specific meaning. An example is Food—Cholesterol content.

Subscribe: A Web term used when joining a discussion group, interest group, *listserv*, or mailing list through the *Internet*. This term is also used when writing commands to join a group and to list a Usenet *newsgroup* on a newsreader. See also *Command*.

Subscription: An arrangement with a *vendor* to supply *online* products, periodicals, newspapers, or other serials for a specified number of issues or period of time, usually one or two years. Payment is made in advance. See also *Subscription agency*.

Subscription agency: A company that offers a wide variety of services to libraries purchasing serials. These services include ordering subscriptions, invoicing the *library*, and following up on missing issues. A subscription agency is often referred to as a *jobber*. See also *Serial* and *Subscription*.

Subtitle: The *title* of an item other than the *title proper* or a *series* title. The subtitle can also be a phrase that expands or limits the title proper. A colon separates a title from a subtitle on a *bibliographic record*.

Subtopic: A secondary or subordinate topic that is included under the major *topic* of an article, a paragraph, or a *book*.

SuDoc number: See *Superintendent of Documents Number*.

Suite: A group, or bundle, of related *computer* applications that are designed to work closely together. These are often called office applications. An example is Microsoft Office, which has *word processing*, a *spreadsheet*, a *graphics* package, and a *database management system*. These full-featured products all work alike and work together as if they were a single *program*. *Text*, *data*, and *graphics* can be linked and combined. See also *Application*.

Summary: A synopsis of the important points of an article or literary *work*.

Summative evaluation: A type of *evaluation* that gives evidence of results and provides a measure of the results for ongoing decision making. See also *Formative evaluation*.

Super video graphics array (SVGA): A set of graphics *standards* that offers greater resolutions than VGA. *Resolution* is 800 pixels horizontally by 600 lines vertically and beyond. SVGA currently begins at 256 colors. An SVGA can also run all other *graphics*. See also *Monitor* and *Video graphics array*.

Supercomputers: *Mainframe* computers that are extremely fast and have a very large *storage* capacity.

Superintendent of Documents: A position within the *Government Printing Office* responsible for distributing public documents to depository libraries and to other institutions and officials authorized by law. Additional responsibilities include the *cataloging* and indexing of government materials and the sale of government publications. See also *Depository library*, *Government document*, and *Superintendent of Documents number*.

Superintendent of Documents number (SuDoc number): A number assigned to each individual federal *document*. The number indicates the issuing agency or office, among others, and is assigned to a *government document* through the *classification system* of the U.S. *Superintendent of Documents*. The documents are printed by the *Government Printing Office*.

Superintendent of schools: The chief executive officer of a *school system*. The person is directly responsible to the *board of education* for the *school district*.

Super-video home system (S-VHS): A high-resolution *video* format that produces a higher quality image for large-screen *television* sets. This version of the VHS format provides a wider luminance *bandwidth* that results in a much sharper picture quality with approximately 400 lines of horizontal resolution. This *format* is capable of capturing the detail and color brilliance of high-resolution signals from *satellite* dish tuners, DVD players, and laser discs. See also *Digital versatile disc*, *Expansion technology*, *Light Amplification by Stimulated Emission of Radiation*, and *Video home system*.

Supplement: A section or part added later or issued separately to *update* or add to the *information* of a *work*.

Supplied title: A *title* supplied by a cataloger to identify the items that do not have titles on the *chief source of information* or its substitute. It is always enclosed with brackets on the *bibliographic record*.

Supply reel: The reel that holds a *cassette tape* or *film* before it is played or recorded. During playback or recording, the film or tape is fed through the proper equipment onto a *take-up reel*.

Surface-mount microphone: A *microphone* with a flat back designed to be mounted on a flat surface such as a table.

Surge: See *Power surge* and *Surge protector*.

Surge protector: A device that protects a *computer* from power fluctuations and compensates for loss of power by directing the surge or spike to electrical ground. See also *Power surge*.

Sustained silent reading (SSR): A *program* implemented in many schools whereby students and staff have a daily period of silent *reading*.

SVGA: See *Super video graphics array*.

S-VHS: See *Super-video home system*.

Switcher: A panel with buttons allowing various *video* sources to be selected through a variety of *transition* devices. Switchers enable technicians to perform a *dissolve*, *fade*, or *wipe*.

Symbology: Refers to the format of the *barcode* structure such as Codabar or Code 39.

Synchronizer: A single-function device that uses a *cassette tape* recorder or other types of playback to operate other equipment. An example is signaling for *slide* changes.

Synchronous: Synchronized *data* communications sent at a fixed rate that is controlled by clock signals in the transmitter and receiver.

Synchronous communication: Electronic communication where two or more parties are communicating simultaneously and interactively; that is, in *real time*. It is the opposite of *asynchronous communication*, where the communication is characterized by a time delay between the posting and the receipt of *information*.

Synonym: A *word* with the same meaning or nearly the same meaning as another word. For example, free is synonymous with gratis. See also *Antonym* and *Homonym*.

Synthesis: A level of *learning* in the *cognitive domain* described in *Bloom's taxonomy*. This level includes the putting together of parts or elements to combine the pieces in a different way, thus forming a new whole.

Synthesizer: A musical device or instrument that generates *audio* electronically. ∎

T1 line: A high-capacity telephone *transmission* line capable of carrying 1.544 *megabits per second* of *data* (equivalent to 24 channels of ordinary telephone signals).

T2 line: A high-capacity telephone *transmission* line capable of carrying 6.312 *megabits per second* of *data* (equivalent to 96 channels of ordinary telephone signals).

T3 line: An ultrahigh-capacity telephone *transmission* line capable of carrying roughly 45 *megabits per second* of *data* (approximately 30 channels of T1 grade signal or 700 channels of ordinary telephone signals). This capacity allows for full-screen, *full-motion video*.

Table: See *Auxiliary table*.

Table of contents: A list, usually located in the front of a *book*, that gives the sections of the book and the corresponding *page* numbers. See also *Contents page*.

Tacking iron: A small, thermostatically controlled heating tool used to attach or tack tissue to the back of a mount board or a print. The tacking will hold the tissue in place while the print is trimmed and heated in a dry-mount press. See also *Dry mounting*.

Tag: A three-character numeric code that identifies each *field* of *information* in a *machine-readable cataloging* record. For example, the tag number 100 identifies the *author* field on a *catalog* record. 2. In an HTML document, a tag is a *command* inserted in a *document* that specifies how various portions of a document should be formatted. A tag consists of a left angle bracket (<), a tag name, and a right angle bracket (>). Tags are generally used in pairs to start and end the tag instructions. For example, <P> indicates the beginning of a paragraph, and </P> (with the slash used in the end tag) indicates the end of the paragraph. See also *Content designators*, *Control field*, and *Metatag*.

Tagged Image File Format (TIFF): A *graphics* file *format*. See also *File*.

Take-up reel: The reel that accumulates a *cassette tape* or *film* as it is played or recorded. During playback or recording, the film or tape is fed through the proper equipment from a *supply reel*.

Tall tales: Exaggerated tales of courage, invention, and optimism with larger than life heroes capable of superhuman feats. Paul Bunyan and Pecos Bill are examples. These tales are sometimes based on historical figures such as Davy Crockett and Johnny Appleseed. Usually, readers or listeners must accept the outrageous facts as true while *reading* or listening to the tales. See also *Folktale*.

Tanka: A Japanese verse form of *poetry* containing 31 syllables arranged in five un-rhymed lines with a 5-7-5-7-7 syllable pattern. This form is similar to *haiku* but with two additional lines of seven syllables each. This type of verse produces a concentrated essence of a single event, image, or mood.

Tape: See *Audiotape*, *Cassette tape*, *Loop tape*, *Magnetic tape*, *Streaming tape*, and *Videotape*.

Tape recording: A strip of *magnetic tape* on which *audio* or *video* can be recorded.

Tattle tape: *Magnetic tape* that is inserted in an item to activate an alarm if the item is removed from the *library media center* without being properly checked out.

Taxonomy: 1. The study of the general principles of scientific classification. 2. A system of classification.

TCP/IP: See *Transmission Control Protocol/Internet Protocol*.

Teacher: 1. An instructor. 2. A role of the school *library media specialist* as delineated by *Information Power* in which the library media specialist collaborates with teachers and students to analyze *information* and *learning* needs and to locate *resources* to be used to meet those needs. See also *Master teacher* and *Roles of library media specialists*.

Teacher evaluation: See *Assessment* and *Performance appraisal*.

Teaching: The process of helping students acquire knowledge, skills, attitudes, or applications by means of a systematic method of *instruction*. Numerous teaching methods are used in classrooms and library media centers, such as *drill-and-practice*, *modeling*, *problem solving*, *role-play*, *simulation*, and *team teaching*. See also *Learning* and *Teaching methodology*.

Teaching methodology: The various methods teachers use to organize classes, present *information* and ideas to students, and use *resources* and materials. These methods vary by student age, *subject*, modes of *learning*, and *teaching* styles. See also *Methodology*.

Team teaching: The sharing of the responsibilities for *teaching* a given class or group by two or more teachers. Each member of the team has unique functions and responsibilities. All team members participate in *planning*, scheduling, and evaluating team activities.

Technical reading: An examination of certain parts of a *library* item that takes place during the *cataloging* process. The *Chief Source of Information* used to locate necessary *bibliographic information* is an example.

Technical services: *Library* services that deal with the *bibliographic control* of library material to ensure that materials are made available for patrons. This work includes acquisitions, *cataloging*, and processing.

Technology: 1. Application of scientific knowledge. 2. Methods of accomplishing certain tasks using technological knowledge and skills such as automated *cataloging*. 3. The use of a wide variety of equipment and *resources* to facilitate *instruction* and the *learning* process in an educational setting. Technology tools offer expanded *access* to educational *information* and resources and deliver education services efficiently and effectively. Technology also assists in meeting the changing educational demands in a rapidly changing world. See also *Instructional technology*.

Technology coordinator: The educator employed for or delegated the administrative authority and responsibility for developing, implementing, and maintaining the *technology* program for a *school*, district, county, region, or state. The coordinator provides leadership in all aspects of the technology *program* including establishing goals and *objectives*, training staff, carrying out student *instruction*, purchasing, installing and maintaining *hardware* and *software*, and administering the *network* system.

Technology Innovation Challenge Grants (TICG): Five-year awards funded by the U.S. Department of Education to develop instructional strategies that integrate new technologies into the *curriculum* and to support *professional development* for teachers. Applications must be submitted by a consortium that includes at least one *local education agency* with a high percentage of children living below the poverty level.

Technology Literacy Challenge Fund (TLCF): Provides formula grants from the U.S. Department of Education to state education agencies. These grants help agencies implement statewide *technology* plans through competitive funding to local education agencies that are using new technologies to improve schools. See also *Local education agency*.

Technology plan: A *document* that describes the goals and *objectives* for incorporating the use of computers and other *technology* in the *school* or *school system*. This includes plans for funding, staff training, *curriculum* integration, student *instruction*, installation, and maintenance.

Teen Read Week: A week in October is designated to promote *reading* by young adults. The *program* began in 1998 and is sponsored by the *Young Adult Library Services Association*.

Telecommunications: The *transmission* of *information* over a public or private *network*. Telecommunications *software* allows a *computer* to communicate through a modem to another computer. Files are uploaded for sending to a computer user and downloaded by the user for receiving and copying. See also *Download, Electronic mail, MOdulator-DEModulator,* and *Upload*.

Teleconferencing: The simultaneous *transmission* of images or *data* via telephone lines, which allows individuals at two or more remote sites to conduct a conference or a meeting. See also *Audioconferencing, Data conferencing,* and *Videoconferencing*.

Telefacsimile (Fax): See *Facsimile*.

Telephoto lens: A *lens* constructed so that it produces a relatively large *image* with a *focal length* shorter than that required by an ordinary lens that produces an image of the same size. Commonly used to photograph or *film* small or distant objects with a device such as a *camera* or *camcorder*.

Television (TV): A combination tuner, picture tube, RF modulator, and *audio* speaker that converts an RF signal into picture and sound. This involves the *transmission* of visual images (*video*) and accompanying sound (*audio*) electronically through the air or through wires. The images and the sound can then be viewed and listened to through a television set. See also *Broadcast television, Cable television, Closed circuit television,* and *Public television*.

Telnet: An *Internet* tool that allows users to *log on* remotely from one Internet site to another. Telnet is useful for accessing *library* catalogs.

Templates: Predefined colors, *text* fonts, and patterns that can be selected for use. Templates are commonly used in authoring systems and presentation systems to ensure good design and consistency.

Tercet: See *Triplet*.

Terminal: A peripheral *input* and/or *output* device that includes a *keyboard* and a *monitor* connected to a *computer*. A terminal allows users to communicate with the computer that houses the *database*.

Terminal host: A *model* of *networking* in which a large "host" *computer* does the computing while users interact through "dumb" devices called terminals. The *terminal* allows interaction through a *keyboard* but has no additional *desktop* intelligence. See also *Dumb terminal*.

Test: 1. A systematic means of *evaluation*, analysis, or *assessment*. 2. A set of questions or problems designed to assess or determine the aptitude, interests, knowledge, performance, or skills of an individual or a group. 3. To conduct an examination or evaluation. See also *Achievement test*, *Aptitude test*, and *Scholastic aptitude tests*.

Tests of General Education Development (GED): See *Certificate of High School Equivalency*.

Text: 1. The printed or written matter on a *page*. 2. The principal body of a *book*, *manuscript*, or *newspaper*, which includes such parts as headings, illustrations, and notes. 3. In *word processing*, data in the form of words, sentences, and paragraphs. 4. In *electronic mail*, the body of the *message*. 5. *Data* consisting of only standard ASCII characters. See also *American Standard Code for Information Interchange*, *Heading*, and *Illustration*.

Text file: A *file* that contains only *text* characters. See also *American Standard Code for Information Interchange file*, *Binary file*, and *Graphics file*.

Thematic instruction: A type of *teaching* in which *instruction* is organized around broad themes that integrate several of the disciplines. For example, a dinosaur *theme* would include music, art, writing, games, *reading*, and history.

Thematic unit: A *lesson plan* that covers a specified time period and incorporates thematic *instruction*.

Theme: The central idea or core of a story and the author's statement about it. It is what the story means. This literary element presents the underlying idea that ties the *plot*, characters, and *setting* together into a meaningful whole. Theme can be stated by characters or through the author's *narrative*. See also *Literary elements*.

Thesaurus: 1. A *specialized book* of synonyms and antonyms. 2. An *index* of terms with cross-references that clarify the relationships among terms. See also *Antonym*, *Cross-reference*, and *Synonym*.

Thesis: A *dissertation* or treatise written for the award of a degree or diploma, usually by postgraduate students.

TICG: See *Technology Innovation Challenge Grants*.

TIFF: See *Tagged Image File Format*.

Tilt: The vertical movement of a *video camera* or a *camcorder* installed on a *tripod*.

Time line: A chronological record of events.

Title: A *word* or phrase that names a *work*, usually identified from the *chief source of information* for the item. It appears in the first *area of description* on a *catalog* record. See also *Alternative title*, *Collective title*, *Parallel title*, *Subtitle*, *Supplied title*, *Uniform title*, and *Variant title*.

Title entry: A catalog *entry* or a *record* of a *work* located under the *title* of a publication.

Title page: The *page* that occurs near the beginning of a *book* and provides the most complete *bibliographic information* about the book. The title page is used as the most authoritative source for *cataloging* an item. The *imprint* is located on the title page.

Title proper: The main *title* of a *bibliographic* item, including alternative titles but excluding all other title *information* such as parallel titles. See also *Alternative title* and *Parallel title*.

Title VI: See *Elementary and Secondary Education Act*.

TLCF: See *Technology Literacy Challenge Fund*.

Toggle: The action of switching between two states or modes, only one of which may be in effect at any given time; e.g., dynamic insert *mode* in *word processing*.

Token ring: A *network* standard that uses a ring *topology* with token-passing techniques to prevent *data* collisions. *Transmission* rates are 4 or 16 *megabits per second*, depending on *interface* cards and type of cable. Faster rates of 100 Mbps and 128 Mbps are emerging. Because of its performance and reliability, this is considered the most cost-efficient of the three types of *network architecture*; however, the materials and maintenance are expensive and can be slower than *Ethernet*. See also *Fiber distributed data interface* and *Ring*.

Toner cartridge: A *cartridge* used with laser printers and photocopy machines. The cartridge contains the toner that is fused to the *page*.

Toolbox: The *menu* component in *hypermedia* programs with tools that allow a user to create *graphics*.

Topic: 1. A term describing content. 2. The *subject* matter of an article, *book*, or other types of *literature*.

Topology: The physical layout of the cables that connect the nodes on a *network*. The topology defines the *hardware* and the means used to connect the parts. See also *Bus*, *Node*, *Ring*, and *Star*.

Touch screen: A device connected to a *computer* screen that permits *data* to be entered by making physical contact with the *screen* or by using a *stylus* to write on the screen.

Tower: A system configuration in which the system components, such as the *power supply* and multiple *storage* devices, are commonly stacked on top of each other. The *computer* is commonly mounted vertically, usually with disks and tape drives arranged to suit. See also *Compact disc-read only memory tower*.

Toy book: A *book* that can be on any *subject* and of any literary *genre* based on the ancient art form of papermaking. Some types of toy books are pop-up, pull-tab, fold-out, and sliding panels. The appeal is visual and tactile with limited *text*. The paper engineering is used to extend the text. See also *Picture book*.

Tracings: A *record* of all the added entries and *subject* headings under which an item is entered in a *catalog*. See also *Added entry*, *Subject entry*, and *Subject heading*.

Track: A concentric circle on a *disk* or other *medium* such as *magnetic tape* along which *data* are recorded. The tracks are divided into sectors on a disk. See also *Sector*.

Tracking: 1. The electronics and sensors in *virtual reality* systems that allow the *computer* to follow the motions of the user. 2. A video control that allows for proper placement of the *videotape* across the *video* and *audio* heads. 3. The practice of grouping students with similar *learning* abilities in a common class or groups within a class. See also *Homogeneous grouping*.

Tractor-feed printer: A type of *printer* with pins for feeding paper on adjustable tractors so that it is capable of printing on paper of different widths.

Trade book: A *book* that is published and sold primarily for public consumption. Generally considered to be of wide reader appeal. Trade books represent 95 percent of a bookseller's stock. The *binding* is often not reinforced and may not be as durable as books with *library binding* for use in a *library media center*.

Traditional literature: Folktales, fables, myths, and legends that have an oral tradition passed down from generation to generation by word of mouth. See also *Fable*, *Folktale*, *Legend*, and *Myth*.

Transition: Visual effects, such as a *dissolve*, *fade*, or *wipe*, that occur as a program moves from one *image* or *screen* of *information* to the next.

Transmission: Transferring *data* over a communications channel. See also *Transmission Control Protocol/Internet Protocol*, *Wireless*, and *Wireless Application Protocol*.

Transmission Control Protocol/Internet Protocol (TCP/IP): The common system of operations and commands or set of *standards* for data *transmission* and error correction that allows the transfer of *data* from one Internet-linked *computer* to another. *Internet* operations conform to the TCP/IP *protocol*.

Transparency: A still *image* recorded on celluloid, acetate, or glass. The image is viewed by projecting light through it. Transparencies are commonly viewed with an *overhead projector* or similar device.

Trigger: The button on a *camcorder* or *video camera* that is depressed as a signal to the recorder to begin or end the recording.

Triplet: A three-line verse of *poetry*, also known as a tercet. This type of poetry is a unit or group of three lines of verse with any two lines rhyming and that are rhymed together or have a rhyme scheme that interlaces with an adjoining triplet or tercet.

Tripod: A three-legged mount for a *video camera* or a *camcorder* that allows for stability during videotaping. See also *Tripod dolly*.

Tripod dolly: A combination *tripod* and *dolly* on which a *camera* is mounted for use in *television* and *video* production.

Truncation: A *search* technique using a special symbol that allows for alternate endings to a *keyword* in accessing an electronic *database*. For example, LIBR- would retrieve records for LIBRA, LIBRARIAN, LIBRARIES, and LIBRARY.

Turnkey system: A *computer* system package comprising *hardware*, *software*, installation, training, and (usually) ongoing maintenance, support, and development.

Tutorial: A type of *instruction* in which a student is guided step by step through a program *application* to a specific skill or task. Most *software* products include a tutorial along with their *computer* programs to assist users with *program* mastery. See also *Documentation*.

TV: See *Television*.

Tweeter: A small speaker used for reproducing high-frequency sounds, usually above 6,000 cycles per second. See also *Woofer*.

Twisted pair cable: Cable made up of a pair of insulated copper wires twisted together or wrapped around each other. This type of cable is less expensive than *coaxial cable* and *fiber optic cable* but has less *bandwidth*. Often, it has been used for telephone communications and for data *transmission* in a *local area network*.

Two-by-six rule: A general rule of thumb for determining *screen* size. Viewers should not be seated closer to the screen than two screen widths or further away than six screen widths.

Types of books: See *Genre*. ■

UHF: See *Ultra high frequency*.

Ultra high frequency (UHF): Television *transmission* on channels 14 through 83 (300–3,000 MHz). See also *Very high frequency*.

Ultrafiche: Micro-images on a flat sheet that are created at reductions more than 90 times the original size. Libraries often use the term loosely to specify fiche created at reductions exceeding 55 times. A special machine is needed to magnify the images. See also *Microform*.

Unidirectional microphone: In recording, a microphone *pickup pattern* in which the *microphone* processes most of its signals from sound collected in front of the microphone.

Uniform Resource Locator (URL): The network *address* commonly used for various *Internet* sites accessed via the *World Wide Web*. URL addresses are formatted as *protocol*:// followed by a code for the host institution identified by the URL.

Uniform title: A *title* assigned by catalogers to various editions and versions of a *work* that appear under different titles proper. The uniform title assigned to an item may be the title by which it is commonly known, the original title of a work published in translation, or a title constructed by the cataloger. For example, all editions and versions of *Alice in Wonderland* would have the uniform title *Alice in Wonderland*. See also *Title proper*.

Uninterruptible power source (UPS): A power source that provides power for a *computer* or *file server* after a power outage. The source is battery powered and provides power for a short time period during which files can be saved and computers can be properly turned off.

Union catalog: A bibliographic *database* that incorporates the holdings of groups of libraries in a city, a school district, regional consortium, a state, or even larger entities.

Unit objectives: Short, precise statements of specific behaviors or skills to be acquired as a result of a *unit study*. One of the unit *objectives* suitable for a unit study on the American Revolution would be that students will identify the major causes of the American Revolution. A *performance objective* is described in terms that can be quantified and measured.

Unit record: A basic *catalog* record of a *work* in the form of a *main entry* record. When duplicated, this *record* can be used as a unit for all other entries of the work in a catalog by adding appropriate headings. See also *Heading*.

Unit set: A set of *card catalog* entries for an item. The cards are identical except for access points or headings. See also *Access point* and *Heading*.

Unit study: A series of related *learning* experiences with purposeful activities developed around a body of knowledge or *topic*, such as the American Revolution, and designed to allow students to achieve previously planned objectives. The unit approach requires a great amount of professional preparation along with creativity, imagination, and initiative. Preplanning, flexibility, and *evaluation* are essential elements for successful unit studies. Most unit studies include daily lesson plans that are developed from the planned objectives. One type of unit study is an instructional *module*, which is available for purchase and often includes lesson plans, *objectives*, and activities, among others. An example is *Pathways to Knowledge*, Follett's Information Skills Model. See also *Lesson plan*.

United States Board on Books for Young People (USBBY): Founded in 1985, the organization is the U.S. section of the *International Board on Books for Young People*. Individual and institutional members promote *literature* for young people and promote interest in international *children's literature*. USBBY publishes the semiannual *USBBY Newsletter*. Annual meetings are held in conjunction with the *American Library Association*, the *International Reading Association*, or the *National Council of Teachers of English*.

United States Machine-Readable Cataloging (U.S. MARC): A *bibliographic* format/standard for *cataloging* materials with automated systems in the United States. This standard, which is used and distributed by the U.S. *Library of Congress*, allows for the interchange of *bibliographic information* across automated systems or networks. See also *Microcomputer Library Interchange Format*.

United States Machine-Readable Cataloging/MicroLIF protocol (U.S. MARC/MicroLIF protocol): A 1991 update to the standard MicroLIF; it is fully compatible with the U.S. MARC that the *Library of Congress* uses and distributes. See also *United States Machine-Readable Cataloging.*

Universal Product Code (UPC): The standard *barcode* symbol used in the retail marketplace with an agreed-upon barcoding for product labels giving country of origin, manufacturer, and other information. In a *library media center*, a barcode is used for *circulation* and *inventory.*

Universal Serial Bus (USB): A *port* in newer computers for connecting modems, printers, and external devices. The USB is designed to replace the parallel ports and serial ports used by most *computer* add-ons. USB add-ons can connect to each other or to multiport hubs for up to 127 connections per socket. See also *Hub, Parallel port*, and *Serial port.*

Universal Service Fund: See *E-rate.*

Unzip: The process of decompressing a *compressed file* to allow a *computer* to manipulate the *file.* See also *Compression.*

UPC: See *Universal Product Code.*

Update: 1. To revise or add *information* later; for example, to publish a *revised edition* of a *book.* 2. To modify a *file*, which could involve adding, *editing*, deleting, or replacing records. See also *Upgrade.*

Upgrade: 1. To bring a *database* or *software* package up-to-date by adding new *information* or a new version of a software package. New software is also used to add functions to an older *application*, making the older application equivalent to a newer one. 2. To improve *hardware* capabilities by adding increased *memory*, new enhancements, or additional ports, for example.

Uplink: A communications channel from an earth station to a *satellite* in orbit. See also *Downlink* and *Telecommunications.*

Upload: The process of transmitting *data* from one *computer* to another, usually at remote sites. The opposite is *download.*

UPS: See *Uninterruptible power source.*

URL: See *Uniform Resource Locator.*

USB: See *Universal Serial Bus.*

USBBY: See *United States Board on Books for Young People.*

Usenet: See *Newsgroup.*

User friendly: A phrase commonly used to describe the interactivity and ease of using a particular *computer*, software *program*, or automated system.

User group: A voluntary association of users of a specific *computer* system or *program* who meet regularly to exchange tips and techniques and to share *public domain software*.

User interface: All the features of a *computer* or a *software* program that combine to create or govern the way users interact with a computer. This includes a combination of menus, *screen* design, *command* language, help screens, *keyboard* commands, mice, touch screens, and other input *hardware*. A successful software *program* must have a well-designed user interface. *Interactive video*, natural *language* understanding, and *voice recognition* are additional features currently being developed or improved, or both.

U.S. MARC: See *United States Machine-Readable Cataloging*.

U.S. MARC/MicroLIF protocol: See *United States Machine-Readable Cataloging/MicroLIF protocol*.

Utility: A software *program* that relates to the management of *computer* operations such as *hard disk* maintenance, *virus* protection, data *compression*, and *data* recovery.

Utopia: A type of *literature* that deals with a place of happiness and prosperity. Generally, the stories are set in the future. Although *technology* plays a role, sociological, psychological, and emotional aspects are the focus of the story. See also *Dystopia*. ■

Validity: The extent to which a *test* measures what it was intended to measure. Gives an indication of the degree of accuracy of predictions or inferences based on test scores. See also *Reliability*.

Variable field: A *field* in the MARC *format* containing *data* that are unrestricted and vary in length and format according to the contents. Most fields in a MARC *record* are variable length. See also *Fixed field* and *Machine-readable cataloging*.

Variant title: A different form of the *title*.

VCR: See *Videocassette recorder*.

VDI: See *Virtual device interface*.

VDT: See *Video display terminal*.

Vendor: A company or a company representative that sells products or services.

Venn diagram: A graphic representational system using overlapping circles to develop reasoning abilities. The circles are used to represent groups. The schematic representation of a set was first used by John Venn in the nineteenth century. See also *Boolean logic*.

Vernacular: The *language* or native speech of a particular location.

Veronica: See *Very Easy Rodent Oriented Net-wide Index to Computerized Archives*.

Version: An adaptation or different *edition* of a *work*.

Verso: The back of a *leaf* of a book or the left-hand *page* of a *book*. The verso of the *title page* usually contains the book's *copyright* date *information*. See also *Recto*.

Vertical file: A *collection* of current materials such as pamphlets, pictures, and *newspaper* clippings. The materials are usually located in a filing cabinet arranged in *subject* order.

Vertical scrolling: A method of displaying *text* on a *video* display unit. Text is scrolled either up or down on the *screen*. When scrolled upward, the text disappears off the top of the screen. When scrolled downward, the text rolls off the bottom. See also *Horizontal scrolling* and *Scroll*.

Very Easy Rodent Oriented Net-wide Index to Computerized Archives (Veronica): A *search engine* or *database* query *software* that executes searches in response to specific user commands. Veronica is a continually updated database of the names of *menu* items on thousands of *gopher* servers.

Very high frequency (VHF): Television *transmission* on channels 2 through 13 (30–300 MHz). See also *Ultra high frequency*.

VGA: See *Video graphics array*.

VHF: See *Very high frequency*.

VHS: See *Video home system*.

Video: The visual portion of a *compact disc*, a *computer*, a *film*, a *television*, a *videodisc*, or a *videotape*. See also *Audio*.

Video adapter card: An *expansion card* designed to enhance the ability of a *personal computer* to manipulate *video*. This type of card works by offloading many of the video processing functions from the *central processing unit* to the card itself. The card is also called the *graphics* adapter board.

Video camera: A component of *video* consisting of a *lens*, a *viewfinder*, and one or more imaging devices that convert light into electrical video signals.

Video display: See *Monitor*.

Video display terminal (VDT): See *Cathode ray tube*.

Video graphics array (VGA): A *graphics* display adapter that originally displayed up to 16 colors simultaneously with a *resolution* of 640 pixels horizontally and 480 lines vertically. See also *Monitor* and *Super video graphics array*.

Video home system (VHS): The standard or dominant home and *library* videotape *format* using half-inch-wide *videotape* encased in a plastic shell. The tapes are played on a *videocassette recorder*. The half-inch format differs electronically from the Beta format and, therefore, is not compatible with Beta. See also *Expansion technology* and *Super-video home system*.

Video noise: Random dots of interference on a display. Also called "snow" in *computer* slang *language*.

Video projector: A *projection* device that uses an LCD panel with a built-in light source to display *video* signals. See also *Liquid crystal display panel* and *Liquid crystal display projector*.

Video recording: A recording generated in the form of electronic impulses and designed primarily for *television* playback. The term includes videodiscs and videotapes. See also *Videodisc* and *Videotape*.

Videocassette recorder (VCR): An electronic component consisting of a tuner, an RF modulator, and a video deck for recording and playback of a *videotape*. *Video* images and *audio* are recorded on *magnetic tape*.

Videocassette tape: See *Videotape*.

Videoconferencing: The simultaneous *transmission* of images that allows individuals at two or more remote locations to conduct a conference or a meeting. A videoconference typically carries *video* images so the participants can see each other while they talk. See also *CU-See Me* and *Teleconferencing*.

Videodisc: A mass *storage* medium using discs that are 12 inches in diameter to *store* pictures, *text*, and video *data*. A *laser beam* is used to read *information* from the surface. This *medium* delivers a high-resolution picture with *digital* sound. More than 100,000 still pictures can be accessed by a *video* player in one second. *Constant Angular Velocity* is a type of videodisc storage *format*.

Videodisc interactivity: The levels of interaction in using a *videodisc* that are determined by the quality of the *hardware*, the *software*, and the *disc* itself.

Videographer: A person who operates a *camcorder* or *video camera*.

Videography: The operation of a *camcorder* or *video camera* during the production of a *video*.

Videotape: Sound and picture signals encoded on a thin strip of plastic tape covered with metal particles. The particles can *record* and *store* a magnetic charge. A *videocassette recorder* is necessary for playback or recording, or both. The term is commonly used interchangeably with videocassette tape.

Videotex: Interactive *transmission* of *text* and *graphics* that links users to a variety of *computer* databases such as home shopping, banking, and news. The text and graphics are delivered by telephone line to a *television* with a decoder box and *keyboard*. Although many marketing strategies have been attempted, this emerging *technology* has not yet been embraced by the public.

Viewfinder: The *camera* component that allows the user to frame the subject being photographed so that the *image* viewed by the *lens* can be seen by the user.

Viewing guidance: See *Reading, viewing,* and *listening guidance*.

Virtual device interface (VDI): A method of speeding *video* playback in a *computer* by using a dedicated video handler to transfer video operations from the *central processing unit* to *graphics* accelerator *hardware*.

Virtual library: 1. *Information* resources that do not physically reside on a *library* shelf but are made available to users through shared *online* databases; e.g., "a library on the *Internet*." An example of a virtual library is the Alabama Virtual Library, a *World Wide Web* electronic library service available throughout the state of Alabama to all citizens through public libraries and to students and teachers through schools, colleges, and universities. A virtual library advances and extends library services to all patrons. 2. A software *program* that contains a *collection* of Internet addresses (URLs) tailored to meet a user's business or professional needs. The program is *user friendly* and intuitive, allowing *access* to the most relevant sites. The virtual library can also be added to a user's *Web site*, which helps to attract visitors and add value to the site.

Virtual reality (VR): An approximation of reality using *technology* to create a three-dimensional simulated environment that appears to be real to the users. See also *Virtual library*.

Virus: A *program* or a segment of code that can be loaded onto a *computer* without a user's knowledge or permission. Most viruses are also able to replicate themselves. All computer viruses are man-made, and a simple virus that can *copy* itself over and over is relatively easy to produce. Even a simple virus is dangerous because it quickly uses all the available *memory* and can stop a computer system. An even more dangerous virus is the type that can bypass security systems and transmit itself across networks. See also *Antivirus software* and *Worm*.

Visual learner: A type of learner who learns primarily by visual methods. Videotapes, films, slides, and written words are useful to this type of learner. See also *Learning style*.

Visual literacy: The ability to perceive, understand, and interpret visual images and to recognize bias, persuasion, propaganda, and other hidden visual messages. See also *Literacy*.

Voice mail: A telephone answering service that takes messages when a person or business is unable to answer directly. Messages are retrieved when a personal code is entered assuring privacy of *information*.

Voice recognition: A technique using special *software* and a *sound card* to allow the user to give spoken commands to a *computer*. This reduces dependence on a *keyboard*, a *mouse*, and other manual devices. See also *Smart phone*.

Volume: 1. A collective issue of a *serial*, usually those published in a 12-month period. A volume can be bound or unbound. 2. A predetermined amount of *memory* on a tape or *disk*. 3. All the material that is contained in one *binding*.

Volunteer: A person who provides time and services without compensation such as a parent or student who assists in a *library media center*.

VR: See *Virtual reality*. ■

WAIS: See *Wide Area Information Server*.

WAN: See *Wide Area Network*.

WAP: See *Wireless Application Protocol*.

Warm boot: A process for resetting a *computer* that is already turned on by pressing a reset switch or a combination of keys without turning off the power. Resetting returns the computer to its initial state, and any *data* or programs in *main memory* are erased. See also *Boot* and *Cold boot*.

Web: See *World Wide Web*.

Web browser: See *Browser*.

Web page: A *document* on the *World Wide Web* that contains *hypertext* links to other Web documents. Every Web page is identified by a unique URL (*Uniform Resource Locator*).

Web site: A site on the *World Wide Web*. Each site contains a *home page*, additional *information* or documents, and files. Sites are maintained by individuals, businesses, organizations, and libraries, among other entities.

Web-based instruction: Planned instructional programs that give students *information*, instructions, helpful strategies, and opportunities to *access* information in a variety of ways on the *World Wide Web*. Learner control is an important component of Web-based instruction because of the wealth of information available on the Web and its anytime, anywhere accessibility. Several characteristics of the Web support the basic forms of learner control, which are control of sequence, control of content/ learning activities, and control of pacing. Control of sequence permits a learner to control the order in which he or she would like to receive *instruction*. The learner may choose to skip or revisit a *topic*. Features of the Web that may be used to foster control of sequence include links, navigational tools, and book-marks. Control of content and learning activities gives learners opportunities to choose the content they wish to explore and the methods they will use. Control of pacing allows learners to adapt instruction to fit their own pace for *learning*.

Webbing: 1. A technique for establishing clear goals for *research* by defining and limiting the direction of the research. The *World Wide Web* becomes the student's guide to locating useful *information* because the Web functions as, in effect, a research *outline*. 2. A way of outlining various *literary elements* of a *book* such as *plot*, *theme*, or *characterization*. Used as a more visual activity than the written book report.

Webliography: A Web-based *bibliography* that lists *resources* on a particular *topic* available on the *World Wide Web*. See also *Mediagraphy*.

Weed: A process for withdrawing obsolete, out-of-date, worn, or unsuitable materials from a library media *collection*.

Western Library Network (WLN): A *bibliographic utility* headquartered in Washington state originally called the Washington Library Network. WLN and OCLC have merged. See also *OCLC Online Computer Library Center, Inc.*

Wet carrel: See *Carrel*.

Wet mounting: A bonding process using adhesives or glue. Items such as a *picture* or a *map* can be sealed onto a cardboard background. See also *Dry mounting*.

What you see is what you get (WYSIWYG): 1. A description for word processors that display a *document* exactly as it will appear when printed. 2. A term often used to describe *hardware* or *software*.

WHCLIS: See *White House Conference on Library and Information Services*.

White balance: 1. The control on a *video camera* or *camcorder* that allows the *videographer* to make minor adjustments in the color output of a *camera*. 2. The process of adjusting a video camera or camcorder's color response to the surrounding light.

White House Conference on Library and Information Services (WHCLIS): Conferences sponsored by the *National Commission on Libraries and Information Science* held in Washington, D.C., approximately every 10 years with a focus on libraries and *information* services. The first conference was held in 1979, and the second and most recent conference was held in 1991. Delegates from all states represented a broad sector of libraries, education, local and state government, and lay leadership. The 700 delegates passed 95 policy recommendations. Several issues were identified as top priorities, including children and youth *literacy*, a national computer *network*, and increased funding for libraries. A report of the conference, *Information 2000: Library and Information Services for the 21st Century,* was presented to the White House in November 1991. This document presented the President and Congress with a set of policy directives to improve the nation's library and information services infrastructure. The summary presentation marked the end of the conference process and the beginning of its implementation phase. A core group of the delegates from all states continues to meet periodically to plan for the next conference and to address continuing *library* concerns.

Whole language instruction: An instructional method of *teaching* reading that integrates oral and written *language* with *learning* across the *curriculum*. This method focuses on students *reading* whole, meaningful texts as opposed to a phonetic approach with the mastery of individual words. See also *Holistic learning* and *Instruction*.

Wide Area Information Server (WAIS): An *Internet* data searching *protocol* that is extremely broad and allows a wide range of Internet-accessible *data* to be searched.

Wide area network (WAN): A system of networked computers or local area networks spanning hundreds or thousands of miles that are interconnected and distributed over a broader area than a single building or institution. This reach can range from local to global and usually requires some form of leased communication line for the long-distance connection. See also *Local area network* and *Network*.

Wide-angle lens: A *camera* lens that permits a wider view of a subject and its surroundings than would be obtained by a normal *lens* from the same position. See also *Zoom lens*.

Wild card: A *search strategy* using a *character* such as an asterisk or a question mark to instruct a *computer* to accept anything in the character's position. Wild cards enable users to select multiple files with a single specification. Many word processors also use wild cards to perform *text* searches. See also *Online searching*.

Window: The portion of a computer *screen* that displays *text*, *graphics,* messages, or documents and represents a particular *application, file,* folder, or *directory* as distinct from the remainder of the screen. See also *Multitasking*.

Windows: An *operating system* with a *user-friendly* graphical *interface* that enables users to quickly and easily *access* and work with files. See also *File, MicroSoft-Disk Operating System,* and *Multitasking.*

Wipe: A *transition* that occurs when one *slide* or *video* source replaces another and one picture seems to "wipe" the other picture off the *screen*. See also *Dissolve* and *Fade*.

Wireless: Radio *transmission* via the airwaves. Various communications techniques are used for this type of transmission, including cellular, microwave, *satellite*, infrared line of sight, and packet radio, among others. See also *Cellular phone, Cellular system,* and *Wireless Application Protocol.*

Wireless Application Protocol (WAP): A standard that enables users to *access* the *Internet* via mobile hand-held devices. *Hyper-Text Markup Language* is translated into text-based content, stripped of the *graphics*, and delivered to a *hand-held device* via a built-in *microbrowser*. See also *Cellular system* and *Wireless*.

Wish file: A *file* of items to be purchased when funds are available. Complete *information* required for ordering is included. Also referred to as a priority purchase or "desiderata."

Withdrawals: Procedures to remove records for materials weeded from the *collection*. All notations about the materials are withdrawn from the *library media center* records. A written policy should specify this process and the disposal of such materials. See also *Weed*.

WLN: See *Western Library Network.*

Wonder tale: A type of *folktale* generally called a fairy tale. Few such stories actually feature fairies, but they might include giants, elves, goblins, or monsters. They deal mainly with magic and the supernatural. Love, kindness, and truth prevail; hate, wickedness, and evil do not. The ending is a recognizable one with "they all lived happily ever after." "Cinderella," "Snow White," "Little Red Riding Hood," and "Jack in the Beanstalk" are examples.

Woofer: A loud speaker used for reproducing low frequency sounds below the treble register. See also *Tweeter*.

Word: 1. A letter or series of letters having meaning and used as a unit of *language*. 2. In *computer* terminology, a word is a grouping of bits that may consist of 8 or 16 bits. Computers *read, store,* and manipulate *data* in words rather than as individual bits. See also *Bit*.

Word processing (WP): A computer *application* that produces written communications. Word processing systems are dedicated to *document* formatting and *text* editing to produce the best possible *output* appearance.

Word wrap: The ability to begin a new line automatically whenever a typed *word* is too long to fit inside the margins of a *word processing* document.

Word-by-word filing: Filing that uses words rather than letters and observes the spaces at the end of each *word*. Spaces between words take precedence over any letter that follows. For example, *New York* appears before *Newark*. See also *Letter-by-letter filing*.

Wordless book: A *book* without *text* that conveys a story through the illustrations. This type of book is designed to encourage a positive attitude toward *reading* and books. Books without words can tell a story and be humorous, fanciful, realistic, and informational. See also *Illustration* and *Picture book*.

Work: 1. An item or intellectual entity. 2. A specific body of recorded *information* in the form of words, sounds, numerals, images, or any other symbols. 3. The informational content of a *bibliographic* entity or an information package.

Work slip: A form or card that accompanies a *book* throughout the *cataloging* and preparation processes. *Information* and instructions needed for preparing *catalog* entries are noted on the work slip by the cataloger and assistants.

Workstation: An individual *desktop computer* on a *local area network* that is used to provide *access* to the *network* and to run *computer* programs.

World Wide Web (WWW or the Web): A hypermedia-based *Internet* information system with a global aggregation of *data* that can be accessed from a vast array of linked *resources* simply by choosing highlighted words or icons on the *home page* or root file of several types of browsers. A *graphical user interface* allows *access* to *text*, *audio*, pictures, or even motion *video* from all over the world. See also *Smart phone*.

Worm: A special type of *virus* that can replicate itself and use *memory* but cannot attach itself to other programs. This is the distinction between viruses and worms. See also *Antivirus software*.

WORM: See *Write once read many*.

WP: See *Word processing*.

Write: To *record* computer *data* through a process of moving the data from *storage* to an *output* device or from main storage to auxiliary storage. 2. To form characters, symbols, or words on a surface with an instrument such as a pen or pencil. See also *Writing*.

Write once read many (WORM): An optical disk *technology* that allows computers to *write* data onto a *disk* only one time. After that, the *data* are permanent and can be read any number of times. WORM technology allows for *storage* of huge amounts of *information*. Use has been hampered because the data can only be *read* by the same type of drive that wrote the data.

Write protect: A method for protecting a *disk* against erasure of *data* already on a disk. This method is accomplished on a *floppy disk* by a notch in the protective sleeve.

Writing: 1. Storing *data* in *memory* or recording data onto a *storage* medium such as *disk* or tape. 2. The act or art of forming visible letters or characters. 3. A written composition. See also *Write*.

Writing process: Process-oriented *instruction* that approaches writing as *problem solving*. A broad range of strategies are used including pre-writing activities, a variety of *resources*, planning the *writing*, writing regularly, drafting, and revising. This type of instruction allows for multiple drafts and time for reflection and revision.

WWW: See *World Wide Web*.

WYSIWYG: See *What you see is what you get*. ∎

YALSA: See *Young Adult Library Services Association*.

Yearbook: A publication issued yearly that contains current *information* in brief, descriptive, or statistical form.

Year-round school: A *school* that has adopted a 12-month school year. Vacation time for students and staff is built into the yearly schedule rather than closing the school for the 3 summer months in the traditional 9-month school year. The extended-year calendar is designed for the way people learn—on a continual basis. However, there are pros and cons on the effectiveness of the plan.

Yellow Book: A common name for CD-ROM *standards*. See also *Compact disc-read only memory.*

Young Adult Library Services Association (YALSA): A division of the *American Library Association* that promotes *library* services for young adults, ages 12 to 18. Members receive *Voices* twice a year and the quarterly *Journal of Youth Services in Libraries*, which is issued jointly with the *Association for Library Service to Children*.

Young adult literature: *Literature* that appeals primarily to individuals between childhood and adulthood who are approximately between 13 and 18 years of age. See also *Children's literature*.

Young Adults' Choice Book Awards: These awards are sponsored by the *International Reading Association*. Teenagers in grades 7–12 in different regions in the United States vote on recently published trade books that have at least two positive reviews from recognized professional journals. The list of winners is published in the November issue of *Journal of Adolescent and Adult Literacy* (formerly *Journal of Reading*). See also *Review* and *Trade Book.* ∎

Z39.50: A national standard that is a client/server-based *protocol* for the network *retrieval* of bibliographic *data*. This protocol was developed by the *National Information Standards Organization* (NISO), which is a unit of the *American National Standards Institute* (ANSI). When using a Z39.50 compatible *application*, a user can frame a query that can be processed on any other *computer* attached to any *network*, including those made by different manufacturers. The protocol precisely specifies the format of the query in such a way that it is ideal for searching *bibliographic* databases such as *library* catalogs.

Zebra code: A black and white striped code that can represent a number and can be read into a *computer* by an optical light *scanner*. The number can be the address to a *record* or it can be an instruction in a *program* or routine.

Zero-based budget: A type of budgeting technique in which every *program* in the *budget* must be justified as to its merit and in comparison to other items in the budget.

Zip: The process of compressing files that are decompressed so that they will use less space on a *disk*. See also *Compression* and *Decompression*.

Zip disk: A *floppy disk* that is somewhat larger than the usual floppy disks and twice as thick. It can hold 100 megabytes of *data* or the equivalent of 70 floppy disks. (The *disk* actually holds 100,431,872 bytes.) A zip disk is used primarily to *backup* and archive large files. It can also be used for exchanging large files with another person, putting a system on another *computer* such as a portable computer, and keeping certain files separate from other files on the *hard disk*. A zip disk requires a *zip drive* for use.

Zip drive: An external *floppy disk drive* used for loading a *zip disk*. Some of the more recent brands will allow a user to *copy* the entire contents of a *hard drive* to one or more zip disks.

Zoom lens: A *lens* with a variable *focal length*. See also *Wide-angle lens*. ■